Managing Digital Governance

"In an era when the term 'digital governance' is often used without definition, thought, or scrutiny, Chen's work is a breath of fresh air and a strong contribution to our thinking about how to build and manage digital governance that best serves and protects the public."

Rosemary O'Leary, *University of Kansas, USA*

Managing Digital Governance provides public administrators with a comprehensive, integrated framework and specific techniques for making the most of digital innovation to advance public values. The book focuses on the core issues that public administrators face when using information and communication technologies (ICTs) to produce and deliver public service, and to facilitate democratic governance, including efficiency, effectiveness, transparency, and accountability.

Offering insight into effectively managing growing complexity and fragmentation in digital technology, this book provides practical management strategies to address external and internal challenges of digital governance. External challenges include digital inclusiveness, open government, and citizen-centric government; internal ones include information and knowledge management, risk management for digital security and privacy, and performance management of information technologies. Unique in its firm grounding in public administration and management literature and its synergistic combination of theory and practice, *Managing Digital Governance* identifies future trends and ways to develop corresponding capacity while offering enduring lessons and time-tested digital governance management strategies. This book will serve as an invaluable resource for students, scholars, and practitioners in public administration, management, and governance who aspire to become leaders equipped to leverage digital technologies to advance public governance.

Yu-Che Chen is Director of the Global Digital Governance Lab and Associate Professor of Digital Governance in the School of Public Administration, College of Public Affairs and Community Service at the University of Nebraska Omaha, USA.

American Society for Public Administration
Series in Public Administration and Public Policy
David H. Rosenbloom, Ph.D.
Editor-in-Chief

Throughout its history, ASPA has sought to be true to its founding principles of promoting scholarship and professionalism within the public service. The ASPA Book Series on Public Administration and Public Policy publishes books that increase national and international interest for public administration and which discuss practical or cutting edge topics in engaging ways of interest to practitioners, policy makers, and those concerned with bringing scholarship to the practice of public administration.

Managing Digital Governance
Issues, Challenges, and Solutions
Yu-Che Chen

The Future of Disaster Management in the US
Rethinking Legislation, Policy, and Finance
edited by Amy LePore

Adaptive Administration
Practice Strategies for Dealing with Constant Change in Public Administration and Policy
Ferd H. Mitchell and Cheryl C. Mitchell

Non-Profit Organizations
Real Issues for Public Administrators
Nicolas A. Valcik, Teodoro J. Benavides, and Kimberly Scruton

Sustaining the States
The Fiscal Viability of American State Governments
Marilyn Marks Rubin and Katherine G. Willoughby

Using the "Narcotrafico" Threat to Build Public Administration Capacity between the US and Mexico
Donald E. Klingner and Roberto Moreno Espinosa

Managing Digital Governance
Issues, Challenges, and Solutions

Yu-Che Chen

NEW YORK AND LONDON

First published 2017
by Routledge
711 Third Avenue, New York, NY 10017

and by Routledge
2 Park Square, Milton Park, Abingdon, Oxon OX14 4RN

Routledge is an imprint of the Taylor & Francis Group, an informa business

© 2017 Taylor & Francis

The right of Yu-Che Chen to be identified as author of this work has been asserted by him in accordance with sections 77 and 78 of the Copyright, Designs and Patents Act 1988.

All rights reserved. No part of this book may be reprinted or reproduced or utilised in any form or by any electronic, mechanical, or other means, now known or hereafter invented, including photocopying and recording, or in any information storage or retrieval system, without permission in writing from the publishers.

Trademark notice: Product or corporate names may be trademarks or registered trademarks, and are used only for identification and explanation without intent to infringe.

Library of Congress Cataloging in Publication Data
A catalog record for this book has been requested

ISBN: 978-1-4398-9091-2 (hbk)
ISBN: 978-1-315-20766-7 (ebk)

Typeset in Sabon
by Sunrise Setting Ltd, Brixham, UK

To my parents: Sheng-I Chen (father) and
Pi-Yun Fang (mother)

Contents

Acknowledgements viii
Preface x

1　Introduction: The Rise of Digital Governance　1

2　A Framework for Managing Digital Governance　20

3　Digital Divide, Digital Inclusion, and Digital Opportunities　42

4　Open Government in the Era of Digital Governance　64

5　Citizen-centric Digital Governance　87

6　Information and Knowledge Management for Digital Governance　113

7　Digital Privacy and Digital Security Management　136

8　Management of ICT Performance for Digital Governance　156

9　Building Management Capacity for Digital Governance　178

10　Conclusion, Trends, and Strategies of Digital Governance　209

Index　236

Acknowledgements

The author would like to acknowledge the support of editors and family members as well as inspiration from colleagues and students. My special thanks to Lara Zoble at the Taylor and Francis Group. She first saw the potential of this book and, more importantly, provided encouragement and support for its development. For the final phase of the book project, the team at Routledge provided me with the necessary structure and editorial assistance. I would like to thank these team members, including Laura Stearns, Misha Kydd, and Brianna Ascher. In addition, I am grateful for the editorial assistance of Gail Jacky and Brenda Sieczkowski, who have helped me polish the chapters.

My colleagues and students are my sources of inspiration. I was privileged to teach and work with the former CIO of the State of Iowa, John Gillispie, who profoundly shaped my orientation to improving the practice of e-government. Drs Barry Rubin and Jon Gant were my mentors while at Indiana University, helping me understand the role of management information systems in transforming the business of government. Stephen Holden, a pioneer in e-government, offered me insights into innovations made in U.S. federal e-government. My colleagues at the Taiwan E-Governance Research Center have been a source of ideas and support. Moreover, the students in my e-government and digital governance courses in the Master of Public Administration programs at the University of Nebraska at Omaha, Northern Illinois University, Iowa State University, and Indiana University-Bloomington, provided me with meaningful motivation to make the knowledge relevant to them as current/future public managers and furnished me with excellent examples of how to leverage information technology to improve public service.

I am particularly grateful to my parents for their unconditional love and support that built the foundation for me as a scholar, educator, and writer. They also taught me the importance of the pursuit of excellence as well as service to the community, which serve as guiding values for this book. My elder brother, An-Che Chen, has shouldered much of the responsibilities for caring for my parents, affording me time for the book. My parents-in-law have been encouraging and supportive of the book project. I am deeply grateful to my wife, who first saw my potential as a graduate student to become a scholar and writer, and who has also provided much-needed impetus to accelerate my intellectual and personal growth. This book project coincided with the transition of my son from a toddler to a fine boy. He has been a great source of joy as well as providing a sense of purpose for shaping a better digital government for his generation of digital natives.

Preface

This book addresses one of the most significant opportunities of our time: leveraging digital technologies for good public governance. This opportunity carries the potential to leverage new and emerging capabilities for providing public information and service as well as interacting with various stakeholders in society via digital and personalized communication channels. This book places public service managers at the center in seizing these digital governance opportunities. These managers can be in government, non-profit organizations, and in collaboratives/networks that produce and/or deliver public information and services. Integration and collaboration are crucial in the effort to provide personalized service and meaningful interactions—important aims for digital governance.

The primary objective of this book is to provide a comprehensive and integrated framework for public service managers to realize the potential of information and communication technologies for improving public service and public governance. This integrated framework, as presented in Chapter 2, considers the engagement and collaboration with stakeholders external to a particular public agency, such as citizens, non-profits, businesses, and other governments. At the same time, this framework helps identify and build capacity internally in resources, risks, and performance as related to information and communication technologies. Ultimately, the framework is a guide for the creation and advancement of public values, including efficiency and effectiveness of public service, transparency and accountability, and democratic governance.

This book further provides specifics on various components of the framework for managers to develop and execute their plans for a better digital future in public service and governance. These components include both external-oriented and internal-focused ones. For working with external stakeholders, the components include digital divide and opportunities (Chapter 3), open government for open data as well as cross-boundary interaction and collaboration (Chapter 4), and citizen-centric service to engage citizens as citizens, customers, and partners (Chapter 5). Internally, this framework puts emphasis on managing information and knowledge resources (Chapter 6), managing risks associated with digital security and privacy (Chapter 7), and managing performance in utilizing information and communication technologies (Chapter 8). In addition, this book reviews capacity-building in digital governance and offers specific recommendations for building the capacity needed to realize the potential of utilizing digital technologies (Chapter 9).

One defining feature of this book is its grounding in both theory and practice. This book specifically builds on the scholarship of public administration in general to aid in our broad understanding of public governance, performance management, and collaborative management, and applies this understanding to inform similar practices in the digital space. In addition, the scholarship on digital governance, e-government, and information management serves as a main source of insights. These scholarly references are documented in the reference section of each chapter. Best practices and lessons learned from the field constitute another major source of reference materials. Field observations and conversations with practitioners further inform the development of the strategies introduced in this book.

This book offers a balanced and long-term perspective in the midst of fast-paced technological innovations. Government and public-service organizations typically have legacy systems dating back to the 1970s and 1980s prior to the explosive growth of the internet. Moreover, the evolution of Web 1.0 (websites), Web 2.0 (social networking platforms), and Web 3.0 (semantic web and internet of things) has resulted in the expansion of technology infrastructure and digital service rather than a direct replacement of technologies employed from the previous era. In response, the strategy and recommendations offered in this book are based on this long-term perspective to offer proven strategies without gravitating to one single strategy or to the newest technological innovations. The risk-management approach to digital security and privacy that combines both technological and institutional solutions is a case in point.

The scholarship and experiences in the United States are the primary sources of information and insight. As the birthplace of the internet and the major capital of technological innovations, the experiences of the United States offer many valuable lessons and strategies. Moreover, a reservoir of strategies and experiences has resulted from innovative digital governance initiatives at the federal, state, and local governments in the United States. At the same time, this book is globally informed through the United Nations' e-government surveys as well as digital governance innovations and development in Asia and Europe.

This book concludes with a glance into the future to guide forward-looking digital governance initiatives while firmly grounding them in the goal of achieving and advancing public values (Chapter 10). The rapid growth and innovation in data and cyberinfrastructure will continue to push the envelope for possible applications of big data, data analytics, and cloud computing in digital governance. Other digital governance trends include personalization of information and services, openness of government data and public governance, emphasis on utilizing information and communication technology for service and scientific innovations, and heightened efforts on safeguarding digital security and privacy. Overall, the framework of digital governance and management strategies as covered in Chapters 2–9 offer the foundation for effective digital governance, for seizing the opportunities to utilize emerging digital technologies to further advance public values.

1 Introduction

The Rise of Digital Governance

The rise of digital governance is fundamentally powered by the new capabilities introduced by advances in information and communication technologies (ICTs) such as social networking platforms and services, smart phones/devices, internet of things (IoT), big data, and artificial intelligence. Citizens and governments around the world are witnessing an unprecedented level of connectedness, user involvement, mobility, usability, and personal computing power. The confluence of citizens' increasing demand to interact with government via a growing array of digital channels and governments' efforts to provide citizen-centric online services raises challenges to 21st-century public managers. The question is no longer whether we will engage in digital governance or not; the challenge is how modern public managers can best create public values via the implementation of strategic digital governance initiatives. Public managers need to first understand the context of digital governance as the initial step in addressing that challenge.

Transformational Development: Web 1.0, Web 2.0 (Social Networking Platforms), and Web 3.0 and Other Emerging Technologies

The rapid growth of the internet in the 1990s ushered in Web 1.0 to make information and service available to anyone with internet access. Participation on the internet has moved from the privilege of the few to a vast majority of populations in the developed world and a majority of the population in the developing world. In the United States, internet use among adults rose from 14 percent in 1995 to 72 percent by the end of 2005. This is a change from a one-in-six minority to a leading majority of 72 percent within a decade. The decade of 2005 to 2015 has continued to see a steady increase from 72 percent to 87 percent.[1] Since 2008, China has become the country with the biggest internet population with a total number of 384 million internet users reported in 2009.[2] By the end of 2010, the number climbed to 457 million according to statistics from the China Internet Network Information Center (CNNIC).[3] Within five years,

2 *Introduction*

China has added another 200 million-plus internet users to reach 688 million internet users by the end of 2015 (CNNIC 2016). That is twice the total U.S. population. Globally, internet use has risen from less than 1 percent of the world population (0.4 percent) in 1995 to 14.7 percent in 2005. That constitutes an increase of 30 times in a decade. The second decade of 2006–15 has witnessed a move from 15 percent to close to half of the world population (47.5 percent).[4]

Starting in the latter part of the first decade in the new millennium, there has been a significant shift from Web 1.0 to Web 2.0, particularly marked by the growth of Facebook. Facebook, as the premium social networking site serving the United States and the world (with the exception of China), has seen exponential growth since 2006. In the United States alone, the number of active Facebook users jumped from approximately ten million in 2007 (*The Economist* 2010, 5) to 168 million in 2012,[5] which is more than a ten-fold increase in a five-year period. In 2016, the number has continued to climb to 191 million and has been projected to experience slight annual increases to 2021.[6] Facebook has reached the vast majority of the population in the United States with a total population of approximately 320 million in 2015 as estimated by the U.S. Census Bureau.[7]

The number of registered Facebook users outside the United States exceeded those in the United States as early as 2007 (*The Economist* 2010, 5) and became five times as large as the number of active users in the United States in 2012 based on information from a Facebook press release (Facebook 2012) and online statistics on users in other countries.[8] The count of active Facebook users passed the one billion mark as of September 2012 (Facebook 2012). In 2015, the number of active Facebook users exceeded 1.5 billion, which is close to five times the U.S. population (*The Economist* 2016a).

The social networking platforms in China have also experienced a phenomenal growth. The exclusion of Facebook from China warrants a separate discussion. According to the report from the CNNIC (CNNIC 2012), the number of registered users for social networking sites reached 244 million (more than all the Facebook users in the United States at the time) by the end of 2011. The number of Chinese users on social networking sites grew by 60 million from 2009 to 2011 (CNNIC 2012). More recently, the development and growth of WeChat, since its birth in 2011, have introduced two important features into social network sites: mobile dominant and all-inclusive service platforms. WeChat has grown from zero to over 700 million active users in less than five years. More impressive is its ability to offer all-inclusive features including advertising, e-commerce, digital content, online-to-offline services, and finance (*The Economist* 2016b, 50).

User-generated content is a main feature introduced in Web 2.0 that barely existed in the Web 1.0 world. In Web 1.0, web content was created by staff members of the organizations behind the official websites. News items, pictures, and documents were posted by the organization.

The growth of Web 2.0 has allowed users to generate and post comments on a blog or a Facebook page. Moreover, peer reviews and rankings have also become popular with products and services such as those seen at Amazon.com, Yelp.com, Angie's List, and various travel websites. In the realm of forming online communities, the Web 2.0 era has offered many free or low-cost tools for individuals to organize and promote awareness of shared concerns. This increasingly user-driven online participation has profound implications for digital governance where the scope, speed, and nature of citizen participation have changed significantly.

Interactivity is another defining feature of Web 2.0. Our social and professional interactions have reached a new level of interactivity given the convenience and pervasiveness of social media as well as smart mobile devices. Facebook users have generated 1.13 trillion "Likes," stamps of approval on online posts of others, since the launch of this feature in February 2009 (Facebook 2012). Users can get Facebook updates through e-mails that are available on their phones. The acquisitions of Instagram in 2012 and WhatsApp in 2014 further expanded Facebook's capability to perform as a social network platform that allows a single sign-on for an array of services and integrated user experiences (*The Economist* 2016a). There are newer possibilities for people to interact with one another through an integrated slew of media (texts, instant messages, photos, videos, etc).

Two of the newer possibilities for interaction are Twitter and LinkedIn. Twitter—with over 100 million active users reported in 2012[9]—can promote interactivity even more instantaneously because Twitter feeds are usually real-time responses to events. The spread of tweets usually follows a subscribed network of interested people who interact with one another. Twitter saw a 300 percent increase over a three-year period, with approximately 300 million active users in 2015.[10] People are increasingly connected professionally with networking sites such as LinkedIn. At the beginning of 2012, LinkedIn had over 150 million registered users.[11] Within a four-year period, the number of active users has doubled to 350 million based on a press release by LinkedIn in 2016 (LinkedIn 2016). Professionals tend to enjoy the ability to search for and connect with their colleagues, with the social network sites providing both connection recommendations and the ability to mobilize a network of professionals. Some people have coined this phenomenon as "hyper-connectivity." For more avid users of social media, the challenge is to keep up with the increasing speed and flow of information and growing expectations for social connectivity.

Both the amount of user-generated content and the level of interactivity are further fueled by the availability of smart mobile devices with a network or internet connection. The abilities of a smart phone to generate a post, take a picture, and shoot a video have continued to be improved. People with smart phones can easily make Facebook posts and upload pictures.

Moreover, the ability to share among friends in the same social circle and colleagues belonging to the same professional network has also increased dramatically with the ease of use of social/professional networking sites. An individual can interact with hundreds or thousands of people via Twitter feeds and Facebook posts. Mobility further feeds into interactivity. As of September 2012, Facebook had 600 million mobile users out of one billion active registered users (Facebook 2012). That accounted for 60 percent of active users. By the end of 2015, the number of active monthly mobile users had exceeded 1.4 billion, accounting for over 90 percent of all active Facebook users.[12] That is a 30 percent increase over (approximately) a three-year period.

The unprecedented growth of smart phone ownership rate among adults in the United States and around the globe created a device platform to enable innovative social networking platforms and shared economy services. In mid-2012, nearly 45 percent of American adults owned a smart phone based on information published by the Pew Internet and American Life Project.[13] The number climbed to 65 percent in 2015, a 20 percent increase in about three years.[14] Around the globe, half of the adult population owned a smart phone in 2015 (*The Economist* 2015). By 2020, it is estimated that approximately 80 percent of adults will have a smart phone (supercomputer) (*The Economist* 2015). Moreover, the growth of an ecosystem of applications as well as services geared toward mobile smart devices will continue to grow. For instance, Uber, as an example of shared economy, relies heavily on the availability and connectivity of smart phones.

Web 3.0 and emerging ICTs will continue to push the envelope of possibilities. One defining feature of Web 3.0 is a growing use of wireless access and networks. The fourth generation wireless network is capable of transmitting 1 gigabyte per second. The fifth generation wireless network will be ten times faster, reaching 10 gigabytes per second (*The Economist* 2016c). Coupled with the high penetration rate of smart phones, the development of the fifth generation wireless network will create an environment of mobile-first to mobile-only ways of accessing information and services. Another defining feature of Web 3.0 is the web as database. The combination of more machine-readable data available on the web with more sophisticated algorithms to process information will make the web into a database. In addition, Web 3.0 will have a growing impact on the IoT. As more and more devices are connected via the internet, Web 3.0 will continue to traffic from smart devices automatically sending information to provide service.

Emerging ICTs will continue to add value to business intelligence, personalization of service, efficiency, and decision-making. The growth of big data, along with big data analytics, is able to provide enhanced business intelligence that draws data from Web 1.0, social networking websites, and semantic web to understand the needs of clients and stakeholders.

The development and utilization of apps on smart phones with their growing penetration rate is likely to reach a new level of personalized service. Technologies for data visualization and augmented reality will increasingly aid in learning, situational awareness, and decision-making. Artificial intelligence powered by supercomputers and developments in machine learning have the potential to leverage big data to power personalized service and transform business processes. Although the specific technologies will likely evolve with new innovations, the values and supporting functionalities are likely to be enduring.

The evolution from Web 1.0 and Web 2.0 (social networking platforms) to Web 3.0 with other emerging technologies gives rise to a growing portfolio of information technologies rather than a replacement of the old with the new. The shift from Web 1.0 to Web 2.0 has not diminished the importance of websites and supporting databases and information systems in providing online information and services. Conventional websites with Web 1.0 features and backend databases are still the mainstay, as they provide a valuable service. People can find information about products, services, and basic contact information. Such websites do not require a high level of interactivity; the keys are availability and usability. These websites are also valuable in terms of online transactions, such as purchasing products and services online, powered by large information systems and databases. Despite this, semantic web (sometimes also called Web 3.0) is emerging. It is the concept of the web as databases, in which the computational power of modern software programs and algorithms can answer your questions with credible sources of information rather than giving you a large number of hits on documents for you to sift through. The emerging technologies on big data analytics and visualization all build on the quality and amount of data collected via Web 1.0 and Web 2.0 (social media platforms).

The adoption of ICTs by governments typically follows the trajectory of the private sector with a cautionary period of observation for innovative ICTs to become mature, stable, and cost-effective. After a decade of rapid growth in internet technologies and e-commerce, local governments in the United States have reached an 83 percent website adoption rate based on the International City/County Management Association (ICMA) 2000 e-government survey (Norris, Fletcher, and Holden 2001). The adoption rate continued to rise in the early 2000s to 91 percent by the end of 2004 (ICMA 2004). Although the rise in website adoption was significant in the late 1990s and early 2000s, the growth in the adoption of online transaction services and more sophisticated informational and transaction services had been relatively slow (Norris and Moon 2005). In 2011, the website adoption rate reached 97 percent. Nonetheless, the progression in more advanced features and the intensity and scope of utilizing these features have been more limited and incremental in nature (Norris and Reddick 2013).

Governments in the United States have gradually adapted to the growing utilization of Web 2.0 tools. The Open Government Initiative emphasizes collaboration and participation as two of its three pillars. The IdeaScale Project is a collaborative project between government and citizens with citizen-generated and ranked policy ideas on a government-hosted website with Web 2.0 features such as posts, comments, and votes. "Challenges and Prizes" programs solicit citizens' and organizations' input on policy challenges, which allows direct participation and collaboration among these individuals and organizations. State governments also have embedded social media features on their websites, such as a Facebook presence, Twitter feeds, and more. At the local level, 67 percent of local government has a social media presence based on a 2011 ICMA national survey of local governments in the United States (ICMA 2011). Facebook was the main social media of choice for those U.S. local governments responding to the survey. Moreover, at the federal level, major U.S. agencies all have a strong social media presence to advance their public service mission—including science exploration, education, transportation, human services, and public health (Mergel 2013). All these efforts reflect a growing recognition that governments need to engage citizens online where they meet (i.e. social media platforms) and adopt a more citizen-centric communication and service model—as characterized in Chang and Kannan (2008) and Goldsmith and Crawford (2014) and exemplified in the e-participation cases documented by Leighninger (2011) as well as in the social media examples mentioned in Zavattaro and Bryer (2016).

Governments around the world have also moved to a more connected governance model. Connections are between organizational and individual members in all sectors of society, including the public (government), nonprofit, and private sector, though emphasis has been placed more on citizens. The United Nations' 2008 E-Government Report captured the notion of connected governance to highlight e-participation as a way to strengthen connections between government and citizens via online channels. The e-rulemaking in the United States allows citizens to comment on a proposed piece of regulation electronically, which allows e-policymaking. The exponential growth in the use of microblog and social networking services (i.e. WeChat) by Chinese governments and public officials in recent years also signifies a move to a more connected governance model.[15] Another example of online connected governance is the Korean e-people portal. This award-winning portal allows a one-stop portal for citizens to register complaints with government, encompassing all relevant central and local government offices.[16]

Moreover, the overall conclusion of the United Nations' 2012 E-Government Report further underscores the need to transform public governance via ICT to promote synergy and coordination among tiers and units of governance structures for "inclusive sustainable development" (United Nations 2012). These findings direct our attention to the synergy and connections needed while interacting with citizens, non-profits, and businesses in the public sector. Integration of government units and systems is required to move to the highest level of e-government (Chen and Hsieh 2009). An example of such integration at the local level is the use of citizen service information systems, known as 311 systems in the United States, as the number to call for all citizen-related services. This 311 system requires the integration of various city departments, or even independently-elected commissions, to integrate their service information and business systems. The integration of healthcare services as seen in England's National Health Service is an example of a highly integrated information system for healthcare.

The United Nations' 2016 E-Government Survey highlights major trends in the use of ICTs by government (United Nations 2016). The use of social media and social networking services has continued to grow and, in some areas, has become the dominant channel of communication between government and citizens. The increasing use of smart phone and mobile devices has introduced many opportunities for government to provide citizen-centric and personalized information and services. In addition, the growth of open data and collaborative governance ushered in a new level of participatory governance. Overall, there is a heightened level of pursuit of public values such as inclusiveness, transparency, and accountability (United Nations 2016).

Digital Governance for Creating Public Values

The overall goal of digital governance is the creation of public values; one such overarching value is sustainability. The United Nations' E-Government Survey reports have articulated the important role that e-government plays in supporting sustainability (United Nations 2012). More specifically, e-government needs to bridge digital divide to provide digital opportunities for vulnerable populations to promote sustainable development. In addition, e-government needs to promote participatory governance as well as prioritize the value of transparency and accountability to foster sustainable good public governance (United Nations 2016).

Inclusiveness is also an important public value, which embodies the notion of social equity (Moore 1995). Inclusiveness deserves special attention in digital governance due to the inherent challenge of digital divide. Such a divide exists both in the general population—between those who have the technology and skills and those who do not—and in various units of governments between those who possess and utilize technologies and those who do not. Digital divide has multiple dimensions, including education, skills, culture, etc. (Mossberger, Tolbert, and Stansbury 2003). The advances of Web 2.0 and smart mobile devices have introduced new types of digital divide between those who can access and utilize these sites and devices vs. those who cannot. Promoting digital inclusiveness needs to address various forms and sources of digital divide. In addition, this value of inclusiveness is a distinctively public social value (Friedland and Gross 2010). Government is designed to serve everyone. In contrast, businesses are driven primarily by profit and by serving their selected customer base.

Additionally, accountability is another important public value. A broad notion of accountability includes efficient and effective use of public resources to advance the welfare of the public. Government can be accountable to citizens for the taxes collected by realizing efficiency gain as the result of introducing e-government functions that shorten the time and effort to obtain government information and services. Effectiveness in addressing complex public problems via the use of ICTs is also about advancing public accountability. Moreover, transparency is an important aspect of accountability (Koppell 2005). Citizens and other stakeholders need to be informed about government operations before they can hold government accountable for those actions.

The advances of ICTs offer opportunities for government to realize sustainability, inclusiveness, and accountability. At the community level, utilization of geographic information systems can aid in understanding the impact of various development proposals on the economy, public finance, transportation, public safety, and the environment. Analytics also shed light on complex interactions between various systems and trade-offs between competing policy objectives. Inclusiveness can be accomplished by the combination of providing broadband access to disadvantaged communities and offering training to bridge the skill gap. Moreover, increasingly user-friendly, powerful, and connected mobile devices can empower a human agent to include all members of a society. E-government is about promoting accountability in managing public resources via the use of ICTs. Online tax filing, online citizen service information systems, online license renewal, among other capabilities, are efforts to provide efficient and effective public services. Making budget and government performance information accessible online is one of many ways to provide virtual accountability to the public.

Digital Governance

Definition of Digital Governance

Digital governance is the use of ICTs to promote public values via government-led initiatives inside government as well as external collaboration among key stakeholders in the public. Defining digital governance in this way emphasizes inclusivity in the ICTs deployed. A more conventional definition of e-government tends to focus only on the internet and websites. The growth of cellular phones and mobile devices allows for interactions and transactions, such as text alerts, without the need for internet access (Bryer and Zavattaro 2011). These technologies also include location-based services and intelligent transportation systems beyond information searches and transactions with governments on their official websites.

Next, this definition places its primary focus on the creation of public values via collaboration. This notion first brings strategic focus to the creation of public values and return on investment. At the same time, utilization of collaborative methods reflects the reality that public services are increasingly produced and delivered via partnerships between organizations in public, private, and non-profit sectors. The participatory and collaborative features of Web 2.0 technologies facilitate such cross-boundary collaboration.

More importantly, this definition captures the central role played by public administrators/managers. The "government-led" notion of digital governance places public administrators/managers at the center of digital governance efforts. This perspective distinguishes itself from a focus on political campaigns utilizing ICTs that places political activities by political parties and election campaigns at the center. The notion of government-led conveys the ultimate responsibility of government to be accountable and is also broad enough to embrace a range of types of production and delivery of public services with collaborators from other governments, businesses, and organizations.

Dimensions of Digital Governance

Digital governance encompasses multiple dimensions that concern public managers/administrators: public values, mode of activities, role of government, and technology. The discussion later builds on the literature on e-government and e-governance. These dimensions of digital governance can best be understood by distinguishing the traditional notion of e-government and digital governance in the era of Web 2.0 and beyond. These distinctions should be treated as a matter of emphasis.

The core values of digital governance include efficiency and effectiveness as well as transparency, sustainability, and inclusiveness. For example, efficiency in service provision, such as electronic filing of tax returns that interfaces directly with citizens, is a core value promoted by e-government. Digital governance extends the list of core values to transparency, which further promotes citizen participation in generating and evaluating policy ideas. The list of core values also includes sustainability and inclusiveness, both of which play more central roles in digital governance than in a conventional notion of e-government.

The primary emphasis in digital governance, as compared to e-government, with regard to activities is integration and interaction. The integration emphasized by digital governance is vertical and horizontal integration in the public sector and across various sectors. In the public sector, digital integration involves inter-agency cooperation in the same governmental unit (such as citizen service information systems) and inter-governmental collaboration across units at multiple levels of government (such as in the area of emergency management). Such integration happens inside government and takes a government-as-a-whole approach (Chen and Hsieh 2009). In addition, digital governance places increasing emphasis on solving public issues by means of intersectoral interactions that involve governments, non-profit (professional) organizations, and businesses. Interaction between government and citizens via online civic engagement is another feature of interactivity embodied in digital governance.

Digital governance ushers in a shift in the role of government in public service production and delivery from a government-centric role to one more invested in partnership or intersectoral collaboration. This trend is consistent with a society that has seen a gradual shift to increased utilization of businesses and non-profit organizations for service production and delivery (i.e. Gray et al. 2003; Milward and Provan 2000). Advances of ICTs make such collaborative networks increasingly easy to coordinate (Bryson, Crosby, and Stone 2015). The traditional notion of e-government puts government at the center of production and delivery of information and services online. A modern notion of digital governance introduces collaborative enterprises that bring government, businesses, non-profit organizations, and citizens together. This emphasis on collaboration and shared ownership is consistent with the need for engaging organizations and individuals from all sectors of a society to solve increasingly complex public problems. For instance, the development of technical data standards for standard business reporting in Australia has needed support from a host of sectors: businesses, professional organizations, and various government agencies. This collaborative consortium helped determine the data standards and how the standards are to be implemented, which, of course, benefits the entire economy (Chen 2010).

The technological emphasis of digital governance is the combination of telecommunication networks, smart mobile devices and applications, cloud computing, Web 2.0 technologies, and future internet. The share of the internet economy will continue to grow in the G-20 countries in the next few years, with three billion people (half of the total population) forecast to be online by 2016, according to the Boston Consulting Group (*Harvard Business Review* 2012). The growing capacity of telecommunications, especially wireless, has offered many opportunities for digital governance (*The Economist* 2016c). This increased capacity provides more and more residents with access to wireless digital networks via phones and/or other mobile devices in various countries, which makes digital communication an increasingly important part of interactions and public governance. For instance, residents of a community can report a neighborhood problem directly from their phones with location information attached for ease of reference.

Cloud computing represents a move from in-house provision of information technology (IT) services to ICT (software applications, web-hosting, databases, e-mails, data analytics) as a service accessible in the cloud anytime and anywhere given an internet connection. The move to cloud computing calls for attention to managing IT resources outside a government agency and the implications of IT outsourcing for privacy and security. Web 2.0 technologies such as social networking, wikis, and "mash-ups" underscore the increasingly cross-sector, integrated, collaborative mode of digital governance. Social media allows for a high level of interactivity, not only between government and citizens, but also among citizens and with other non-governmental organizations. Another feature of Web 2.0 is the emphasis on user-generated content and leverage of collective knowledge. Advances in internet and other digital technologies will continue to enable digital governance. For instance, the developments in semantic web (Web 3.0) offer additional integration and interoperability of data on specific topics, also known as the web of things. The growth in big data and data analytics will also help bring tools to citizens to monitor government actions and for government to provide citizen-centric government information and services.

Managing Digital Governance

The mission of this book is to provide managers of public services with a conceptual framework for making informed digital governance decisions. Digital governance is a critical issue facing 21st-century governments and public service organizations around the world. We have witnessed recent rapid developments in Web 2.0 social networking technologies and growth in the adoption and use of mobile devices among an array of ICTs for public service and engagement with individuals and organizations in all sectors of a society. Although a number of edited volumes currently provide surveys of technological developments and e-government applications, few have offered an issue-focused, coherent framework for improving the management of digital governance. Publication on e-government and e-governance has grown steadily; however, it may be difficult for a reader to distill concrete knowledge to inform practice from these research articles or chapters. The coherent framework proposed in this book integrates research insights from a diverse body of literature and provides an integrated view of digital governance to aid in formulating a comprehensive strategy and in generating and implementing actionable recommendations.

This management framework of digital governance is grounded in a socio-technical perspective that puts IT deployment in a societal context. Garson (2006) has presented four theories on the relationship between IT and society: namely, technological determinism theory, reinforcement theory, socio-technical theory, and system theory. The empirical evidence has suggested the relevance of a socio-technical perspective that emphasizes the interactions between socio-organizational context and technology rather than one that emphasizes the domination of one over the other.

The deployment of ICTs should be framed in the dynamics of these interactions rather than developed in isolation from organizational, institutional, and political contexts (Fountain 2001; Ahn and Bretschneider 2011).

More specifically, this book's management framework is based on the notion that management actions matter in advancing digital governance. This notion is built on the technology enactment theory proposed by Fountain (2001), which underscores the active role played by organizations and decision-makers in deciding which technology to deploy and which objectives to achieve with that technology. This management framework also builds on the findings of the broad digital governance literature on digital divide and opportunities (i.e. Helsper 2012; Mossberger, Tolbert, and Stansbury 2003), open government and e-participation (i.e. Evans and Campos 2013; Fishenden and Thompson 2013), information and knowledge management (i.e. Dawes 2010; Dawes, Cresswell, and Pardo 2009), e-government outsourcing and integration (i.e. Young 2007; Chen and Perry 2003; Scholl and Klischewski 2007), IT innovation management and leadership (i.e. Ahn and Bretschneider 2011; Ho and Ni 2004; Moon and Norris 2005), strategic and performance management (i.e. Yu and Janssen 2010; Dufner, Holley, and Reed 2003; Desouza 2015), and management capacity-building (i.e. Ganapati and Reddick 2016; Melitski 2003).

Moreover, this framework draws from the theory and practice of digital governance in the United States as well as in countries around the world. This book's perspective, although grounded in the experience of the United States as one of the leaders in the field of digital governance, is global in nature. Special attention has been paid to Asia and Europe. For instance, a discussion of China is included to aid the understanding of major developmental forces in digital governance, given that it has the largest internet population in the world coupled with large and dynamic social networking platforms and services. The Republic of Korea, as the top ranked e-government country according to the United Nations' e-government surveys (United Nations 2010, 2012, 2014), also offers innovative digital governance practices. In addition, the experiences of European countries are informative in advancing digital governance, particularly in the area of democratic participation, protecting personal data, and using ICTs to foster innovations in communities (United Nations 2016).

The issue-based approach to the management of digital governance adopted by this book is flexible to keep pace with rapid technological development. The core issues remain relatively stable while the technologies are evolving. For instance, the challenge of digital divide is about digital inclusion via bridging not only the divide in technology but also in skills and orientation. Since this is the case, a digital inclusion management strategy should at least have both technology and training components. Similarly, the tension between information access/utilization and personal privacy is an enduring issue, and a management approach focusing on an enduring issue is likely to provide guiding principles that will be relevant to new technologies. For instance, a risk management approach has been the mainstay for managing digital security. These issue-based management approaches and guiding principles will remain relevant for an extended period of time and be effective in managing a growing portfolio of ICTs developed in different eras.

In sum, this book offers management strategies that advance digital governance. Public administrators/managers can develop an overarching strategy that cuts across various issue areas such as digital inclusion, cyber infrastructure, integration, and open government. At the same time, they will gain the flexibility to focus directly on each issue area, as the book offers management strategies and practices for each of them. Moreover, this book incorporates an understanding of the larger political, institutional, and organizational contexts that public managers operate in while creating public values in digital governance. This management-focused approach is sustainable because even the newest technological innovations can be evaluated and placed in their issue-specific decision-making context.

Organization and Plan

This book focuses on the core issues that public administrators face when using ICTs to produce and deliver public service and to facilitate public governance. These issues include digital inclusion and opportunities, digital open government, information and knowledge management, citizen-centric ICT services, digital privacy and security, performance management of ICT, and ICT management capacity-building to address these issues. The organization of the book follows these core issues.

The next chapter, Chapter 2, provides a digital governance management framework that identifies and illustrates the main components. This framework integrates technical and institutional considerations (digital inclusion and digital infrastructure) with the objectives and strategies for creating public values. It also provides an overarching strategy for effectively addressing various digital governance issues and building long-term capacity to fully realize the potential of digital governance.

Chapter 3 discusses strategies for assessing and improving digital inclusion and opportunities. Such assessment includes studying the demographics of online vs. off-line populations as well as the factors determining the use of e-government. Public managers first need to know the degree of digital inclusion and the various factors affecting inclusion before formulating strategies for digital governance. This chapter then presents various strategies for digital inclusion and opportunities to bridge digital divide and enhance digital opportunities.

The focus of Chapter 4 is open government in the digital age. This chapter presents the main components of open government: transparency, participation, and collaboration. It also introduces pertinent institutions supporting open government, including laws, regulations, and policy

14 Introduction

memorandums. More importantly, this chapter presents recent developments in open government and the open-data movement and proposes a management strategy for realizing public values embodied in open government.

Chapter 5 is on citizen-centric electronic services with a focus on cross-boundary collaboration and integration via ICTs. Providing citizen-centric electronic services constitutes an important goal of digital governance. This chapter outlines and discusses management issues facing the provision of citizen-centric electronic services, including integration of government information systems and sharing of data that bring agency-specific services together to serve individual citizens. Moreover, true citizen-centric electronic services require management strategies to work across levels of governments as well as across sectors (public, private, and non-profit) in the increasingly networked form of public services.

Chapter 6 addresses the challenge of managing information and knowledge for digital governance. This chapter begins with an introduction of the main concepts as well as policies and principles of information and knowledge management. It then focuses on knowledge management for digital governance with regard to processes and management principles. Against the backdrop of recent developments in big data and data analytics, this chapter concludes with overarching leadership and management strategies to further advance information and knowledge management for digital governance.

Chapter 7 introduces the issues and challenges associated with digital privacy and digital security. This chapter focuses on the laws and regulations that govern the protection of digital privacy and digital security. Moreover, it offers a management strategy for protecting digital privacy with the combination of institutional and technical solutions. For digital security, this chapter outlines a comprehensive risk management approach with various components for risk minimization.

Performance management of ICTs is the focus of Chapter 8. This chapter describes human, technological, and financial resources that need to be invested in so as to improve performance. The discipline of project and program management, especially with agile methodology, provides the structure and processes for successful development and implementation of digital governance projects. Moreover, this chapter offers a digital governance performance management strategy. This strategy embodies the principles of being stakeholder-focused, strategically aligned, data and outcome driven, user-centric, and agile.

Chapter 9 provides a list of core management competencies for digital governance and strategies for developing them. Building relevant management capacities is critical for succeeding in implementing the issue-based management framework proposed in this book. This chapter also outlines a strategy for building relevant management capacities such as strategic IT planning, development and implementation of technical

Introduction 15

standards, evaluation of digital governance projects, cross-boundary collaboration, civic engagement, risk management, etc. The focus is on building the capacity to provide systems and processes for successful digital governance implementation.

The concluding chapter, Chapter 10, summarizes the main points of the book and highlights the unique challenges and opportunities of 21st-century digital governance. Challenges lie in public managers' ability to keep pace with the advent of Web 2.0, Web 3.0, and mobile devices and to serve an increasingly online and diverse group of stakeholders as well as maintain traditional channels of communication because governments serve everyone, including those who do not have access to technology and/or the internet. At the same time, opportunities for managers delivering high-impact digital governance abound. High-quality, personalized citizen-centric services are possible with the integration of disparate sources of government information and utilization of emerging technologies to create value for citizens. Engagement with citizens and other stakeholders (businesses, non-profits, civil groups) provides governments with opportunities to collaborate with them to solve complex public service problems.

Notes

1 The source of statistics is the Pew Internet and American Life Project. More details are available on www.pewinternet.org/data-trend/internet-use/internet-use-over-time/, accessed September 2, 2016.
2 The statistics are based on the number available in an article published by the Pew Internet and American Life Project, www.pewresearch.org/fact-tank/2013/12/02/china-has-more-internet-users-than-any-other-country/, accessed September 2, 2016.
3 More details, see cnnic.com.cn/IDR/BasicData/, accessed September 1, 2016.
4 More details, see www.internetworldstats.com/emarketing.htm, accessed September 2, 2015.
5 Source of data: www.socialbakers.com/facebook-statistics/, accessed July 20, 2012.
6 Data source: www.statista.com/statistics/408971/number-of-us-facebook-users/, accessed August 20, 2016.
7 Source: www.census.gov/quickfacts/table/PST045215/00, accessed July 1, 2016.
8 Data source: www.socialbakers.com/facebook-statistics/, accessed November 1, 2012.
9 Data source: www.digitalbuzzblog.com/social-media-statistics-stats-2012-infographic/, accessed November 2, 2016.
10 Data source: www.statista.com/statistics/282087/number-of-monthly-active-twitter-users/, accessed August 28, 2016.
11 Data source: www.statista.com/statistics/274050/quarterly-numbers-of-linkedin-members/, accessed August 31, 2016.
12 Data source: www.statista.com/statistics/277958/number-of-mobile-active-facebook-users-worldwide/, accessed August 30, 2016.
13 Data source: pewinternet.org/Infographics/2012/Our-Smartphone-Habits.aspx, accessed November 1, 2012.

14 For more details, visit www.pewinternet.org/2015/04/01/us-smartphone-use-in-2015/, last accessed July 29, 2016.
15 In China, the number of microblogs surpassed the 50,000 mark by the end of 2011, with the growth in 2011 alone exceeding 25,000 (Chinese Academy of Governance 2012).
16 For details, visit www.epeople.go.kr/jsp/user/on/eng/whatsnew.jsp, accessed July 20, 2014.

References

Ahn, Michael J., and Stuart Bretschneider. 2011. "Politics of E-Government: E-Government and the Political Control of Bureaucracy." *Public Administration Review* 71 (3):414–24.

Bryer, Thomas A., and Staci M. Zavattaro. 2011. "Social Media and Public Administration: Theoretical Dimensions and Introduction to the Symposium." *Administrative Theory & Praxis* 33 (3):325–40.

Bryson, John M., Barbara C. Crosby, and Melissa Middleton Stone. 2015. "Designing and Implementing Cross-Sector Collaborations: Needed and Challenging." *Public Administration Review* 75 (5):647–63.

Chang, Ai-Mei, and P. K. Kannan. 2008. "Leveraging Web 2.0 in Government." Washington, DC: IBM Center for the Business of Government.

Chen, Yu-Che. 2010. "Realizing the Full Potential of XBRL in Government: Case Studies of XBRL Implementation." Washington, DC: IBM Center for the Business of Government.

Chen, Yu-Che, and James Perry. 2003. "Outsourcing for E-Government: Managing for Success." *Public Performance & Management Review* 26 (4):404–21.

Chen, Yu-Che, and Jun-Yi Hsieh. 2009. "Advancing E-Governance: Comparing Taiwan and the United States." *Public Administration Review* 69 (Supplement 1): S151–8.

China Internet Network Information Center (CNNIC). 2012. "2011 Research Report on Application of Social Networking Sites in China" (in Chinese). Beijing, China: China Internet Network Information Center.

China Internet Network Information Center (CNNIC). 2016. "Statistical Report on Internet Development in China (January 2016)." Beijing, China: China Internet Network Information Center.

Chinese Academy of Governance. 2012. "Evaluation Report on Chinese Government Microblogs in 2011" (in Chinese) (2011 nian zhongguo zhengwu weibo pinggu baogao). Beijing, China: Electronic Government Research Center, Chinese Academy of Governance.

Dawes, Sharon S. 2010. "Stewardship and Usefulness: Policy Principles for Information-based Transparency." *Government Information Quarterly* 27 (4): 377–83.

Dawes, Sharon, Anthony Cresswell, and Theresa Pardo. 2009. "From 'Need to Know' to 'Need to Share': Tangled Problems, Information Boundaries, and the Building of Public Sector Knowledge Networks." *Public Administration Review* 69 (3):392–402.

Desouza, Kevin C. 2015. "Creating a Balanced Portfolio of Information Technology Metrics." Washington, DC: IBM Center for the Business of Government.

Dufner, Donna, Lyn M. Holley, and B. J. Reed. 2003. "Strategic Information Systems Planning and U.S. County Government." *Communications of the Association for Information Systems* 11:219–44.

Evans, Angela M., and Adriana Campos. 2013. "Open Government Intiatives: Challenges of Citizen Participation." *Journal of Policy Analysis and Management* 32 (1):172–203.

Facebook. 2012. "Facebook Reached 1 Billion Monthly Active Users on September 14". Press Release.

Fishenden, Jerry, and Mark Thompson. 2013. "Digital Government, Open Architecture, and Innovation: Why Public Sector IT Will Never Be the Same Again." *Journal of Public Administration Research and Theory* 23 (4):977–1004.

Fountain, Jane. 2001. *Building the Virtual State: Information Technology and Institutional Change*. Washington, DC: Brookings Institution Press.

Friedland, Carsten, and Tom Gross. 2010. "Measuring the Public Value of e-Government: Methodology of a South African Case Study." The IST-Africa 2010 Conference, Durban.

Ganapati, Sukumar, and Christopher Reddick. 2016. "Symposium Introduction: Information Technology and Public Administration Education." *Journal of Public Affairs Education* 22 (2):156–60.

Garson, David. 2006. *Public Information Technology and E-Governance: Managing the Virtual State*. Sudbury, MA: Jones and Bartlett Publishers, Inc.

Goldsmith, Stephen, and Susan Crawford. 2014. *The Responsive City: Engaging Communities Through Data-Smart Governance*. San Francisco, CA: Jossey-Bass.

Gray, Andrew, Bill Jenkins, Frans Leeuw, and John Mayne. 2003. *Collaboration in Public Services*. In Vol. X, *Comparative Policy Analysis Series*, edited by Ray C. Rist. New Brunswick (USA) and London (UK): Transaction Publishers.

Harvard Business Review. 2012. "Vision Statement: It Keeps Growing... and Growing." *Harvard Business Review* 90 (10):32–3.

Helsper, Ellen Johanna. 2012. "A Corresponding Fields Model of Digital Inclusion." *Communication Theory* 22 (4):403–26.

Ho, Alfred Tat-Kei, and Anna Ya Ni. 2004. "Explaining the Adoption of E-Government Features: A Case Study of Iowa County Treasurers' Offices." *American Review of Public Administration* 34 (2):164–80.

International City/County Management Association (ICMA). 2004. *2004 E-Government Survey*. Washington, DC: International City/County Management Association.

International City/County Management Association (ICMA). 2011. *Electronic Government 2011*. Washington, DC: International City/County Management Association.

Koppell, Jonathan GS. 2005. "Pathologies of Accountability: ICANN and the Challenge of 'Multiple Accountabilities Disorder'." *Public Administration Review* 65 (1):94–108.

Leighninger, Matt. 2011. "Using Online Tools to Engage—and be Engaged by—The Public." Washington, DC: IBM Center for the Business of Government.

LinkedIn. 2016. "About LinkedIn." LinkedIn. Available at: press.linkedin.com/about-linkedin (accessed September 1, 2016).

Melitski, James. 2003. "Capacity and E-Government Performance: An Analysis Based on Early Adopters of Internet Technologies in New Jersey." *Public Performance and Management Review* 26 (4):376–90.

Mergel, Ines. 2013. *Social Media in the Public Sector: A Guide to Participation, Collaboration and Transparency in the Networked World.* San Francisco, CA: John Wiley & Sons.

Milward, H. Brinton, and Keith Provan. 2000. "Governing the Hollow State." *Journal of Public Administration Research and Theory* 10 (2):359–79.

Moon, Jae, and Donald Norris. 2005. "Does Managerial Orientation Matter? The Adoption of Reinventing Government and E-Government at the Municipal Level." *Information Systems Journal* 15 (1):43–60.

Moore, Mark H. 1995. *Creating Public Value: Strategic Management in Government.* Cambridge, MA: Harvard University Press.

Mossberger, Karen, Caroline Tolbert, and Mary Stansbury. 2003. *Virtual Inequality: Beyond the Digital Divide.* Washington, DC: Georgetown University Press.

Norris, Donald, and Christopher Reddick. 2013. "Local E-Government in the United States: Transformation or Incremental Change?" *Public Administration Review* 73 (1):165–75.

Norris, Donald, and M. Jae Moon. 2005. "Advancing E-Government at the Grassroots: Tortoise or Hare?" *Public Administration Review* 65 (1): 64–74.

Norris, Donald F., Patricia D. Fletcher, and Stephen H. Holden. 2001. Is Your Local Government Plugged In? Highlights of the 2000 Electronic Government Survey. Washington, DC: ICMA.

Scholl, Hans J., and Ralf Klischewski. 2007. "E-Government Integration and Interoperability: Framing the Research Agenda." *International Journal of Public Administration* 30 (8/9):889–920.

The Economist. 2010. "A World of Connections: Special Report on Social Networking." *The Economist*, January 30.

The Economist. 2015. "Planet of the Phones." *The Economist*, February 28–March 6, 9.

The Economist. 2016a. "Briefing: The New Face of Facebook." *The Economist*, April 9, 21–4.

The Economist. 2016b. "China's Mobile Internet: WeChat's World." *The Economist*, August 6, 50–2.

The Economist. 2016c. "Wireless: The Next Generation." *The Economist*, February 20, 53–4.

United Nations. 2010. United Nations 2010 Global E-Government Survey: Leveraging E-government at a Time of Financial and Economic Crisis. New York: United Nations.

United Nations. 2012. United Nations E-Government Survey 2012: E-Government for the People. New York: United Nations.

United Nations. 2014. United Nations E-Government Survey 2014: E-Government for the Future We Want. New York: United Nations.

United Nations. 2016. United Nations E-Government Survey 2016: E-Government in Support of Sustainable Development. New York: Department of Economic and Social Affairs, United Nations.

Young, Suzanne. 2007. "Outsourcing: Uncovering the Complexity of the Decision." *International Public Management Journal* 10 (3):307–25.

Yu, Chien-Chih, and Marijn Janssen. 2010. "The Need for Strategic Management and Business Model Design in Government and Public Administration." *Electronic Government, An International Journal* 7 (4):299–315.

Zavattaro, Staci M., and Thomas A. Bryer, eds. 2016. *Social Media for Government: Theory and Practice*. New York: Routledge.

2 A Framework for Managing Digital Governance

Introduction

This chapter introduces a coherent management framework that guides public administrators and managers in their efforts to manage digital governance. The objective of this framework is to identify the main elements of digital governance and their interactions for the purpose of creating public values. As shown in Figure 2.1, the goal of digital governance should be the pursuit of public values, and these values should constitute the relevant measures of success.

Strategy and policy decisions should be made first, taking into account opportunities presented by interacting with organizations and citizens outside a governmental unit and internal management capacity. An overarching digital governance strategy will engage and interact with key stakeholders, seek cross-boundary collaboration, and utilize innovative information and communication technologies (ICTs) as represented by the two-way arrows in Figure 2.1.

The management layer covers three main areas of digital governance management. The first is resource management including information, financial, and technology resources. Digital governance performance management is another area that includes performance management as well as business process/project management. The third area is management of digital privacy and security. The priority and interaction between these three management areas should follow the digital governance strategy and policies established in the strategic layer.

This chapter will first introduce the core public values for digital governance and then go into the strategies and policy of digital governance from an enterprise perspective. Next, it will present the guiding principles for managing external stakeholders and forces. The remainder of the chapter is a detailed presentation of three management areas, including resources, risks, and performance as well as recommendations for capacity-building. This chapter will conclude with core ideas for this framework.

Public Values

The strategic imperative of digital governance for 21st-century public managers and administrators is the creation of public values. These core

Figure 2.1 Digital Governance Management Framework: Advancing Public Values

values should be broad and relevant to people around the world and in various socio-economic conditions. In addition, these values should reflect the unique opportunities presented by the ICTs in this new millennium. The strategic focus of ICT-driven digital governance reflects the general strategic notion of public value creation as articulated by Moore (1995).

Inclusiveness should be one of the core public values of digital governance. The advances of ICTs have created opportunities for some countries and communities to leapfrog by adopting the newest technologies, such as dramatically increasing the phone penetration rate by skipping landlines to adopt cellular phone services and offering internet connectivity at the same time. However, any introduction of ICTs also creates some form of digital divide between the haves and have nots, such as that between those with broadband access and those without. Given the tension between ICT adoption and digital divide, public managers should make their best effort to promote digital inclusion.

Sustainability is another overarching core value for digital governance. Digital governance should help address complex and long-term challenges facing countries and communities around the world. The use of ICTs by government has the potential to enhance our understanding of the nature of complex problems and the prospect of finding appropriate solutions. For example, environmental sustainability can be improved by implementing smart electric grids and intelligent water supply. In addition, the use of ICTs for collecting and analyzing financial information could aid government in monitoring financial markets and making informed decisions on financial sustainability (Chen 2012).

Public accountability is another core value. Governments are ultimately accountable to citizens in their countries or communities for the public resources entrusted to them. Accountability is at minimum about efficiency and effectiveness in the production and delivery of public information and services. Since the inception of the internet, more and more public information and services are being delivered online. Public managers should strive to improve efficiency and effectiveness as part of digital governance. A higher level of transparency via the use of ICTs by citizens also plays an important role in ensuring public accountability. Such transparency aids in reducing corruption and making government accountable (Bhatnagar 2003; Shim and Eom 2008).

More specific public values could be delineated under the three overarching values articulated above. For a three-to-five-year strategic digital government plan, a government can aspire to achieve more specific public values such as improved quality of public services, networks, and telecommunication infrastructure, as well as creation of economic opportunities. For instance, Chattanooga, Tennessee, in the United States touted itself as a Giga city with a fiber-to-home network spanning 600 square miles of the city. Such a move can help improve economic opportunities, offer workforce training, and increase efficiency and effectiveness of public services (Williams 2012). The City of Pueblo, Colorado, has set service improvement as one of the values its strategic information technology (IT) plan strives to accomplish. Such services expand beyond what an IT department provides to internal customers to include network infrastructure and services, external customers/citizens, and innovation (Information Technology Department 2011).

Strategic/Policy Layer

Strategic IT Management

This digital governance framework emphasizes enacting a strategic IT plan for a government. Strategic planning requires a government to articulate its mission and goals and how its actions support the achievement of those goals (Bryson 2011). Ensuring strategic alignment is beneficial for getting the best return on investment in advancing organizational goals. A strategic IT plan follows the same logic by aligning IT initiatives with the missions and goals of the organization as a whole (Dufner, Holley, and Reed 2003; Rocheleau 2006). Without such alignments, ICT projects could be driven by the preferences of separate departments, which typically results in lack of interoperability and redundancy in the technologies or information systems deployed. Moreover, having a strategic IT plan under the broader framework of an organizational strategic plan is important because the use of ICTs has become more pervasive in all aspects of government operation.

A digital governance strategic plan should take an enterprise and government-as-a-whole perspective. The ideal digital governance is highly integrated for serving and engaging its main stakeholders. It should include various departments of a government working together to provide stakeholder-centric public information and services rather than stakeholders having to negotiate or navigate various layers and departments of a government. For instance, a citizen service information system such as a 311 system in the United States allows integration of service information across various departments (Fleming 2008). Such a high level of integration is marked as a defining feature of digital governance (Chen and Hsieh 2009). This type of integration is also called for by advocates of holistic governance in order to instigate institutional reform to help solve complex public problems and improve public accountability (6 et al. 2002).

Public managers need to be aware of the differences in strategic IT planning between the public and private sectors. Strategic IT planning in the public sector tends to have a shorter time horizon than that in the private sector because of the election cycle, multiple and competing policy objectives, and a broader set and higher level of stakeholder involvement (Dufner, Holley, and Reed 2002). As a result, public managers need to address these unique features of strategic IT planning for digital governance by being flexible, making trade-offs, and involving key stakeholders.

A strategic digital governance plan must start with identifying and mobilizing key stakeholders in the first stage of setting strategic objectives. Key stakeholders should include internal ones—such as policy makers, managers, and employees—and external ones, such as representatives of citizens, businesses, and non-profit organizations. The setting of strategic objectives should strive to align them with the mission of the organization. Once the main objectives are set with a specific timetable, the core group should develop a plan to achieve these goals. This plan needs to include an inventory of existing ICT assets, more specific objectives in various areas of technologies, and implementation plans. Moreover, this plan should have a mechanism for periodic review and revision, as the landscape of technologies changes relatively quickly.

Leadership and Governance Structure

Top management support and leadership are critical in providing the foundation for strategic digital governance planning and management. Political will has been identified as one of the key driving factors for the use of ICTs in government (Ahn 2010; Ahn and Bretschneider 2011). This political will can be grounded in the perception of citizen demands (Ho and Ni 2004) or established as part of a political reform agenda (Ahn and Bretschneider 2011). Political appointees for a governmental agency, city council, or any legislative body can help instill the needed political support for digital governance with a focus on core public values. The critical role of top management support is evident in the implementation of large information systems such as enterprise resource planning software and citizen-centric information systems (Chen 2010).

Leadership is critical in finding and maintaining the strategic focus of a governmental agency/enterprise. Developing a shared understanding of the mission and goals of a public-sector organization takes a considerable amount of leadership (Bryson 2011). Each sub-unit of a government tends to have its own priorities influenced by its mission and the preferences of key decision-makers and stakeholders. These different priorities could lead to turf issues that have been identified in the e-government literature as one of the barriers to information-sharing across boundaries (Dawes 1996; Dawes, Cresswell, and Pardo 2009). Leadership can put organizational goals and objectives above the interests of individuals or departments (Enns, Huff, and Higgins 2003).

Establishing a governance structure in support of the central role of ICT in government helps to maintain the strategic focus of digital governance and its alignment with core public values. The elevation of a chief information or technology officer to a cabinet (department) level position provides needed participation by the chief person responsible for information and IT in various aspects of government operation. This role can be further differentiated in the creation of chief digital security officers, chief knowledge officers, chief innovation officers, and other sub-roles that meet the needs of a particular government or public-service organization.

An important governance structure that fits a more federated government structure is a chief information officer (CIO) council. This council will allow coordination among various governmental agencies in advancing the collective interests and considerations of government as a whole above the interests of individual agencies. Such a governance structure is needed for the formulation and implementation of digital governance policies and procedures such as digital inclusion, open government, and digital privacy and security.

Strategic Alignment for Policies

With regard to policy, the attention of the digital governance leadership should be on achieving alignment with core public values and missions. The goal of a digital governance policy should help advance a specific core public value. The main governance body for digital governance, either a council or a CIO office, needs to ensure policy objectives are in alignment with the core values of digital governance. To achieve the stated policy objectives, governments must possess a specific implementation plan with allocated resources. For instance, an open digital government policy should have online transparency as one of the main policy objectives for improving virtual accountability. This policy should connect to the strategic information technology plan for the organization and be further developed with implementation details. The role of leadership is to ensure the needed resources and to resolve potential conflict for successful implementation.

An example of aligning digital governance goals with core values is demonstrated by achieving accountability via formulation and implementation of digital privacy and security policies. These policies should be included as part of a strategic information technology plan for the organization. In addition, appropriate resources should go into securing government servers and databases to safeguard citizens' personal information entrusted to government to ensure implementation. Failure to do so has severe consequences, as seen in the security breaches in the U.S. Office of Personnel Management reported in 2015 that compromised the records of more than 22.1 million affected people.[1] Successful implementation of these policies is likely to earn the trust of citizens because they see loss of personal information as a main concern. Another example of such alignment involves advancing inclusiveness as a strategic public value. A policy making government websites, social media, and other online communication channels available to all segments of demographics can help advance inclusiveness. The specific policy measures could be about accommodating those who are visually impaired or those who can only access the internet via smart phones. These measures are in alignment with achieving digital inclusion as an overarching core policy value.

Guiding Principles for Managing External Environment

Stakeholder-focused Online Interactions

Stakeholders are central to the interaction enabled by ICT between a government and its external environment. Citizens constitute the primary group of stakeholders because government exists to provide services to them. In addition to citizens, a successful digital governance strategy should also include businesses, non-profits (non-governmental), and other governments. Governments' regulatory obligations drive interactions between government and businesses, including business registration, regulatory compliance, and taxes, among others. Interaction with businesses could be a prime area for realizing the efficiency gain of ICT use (Chen and Thurmaier 2008). The user fees charged for online business services are an important source of revenue to pay for the establishment of e-government services that are beneficial not only to businesses, but also to citizens and non-profit organizations.

Non-profit (non-governmental) organizations have become increasingly involved in the delivery of public services, especially in the social-service area. A digital governance strategy should also engage these non-profit organizations to realize core public values such as inclusiveness. Other governments are main stakeholders because of the need for inter-governmental collaboration for cross-boundary public problems such as cybersecurity, public safety, natural disasters, etc. A coherent digital governance strategy should take into account all stakeholders and produce synergy among digital governance development that leverages cross-sector collaboration.

Governments should be responsive to stakeholder needs for successful interaction. This responsiveness could take the form of putting needed public information and services online for citizens, businesses, non-profit organizations, and other governments. Such responsiveness could also involve providing a mechanism for two-way communication or even an electronic forum for these stakeholders to voice their concerns. Stakeholder demands can help guide prioritization of digital governance initiatives. Moreover, responsiveness in digital governance should help provide access to online government information and services because digital access is a basic requirement for any online interaction with government. Governments should address digital divide issues not only among citizens, but also businesses and non-profits.

Creation of public values should guide stakeholder interactions, and such interactions should serve the purpose of advancing public values. Efficient and effective public services free of favoritism and corruption are desirable public values for all stakeholders. Additionally, digital inclusion is likely to advance inclusiveness. Smart city/smart government initiatives can help with sustainable management of natural, financial, and human resources.

Cross-boundary Collaboration

When working with external stakeholders for cross-boundary collaboration, governments should act increasingly as a partner or network manager that leverages resources rather than remains solely responsible for production and delivery of public services. Governments can be a partner in a consortium to address cybersecurity issues that cut across various levels of government and require cooperation of information-sharing across jurisdictions, as seen in the Multi-State Information Sharing and Analysis Center (MS-ISAC). Alternatively, governments can be a network manager to organize a network of geographic information systems (GIS) experts in pursuing innovative ways of leveraging GIS for improving government services (Agranoff 2007).

Governments can enable innovation for open collaboration. For instance, the Challenges and Prizes Program in the United States is a government-led effort to promote open innovation and competition to provide the best solutions to public problems. Governments can also enable innovations by providing common data standards, such as resource description framework (RDF) documents for data mesh-ups.[2] These kinds of data and application programming interface (API) standards, as well as technical frameworks, will enable software developers to combine various data resources to better understand public problems such as the relationship between energy use and demographics.

The goal of cross-boundary open collaboration should be the creation of public values. The role of government should be to motivate individual and organizational collaborators to focus on realizing public values and to measure progress accordingly. Since governments are ultimately accountable for the results of these open-collaboration initiatives, governments should devote energy to ensuring realization of public values such as inclusiveness, sustainability, and accountability.

Innovative ICT Utilization

Governments can utilize innovative ICTs in leveraging advances in the telecommunication and IT industries. The development of cloud computing offers a new opportunity for governments to leverage economy of scale and industry expertise with a reduced cost for producing the same level of IT services in-house. The availability of mobile devices and tablet computers also offers an array of new opportunities for governments to increase the effectiveness of their field workers and delivery of public services in interacting with community members on site.

Innovative use also entails ICT-enabled business process reengineering. Governments can use an electronic government information exchange system to facilitate the exchange of government information and streamline the approval process of permits and licenses. Such innovation can bring efficiency and effectiveness to public services. Another innovative use of IT is a cloud-based case management system that allows providers of human services (i.e. mental health, job training, and homeless shelter) to create a holistic view of individuals and help them to more effectively reach independence.

The more recent development of semantic web also offers governments opportunities for innovative utilization. One example is the use of XBRL, a semantic web (a.k.a. Web 3.0) language, for increasing financial transparency and accountability in the United States and the enabling of standard business reporting in Australia. Moreover, the amount of government data in digital format has grown exponentially with access to real-time information in various formats (i.e. text, images) and types (i.e. location, transaction). These data tend to be more about actual behavior (i.e. online transactions) than opinions (survey data).

Big data and big data analytics offer governments opportunities to generate business insights and intelligence to improve the efficiency and effectiveness of public service (Desouza 2014). Moreover, such use of big data analytics holds the promise of making government more responsive to the needs of citizens and other stakeholders as well as providing a more personalized service to them (Goldsmith and Crawford 2014). The growing trend of developing an innovation ecosystem to serve as a platform for the development and application of ICT innovations holds potential to further improve public service (Greenberg 2015). The rise of artificial intelligence, virtual reality, and other innovative technologies will continue to push the envelope of ICTs and their applications for public service.

Managing Resources for Digital Governance

Information Resources

Information should be treated as a strategic resource. Such thinking is a departure from treating information as something generated in the course of production and delivery of public services as opposed to using that information to help accomplish a strategic objective. The Clinger-Cohen Act of 1996 (formally known as the Information Technology Management Reform Act) emphasizes the strategic nature of information as a resource. The strategic relevance of information has become increasingly apparent recently with more and more information available in electronic formats across departments to create a government-wide view. For instance, a citizen service information system (also known as a 311 system) allows government to gauge efficiency and effectiveness in delivering public services to citizens and strategic allocation of resources to under-performing areas of public services.

A cabinet-level position to advocate information as a resource for all areas of government operation is critical for strategic information resource management. The mandated designation of CIOs for all federal agencies by the Clinger-Cohen Act of 1996 is such an effort to ensure a strategic consideration of utilizing information for improving government operations in all areas of public services—such as finance, education, public safety, transportation, human services, etc. State governments and large local governments in the United States tend to have a designated CIO position for the same exact purpose. For instance, a strategic use of information could be about improving accountability by making government performance information available online while attending to protection of individual privacy.

Information resource management needs to follow the two mega principles as articulated by Dawes (2010): stewardship and usefulness. Stewardship, at minimum, is about ensuring the quality and availability of information. Since government services and operation depend on correct information, information quality such as accuracy and integrity is critical in government information resource management. For instance, an erroneous piece of information could result in denying a senior citizen social security benefits that he/she depends on for survival. Availability requires preservation of information and access to information as deemed appropriate. As a result, archiving government information, such as the role of the National Archive in the United States, is critical for government since citizens and all other organizations depend on government for storing these vital records for their operation. Information access should also be part of stewardship; government should provide governmental employees and citizens with access to vital information.

Utility of information is a vital quality for turning information into a resource. Usefulness is about the experience of information users (Dawes 2010, 380), and usually involves allowing the information users to improve job performance in a work situation. For instance, a public employee will find the estimated time for processing a building permit useful when asked by a contractor. Citizens are likely to find information about vital records useful when they are experiencing life events (such as marriage, the birth of a child, etc.). Information resource management should attend to usefulness from the perspective of information users.

Financial Resources

Financing digital government projects has consistently been identified as one of the two most serious challenges facing e-government for U.S. local governments (International City/County Management Association (ICMA) 2004, 2011). The fiscal challenges facing governments around the world further highlight the need to address this issue. A range of funding options is available for governments to pay for digital governance projects. User fees are considered one of the funding options as users pay for the convenience of transacting with government electronically. Another option is the so-called self-funding model in which government does not pay for any of the development and hosting of e-government services. The initial development and later operating cost is borne by an e-government website-hosting company and such cost is recovered by charging a user fee. In addition, funds for technology can also come from the general fund, as technology is an integral part of all government operation. Governments can also issue bonds for technology-related infrastructure projects. Partnership (shared services) is also an option for finding financial resources for digital governance projects. Such a partnership could be with a community organization or individuals that provide WiFi services with no cost to government. Governments can also form a consortium for shared IT services, such as a GIS.

Public finance principles can help choose the appropriate funding mechanism. The benefit principle of public finance establishes the relevance of user fees for e-government services that benefit a select group of individuals and/or organizations. In contrast, basic required services that are provided electronically for all residents should be paid by broad-based revenue sources such as property taxes rather than charging additional user fees. Moreover, government should look for projects with positive production and consumption externalities that yield the most return on investment (Chen and Thurmaier 2008). This is a way to leverage limited financial resources for digital governance projects. The issuance of bond or capital financing is appropriate for telecommunication infrastructure projects such as laying fiber optics for community anchor organizations (schools, public libraries, community centers, etc.) due to the need for a large initial investment for long-term economic returns.

Technology Resources

Governments also need to manage their technology resources wisely. Governments typically face two challenges associated with their information technologies. First is the proliferation of information technologies and systems as each department in a government tends to buy systems, databases, and technologies optimized for their own independent departments. As a result, there are silos and a growing array of systems, data, and technologies for IT directors (or CIOs) to manage. The second main challenge is the existence of legacy systems. Legacy systems refer to antiquated software programs, hardware, computers, and information systems that were created decades ago and are difficult to maintain and upgrade. Modernization can be relatively difficult to come by when governments are under budget constraints for major system changes. As a result, usually only patchwork is put in place to meet a pressing need. Legacy systems are difficult to maintain, as the parts and requisite programming skills are in short supply. It is also challenging to extract timely and relevant service information because of the antiquated data structure and the need for extensive programming for such information extraction.

A portfolio approach is productive in addressing the problem of proliferation and fragmentation of government information technologies and systems. This approach aims to curb the multiplication of specialized systems and the associated maintenance costs, and to promote IT procurement with benefits to the entire government rather than a single department. Such a portfolio begins with an inventory of existing technologies and systems by taking an enterprise point of view (McKeen and Smith 2002). Top government executives and managers then have a more comprehensive view of the organization's technology assets. A desired future state of the portfolio needs to be articulated to guide future purchases and the phase-out of technologies and systems in alignment with government's strategic goals. The development of a strategic IT plan for a government can accomplish both the inventory and plan for a strategically focused inventory. The implementation of such a portfolio requires a decision body that puts the interest of the government as a whole above individual departments. This governance structure could be a CIO that oversees all technology-related purchases for a small local government or a CIO council for a state government that helps coordinate and prioritize technological assets to maintain a healthy portfolio.

A conscious effort to modernize and integrate government information technologies and systems helps address the challenges of legacy systems. This effort is best guided by a strategic vision for digital governance, which could be a gradual move to put all the disparate systems onto the same platform (such as .net). Alternatively, it could be a slow transition to cloud computing by treating software as a service (SaaS). Funding should give priority to those modernization and integration projects that are consistent with the strategic direction of the entire government.

The portfolio approach has become even more relevant with the growing use of a variety of social media and social networking services. The growing array of social media and their use require a more comprehensive and coherent approach (Mergel 2013). More importantly, social media should be incorporated into an overall online communication and engagement strategy that includes social media, website, texting, and other aspects to advance public value (Dumont 2013). Moreover, such an inclusive online communication and engagement technology portfolio should be further integrated into a larger portfolio that includes a customer relationship management system, enterprise resource management system, and other legacy ICT systems.

Managing Privacy and Security Risks for Digital Governance

Protecting Digital Privacy

Digital privacy is an important consideration of digital governance as governments around the world wish to earn the trust of their citizens. The amount of information citizens provide online in digital format has increased dramatically over the last few years due to the use of social media, e-commerce, and e-government. However, the salience of digital privacy concerns varies from country to country due to differing cultures, history, and ICT use. In the United States, digital privacy is not construed as an absolute right of citizens, but an important protection that government offers to avoid unnecessary intrusion of others into one's personal life (Cullen 2009). In Europe, there is an established practice of personal data protection that aims to limit the use of personal data only to the intended purposes (OECD 1980), and such protection has been extended to data in digital format. In Asia, digital privacy is a relatively new concept, as the notion of privacy does not have an established history in a more centralized administrative system and communal culture. Despite the variation in the level of concerns about digital privacy, the shared goal is for governments to provide citizens with privacy protection proportional to their concerns in order to earn their trust.

For public administrators, one of the main policy challenges is to balance privacy and access. The move to making more public information online, as some e-government initiatives do, presents challenges to digital privacy. For instance, the publication of property information online (public records in the United States) may compromise privacy as one can search for the property holding of an individual in a community by going online. The e-government's move to provide more personalized services to citizens would require data linkages to create a profile, which poses the risk of exposing a large amount of an individual's personal information in the event of a security breach. The disclosure of raw government data sets as part of open government initiatives for citizens and civil groups to use also poses privacy concerns if the information is not screened properly. The challenge is to find a way to maximize the benefits of integrated e-government service and open government while minimizing the risk of invasion into privacy.

An appropriate approach to the protection of digital privacy includes both institutional and technical solutions. Digital privacy issues continue to evolve with advances of ICTs such as drones and surveillance technologies. As a result, an appropriate protective measure should have an institutional mechanism such as periodic review and active monitoring of new privacy threats to keep up with technological developments. Moreover, a board or an individual should be designated to safeguard digital privacy with regard to information that a government is responsible for. It could be a privacy officer, privacy review board, or a national commission whose primary responsibility is to safeguard informational privacy.

Technical solutions are evolving. Some basic ones include de-identification to remove identifiable personal information from the records (such as social security numbers) before sharing or releasing them to the public. For releasing information with patterns, such as census tracking, caution can be taken by scrambling the information but preserving the main pattern for decision-making. More sophisticated approaches include embedding privacy rules in an enterprise resource planning/management system. With a unique employer identification number and access control, personal information such as health records, social security number, and other information is less likely to be released or captured by unauthorized access.

Digital Security (Cybersecurity)

Digital security (cybersecurity) has become an increasingly important digital governance issue (Deloitte-NASCIO 2014; Government Accountability Office (GAO) 2012). Digital security is a broad conceptualization that deals with both internal and external security threats to data and information in electronic/digital format. Some people put more emphasis on cybersecurity or cyberterrorism to link digital security to national security and cyberspace. Others pay more attention to internal operations within private networks, servers, and internal computer systems. Digital security is foundational to digital privacy because secured personal data is a basic requirement for privacy. The main objective of digital security is to achieve confidentiality, integrity, and availability of digital information (Bishop 2002; Radl and Chen 2005).

The policy and management challenges associated with digital security include the evolving nature of security threats, the human element, the balance between security and access, and the resource investment. Security threats change with new developments in ICTs. The increasing popularity of mobile devices introduces a new set of security threats when they are connected to secure networks (Opsahl 2011; Deloitte-NASCIO 2014). Humans are the weakest link in any defense against digital security threats, and human errors, either intentional or accidental, are responsible for the majority of digital security issues (Reddick 2009). The tension between security and access presents a particular challenge to public managers who wish to provide integrated and open online public services because easy and open access to digital information poses security risks. In addition, securing digital information requires resources. Governments need to make the necessary resource investment both in the technologies and organizational processes to mitigate the risks associated with cybercrime and cybersecurity threats.

The overarching solution to the management challenges of digital security is the adoption of a risk management approach as utilized by the U.S. Federal Government (mandated by the Federal Information Security Management Act). Digital security should not be viewed as an absolute standard to achieve, but, instead, a portfolio of risks to be managed. Such a management approach first requires identification and prioritization of risks, and then a management plan for risk mitigation. Such a plan typically involves awareness, education, and training crucial to reducing the number of human errors. In addition, this type of plan utilizes intrusion detection systems, security patches, and other technologies to mitigate cybersecurity threats. More importantly, the evolving nature of digital security threats requires a governance body that conducts periodic reviews of digital security threats and implements measures to address them.

Managing Performance of Digital Governance

Performance Management Systems

Public managers need to manage the performance of digital governance to realize the public value propositions. Overarching values such as inclusiveness, sustainability, and accountability should first be translated into concrete strategic goals and objectives for the medium-term of three to five years. For instance, a strategic objective for inclusiveness can be offering broadband access to 95 percent of the population in two years. Once such a specific, measurable, and feasible objective is set, public managers can track progress. Another example is the use of IT for sustainability by cutting water waste by 10 percent.

The use of key performance indicators (KPIs) is critical to the success of performance management systems for digital governance. The process of creating KPIs should involve key stakeholders of digital governance, including government, citizens, businesses, non-profits, etc. These KPIs should include both internal and external perspectives. An internal perspective focuses more on the performance of IT services provided to and perceived by government employees such as satisfaction with IT support and a quality rating for information systems. An external perspective will incorporate citizen and business satisfaction with online government information and services. For instance, citizens measure e-government performance by ease of navigation, ability to find relevant information, likelihood to revisit the site, overall satisfaction, etc. (Morgeson 2012). These performance indicators could also include the level of transparency as measured by the type and details of government information made available online.

These performance scores, when feasible, should be linked to cost to understand return on investment. Such a focus on return on investment is consistent with the notion of accountability for efficient and effective use of government resources. Given the nature of digital governance projects, return should be measured more broadly to include both tangible and intangible benefits. Tangible benefits typically include reduction in staff time, savings in printing and mailing costs, reduced time for processing service requests, provision of personalized and efficient services, etc. Intangible benefits are those more difficult to quantify, but linked to overarching values that digital governance intends to promote. These benefits include more citizen involvement, higher level of transparency, open innovation, etc.

Business Process and Project Management Systems

Major performance improvement usually comes from reengineering business processes. The introduction of ICTs typically offers opportunities for streamlining and, if done properly, reengineering business processes. For instance, sequential approval of government-issued student loans relying on regular mail can be streamlined using electronic submission of these applications and web-based access for approval. Reengineering of the process could take the form of joint approval rather than a sequential one and electronic exchange and approval rather than a paper-based process, such as seen in local governments in Britain (Dhillon, Weerakkody, and Dwivedi 2008).

Digital governance needs to take a step further by adopting an enterprise view of business process reengineering, also known as business process management (BPM) (Schurter 2005). The BPM perspective allows public managers to observe the variety and interdependence of existing business processes such as permitting, zoning, and online payment. This perspective will further the goal of identifying high return on investment ICT projects that have the potential to enable and transform business processes for the entire government.

The implementation of these transformational and high-performing projects requires the discipline of project management. Project management has established itself as a discipline with its concepts, tools, and techniques, and the basic components of project management include project goals, tasks, resources, schedule, and contingency plan. Project management also requires a holistic view of how various components come together to produce the project deliverables as captured by a Gantt chart. A project manager oversees the entire project and is ultimately accountable for the result. Moreover, IT project management in digital governance is influenced by various contextual forces in the public sector such as election cycles and the resultant changes in leadership and priorities, rules for administrative procedures and civil servants, etc. The advice is to maintain focus on the overall direction of the project (i.e. providing integrated e-government services) rather than on specifics (i.e. when to bring what system online) (Miller 2006).

Capacity-building for Digital Governance

Strategic Digital Governance Planning and Execution

One overarching leadership and management skill for successful digital governance is strategic digital governance management. This strategic perspective allows the lead public manager, usually a CIO, to plan and execute digital governance initiatives from an enterprise (government-as-a-whole) perspective while taking into account both internal management and external relationships with various stakeholders.

More specifically, a CIO or IT manager should be skilled in strategic management in general and strategic IT planning in particular (Dawes 2004). This strategic perspective will require an environmental scan to identify the comparative advantage of his/her government as well as the strengths, weaknesses, opportunities, and challenges facing it. The formulation of a strategic vision should take into account the main stakeholders of digital governance, including citizens/residents, businesses, and non-profit organizations. This also requires a keen understanding of the political and institutional realities facing governments.

Execution of a strategic plan is as crucial as its formulation. A successful execution requires CIOs to be skillful in leadership and communication. Leadership skills are needed to align management plans and operational tasks with strategic priorities of the organization. Such leadership needs to be grounded in a clear understanding of the institutional constraints and incentives facing various departments/units of a government and how to align departmental goals and incentives to the government as a whole. For instance, the CIO training at the federal government in the United States puts emphasis on familiarity with the relevant laws and regulations that shape institutional constraints and incentives (CIO Council 2012).

Managing External Stakeholders and Relationships

An effective leader for digital governance can skillfully manage external stakeholders and relationships with them. The guiding principle articulated earlier calls for stakeholder-focused interactions. For digital governance, the stakeholders include citizens, businesses, other governments, and non-profit organizations. An effective digital governance manager needs to gather information on stakeholders' expectations for digital governance, such as electronic participation and availability of online services. Moreover, such a manager needs to find synergy in diverse expectations of stakeholders to advance digital governance. In pursuing synergy, a CIO can introduce an online platform for public affairs dialogues that benefit various stakeholders.

Increasingly, digital governance requires collaboration of organizations and individuals across organizational boundaries and sectors (public, private, and non-profit). For instance, a shared service model for GIS requires collaboration between various governments. Collaborative governance requires public managers to activate and mobilize key organizations and individuals and keep them focused on the shared goals (McGuire 2002). Effective collaborative governance also needs to consider the appropriate form of governance to fit the resource endowment and implementation realities of collaboration (Provan and Kenis 2008).

Another important skill in managing external relationships is facilitating open innovation for digital governance. This skill is particularly relevant given the enabling effect of ICTs to reach national and international audiences for providing innovative solutions to public problems. A CIO needs to understand the nature of problems most suitable for open innovation, such as the generation of policy ideas. Managing the innovation process requires careful design of incentives and execution. For example, the lessons learned from the Challenges and Prizes Program in the United States are instructive.

Skills in Managing Resources, Performance, and Trust for Digital Governance

An effective public manager for digital governance needs to possess skills in managing resources, performance, and trust for enabling ICTs. The first set of skills concerns managing financial, information, and technology resources. Skills in leveraging information as a strategic resource, as articulated in the Clinger-Cohen Act, are critical. The ability to find financial resources for digital governance projects is equally important, as lack of funding is an enduring issue for improving digital governance. Lastly, the ability to manage a diverse and sometimes dated technology portfolio is essential for digital public governance because governments tend to have an array of information systems and technologies.

An effective CIO would be able to improve the performance of digital governance projects. At minimum, a performance review body is required to conduct reviews of digital governance proposals and existing digital governance projects. KPIs need to be included in the evaluation, with strategic objectives as one of the indicators. An enterprise perspective is critical to conduct BPM that spans from a single business process to include multiple core business processes for government to leverage ICTs to transform public services. Moreover, a CIO needs to develop and implement performance measures for digital privacy and security to earn the trust of citizens, businesses, non-profit organizations, other governments, etc. Adoption of an overarching risk management approach would be productive in this endeavor.

Conclusion

This chapter introduced a digital governance framework that is driven by guiding core public values. This framework is organized around an enterprise (government-as-a-whole) strategic perspective that simultaneously considers external stakeholders and relationships with them as well as the internal management of resources, performance, and privacy and security. The enterprise strategic perspective highlights the importance of strategic IT management, the leadership and governance structure, and the strategic alignment of major policies and implementation plans.

Effective management of external relationships with a multitude of stakeholders requires some core guiding principles. One principle is to conduct stakeholder-focused interactions in which a government regularly interacts with key stakeholders (citizens, businesses, other governments, and non-profits) to understand their digital governance concerns and priorities. Another principle is to foster cross-boundary collaboration through which a government can serve as a focal organization to leverage partnerships between citizens, businesses, and non-profit organizations. The third principle is to promote and utilize ICT innovations. To that end, an open innovation model with rapid adoption is productive.

Simultaneously, this digital governance framework pays attention to internal management and operation. First, digital governance is about better managing information, financial, and technology resources. Information should be treated as a strategic organization resource rather than a by-product. Developing appropriate business models and finding sources of revenue for digital governance initiatives are equally important for governments facing fiscal challenges. A portfolio approach to managing diverse technology assets is recommended.

Second, a governance structure and a performance information system need to exist to track and improve performance of digital governance initiatives. One of the KPIs should be the extent to which such an initiative realizes the core public values espoused in the strategic plan. Performance improvement can be further achieved by the discipline of project management and by the transformational potential of BPM.

These elements of successfully managing digital governance underscore a set of competencies for leaders and managers. These include the ability to conduct strategic digital governance planning for the entire organization and to execute it with superior communication skills for achieving strategic alignment of various priorities of stakeholders. Next, the skills to manage external stakeholders and build relationships with them are equally important because governments are increasingly relying on collaboration/partnership with organizations and individuals outside government for the production and delivery of public services online. Finally, the core skill set for managing information, finances, and technology as resources, along with the ability to manage performance and engender trust via protecting digital privacy and security, are important.

The next few chapters will examine the various goals and challenges of digital governance with a focus on digital inclusion, digital infrastructure, and integrated citizen-centric digital government services. The framework proposed in this chapter will serve as a guide for developing a digital governance strategy to accomplish these goals. Then, the next few chapters will cover internal management and external relationship building, with the last substantive chapter on capacity-building. The concluding chapter will summarize the challenges as well as solutions to advance to the next level of digital governance.

Notes

1 This is based on a news article published in the *Washington Post*. For more details, see www.washingtonpost.com/news/federal-eye/wp/2015/07/09/hack-of-security-clearance-system-affected-21-5-million-people-federal-authorities-say/, accessed January 20, 2016.
2 For details, see www.data.gov/developer/page/semantic-web, accessed November 10, 2012.

References

6, Perri, Diana Leat, Kimberly Seltzer, and Gerry Stoker. 2002. *Toward Holistic Governance: The New Reform Agenda*. New York: Palgrave.

Agranoff, Robert. 2007. "Managing within Networks: Adding Value to Public Organizations." In *Public Management and Change Series*, edited by Beryl Radin. Washington, DC: Georgetown University Press.

Ahn, Michael. 2010. "Adoption of E-Communication Applications in U.S. Municipalities: The Role of Political Environment, Bureaucratic Structure, and the Nature of Applications." *American Review of Public Administration* 71 (4):428–52.

Ahn, Michael J., and Stuart Bretschneider. 2011. "Politics of E-Government: E-Government and the Political Control of Bureaucracy." *Public Administration Review* 71 (3):414–24.

Bhatnagar, S. 2003. "E-government and Access to Information." In *Global Corruption Report* 2003. Washington, DC: Transparency International.
Bishop, Matt. 2002. *Computer Security: Art and Science.* Boston, MA: Addison-Wesley.
Bryson, John M. 2011. *Strategic Planning for Public and Nonprofit Organizations: A Guide to Strengthening and Sustaining Organizational Achievement.* Fourth edition. San Francisco, CA: Jossey-Bass.
Chen, Yu-Che. 2010. "Citizen-Centric E-Government Services: Understanding Integrated Citizen Service Information Systems." *Social Science Computer Review* 28 (4):427–42.
Chen, Yu-Che. 2012. "A Comparative Study of E-Government XBRL Implementations: The Potential of Improving Information Transparency and Efficiency." *Government Information Quarterly* 29 (4):553–63.
Chen, Yu-Che, and Jun-Yi Hsieh. 2009. "Advancing E-Governance: Comparing Taiwan and the United States." *Public Administration Review* 69 (Supplement 1): S151–8.
Chen, Yu-Che, and Kurt Thurmaier. 2008. "Advancing E-Government: Financing Challenges and Opportunities." *Public Administration Review* 48 (3):537–48.
CIO Council. 2012. *2012 Clinger-Cohen Core Competencies & Learning Objectives.* Washington, DC: CIO Council.
Cullen, R. 2009. "Culture, Identity and Information Privacy in the Age of Digital Government." *Online Information Review* 33 (3):405–21.
Dawes, Sharon. 1996. "Interagency Information Sharing: Expected Benefits, Manageable Risks." *Journal of Policy Analysis and Management* 15 (3): 377–94.
Dawes, Sharon. 2004. "Training the IT-Savvy Public Manager: Priorities and Strategies for Public Management Education." *Journal of Public Affairs Education* 10 (1):5–17.
Dawes, Sharon S. 2010. "Stewardship and Usefulness: Policy Principles for Information-based Transparency." *Government Information Quarterly* 27 (4): 377–83.
Dawes, Sharon, Anthony Cresswell, and Theresa Pardo. 2009. "From 'Need to Know' to 'Need to Share': Tangled Problems, Information Boundaries, and the Building of Public Sector Knowledge Networks." *Public Administration Review* 69 (3):392–402.
Deloitte-NASCIO. 2014. "2014 Deloitte-NASCIO Cybersecurity Study: State Governments at Risk: Time to Move Forward." Deloitte and the National Association of State Chief Information Officers (NASCIO).
Desouza, Kevin C. 2014. "Realizing the Promise of Big Data." Washington, DC: IBM Center for the Business of Government.
Dhillon, Gurjit Singh, Vishanth Weerakkody, and Yogesh Kumar Dwivedi. 2008. "Realising Transformational Stage E-Government: A UK Local Authority Perspective." *Electronic Government: An International Journal* 5 (2):162–80.
Dufner, Donna, Lyn M. Holley, and B. J. Reed. 2002. "Can Private Sector Strategic Information Systems Planning Techniques Work for the Public Sector?" *Communication of the Association for Information Systems* 8:413–31.
Dufner, Donna, Lyn M. Holley, and B. J. Reed. 2003. "Strategic Information Systems Planning and U.S. County Government." *Communications of the Association for Information Systems* 11:219–44.

Dumont, Georgette. 2013. "Transparency or Accountability? The Purpose of Online Technologies for Nonprofits." *International Review of Public Administration* 18 (3):7–29.

Enns, Harvey G., Sid L. Huff, and Christopher A. Higgins. 2003. "CIO Lateral Influence Behaviors: Gaining Peers' Commitment to Strategic Information Systems." *MIS Quarterly* 27 (1):155–76.

Fleming, Cory. 2008. "Call 311: Connecting Citizens to Local Government Case Study Series: Minneapolis 311 System." Washington, DC: International City/County Management Association.

Goldsmith, Stephen, and Susan Crawford. 2014. *The Responsive City: Engaging Communities Through Data-Smart Governance*. San Francisco, CA: Jossey-Bass.

Government Accountability Office (GAO). 2012. *Cybersecurity: Threats Impacting the Nation*. Washington, DC: Government Accountability Office.

Greenberg, Sherri. 2015. "Using Innovation and Technology to Improve City Services." Washington, DC: IBM Center for the Business of Government.

Ho, Alfred Tat-Kei, and Anna Ya Ni. 2004. "Explaining the Adoption of E-Government Features: A Case Study of Iowa County Treasurers' Offices." *American Review of Public Administration* 34 (2):164–80.

Information Technology Department. 2011. Information Technology Strategic Plan Revision 4.0. Pueblo, CO: City of Pueblo.

International City/County Management Association (ICMA). 2004. 2004 E-Government Survey. Washington, DC: International City/County Management Association.

International City/County Management Association (ICMA). 2011. Electronic Government 2011. Washington, DC: International City/County Management Association.

McGuire, Michael. 2002. "Managing Networks: Propositions on What Managers Do and Why They Do It." *Public Administration Review* 62 (5):599–609.

McKeen, James, and Heather Smith. 2002. "New Development in Practice IV: Managing the Technology Portfolio." *Communications of the Association for Information Systems* 9:77–89.

Mergel, Ines. 2013. *Social Media in the Public Sector: A Guide to Participation, Collaboration and Transparency in the Networked World*. San Francisco, CA: John Wiley & Sons.

Miller, Emory. 2006. "Limp Kites and Unfulfilled Projects." *Public CIO* 4 (3):32–7.

Moore, Mark H. 1995. *Creating Public Value: Strategic Management in Government*. Cambridge, MA: Harvard University Press.

Morgeson, Forrest V. III. 2012. "E-Government Performance Measurement: A Citizen-Centric Approach in Theory and Practice." In *Electronic Governance and Cross-Boundary Collaboration: Innovations and Advancing Tools*, edited by Yu-Che Chen and Pin-Yu Chu, 422. Hershey, PA: IGI Global.

OECD. 1980. Recommendation of the Council Concerning Guidelines Governing the Protection of Privacy and Transborder Flows of Personal Data. Paris, France: OECD.

Opsahl, Andy. 2011. "CIOs Cope with Personal iPads and Smartphones on Secure Networks." *Government Technology* 24 (8).

Provan, Keith, and Patrick Kenis. 2008. "Modes of Network Governance: Structure, Management, and Effectiveness." *Journal of Public Administration Research and Theory* 18 (2):229–52.

Radl, Alison, and Yu-Che Chen. 2005. "Computer Security in Electronic Government: A State-Local Education Information System." *International Journal of Electronic Government Research* 1 (1):79–99.

Reddick, Christopher G. 2009. "Management Support and Information Security: An Empirical Study of Texas State Agencies in the USA." *Electronic Government, An International Journal* 6 (4):361–77.

Rocheleau, Bruce. 2006. *Public Management Information Systems*. Hershey, PA: Idea Group Publishing.

Schurter, Terry. 2005. "Business Process Management." In *Technologies for Government Transformation*, edited by Shayne Kavanagh and Rowan Miranda, 235–47. Chicago: Government Finance Officers Association.

Shim, Dong Chul, and Tae Ho Eom. 2008. "E-government and Anti-corruption: Empirical Analysis of International Data." *International Journal of Public Administration* 31 (3):298–316.

Williams, Matt. 2012. "King of the Hill." *Government Technology* 25 (4):12–17.

3 Digital Divide, Digital Inclusion, and Digital Opportunities

Introduction

The development of telecommunication over the last century has afforded the populations in most developed countries almost ubiquitous access to telephone, with a reported 97 percent penetration rate by the International Telecommunication Union as early as 2007.[1] In contrast, internet access in the United States, even with the rapid development of internet technologies and social media over the last two decades, is still below a 90 percent penetration rate as of 2015.[2] Ideal digital governance requires the ability of citizens, businesses, and non-profits to connect and communicate with governments via digital means. Therefore, governments around the world are particularly concerned with the issue of access because e-government, like other public services, should strive for universal access.

The digital divide has been a concern for public administration scholars and practitioners alike because of its implications for social equity and economic development. As a result, it is important to understand the type and nature of such a divide. Typically, digital divide is primarily viewed as an access divide between people who have internet access and those who do not. However, digital divide, as argued by Mossberger, Tolbert, and Stansbury (2003) and Helsper (2012), extends beyond access to include skills, economic opportunities, and democratic participation. A careful examination into these aspects of digital divide suggests the need to consider education, income, race, culture, location, and other issues.

In managing digital governance, public managers need to confront the digital divide seen in their jurisdictions. A strategy for digital inclusion to address digital divide should be part of the overall digital governance strategy. The nature of digital divide seen in a country or community is likely to determine the composition of an appropriate strategy. For instance, when access divide is the predominant form of digital divide, making internet access available should be the focus. Similarly, a skill divide for virtual inequality would call for appropriate educational and training programs. For serving the hardest-to-reach populations, such as the elderly and disabled, a human agent equipped with mobile technology powered by an integrated government service information system is probably more effective than offering training workshops to this particular population. Overall, this strategy should focus on delivering public values (as suggested in the management framework mentioned in Chapter 2) while taking into account all external interactions and internal capacity-building.

An inclusive program to bridge digital divide will provide citizens and other stakeholder groups with digital opportunities. On the most basic level, citizens should be able to receive public services in a way that is more convenient for them (24/7) and in a more integrated manner (via a single portal or system). The use of human agents empowered with technology could help provide digital opportunities even for people who do not use any technology to benefit from e-government services. These are opportunities for governments to improve their relationship with citizens by providing high-quality services. Moreover, a digital opportunity program focusing on public education and universal access could further economic and civic engagement opportunities for all to create digital citizenship (Mossberger, Tolbert, and McNeal 2008).

This chapter will first describe the state and nature of digital divide to increase our understanding and knowledge about various aspects of digital divide and their sources. In addition to the general internet access divide, special attention is given to the divide seen between internet users who utilize e-government and those who do not, as well as the divide between governments with high-level vs. low-level e-government services. Then, this chapter turns to policies, programs, and management strategies for digital inclusion with examples of specific digital opportunity programs. This chapter concludes with a summary of the main points and their connection to the framework of managing digital governance detailed in Chapter 2.

Digital Divide

State of the Divide

Digital divide is an important issue for the public managers who bear the responsibility of advancing digital governance. People who do not have access to the internet are in a disadvantageous position compared to those who can participate in the internet economy. More importantly, as more and more government information and services are moved online, the lack of access creates a growing divide between those who have access and those who do not. Such a divide is directly contrary to social equity and equal opportunities pursued by governments. Moreover, as technologies advance, new types of digital divide emerge, and some old problems of divide are alleviated. For instance, some people in the United States are concerned about a broadband divide between those with fast connections and those without, as more and more content and services online demand more bandwidth. The rise of social media and smart phones helped reduce some of the gaps in accessing the internet. However, some differences in access still persist in terms of age and education levels (Zickuhr and Smith 2012).

According to the statistics generated by the Pew Internet and American Life Project, in the United States, digital divide in internet use can be seen in various demographic dimensions as shown in Table 3.1. Both the 2012 and 2014 statistics are included in the table as the basis for discussion. About 95–7 percent of younger adults (18–29) used the internet in the last six months. In contrast, approximately 52–7 percent of senior citizens (65 plus) had used the internet. Income is another major factor when considering that approximately 97–9 percent of people in the annual household income group of $75,000 or above used the internet versus 68–77 percent of people in the income group of less than $30,000. Education level is another important factor; the percentage of internet users with a college degree or more education is 96–7 percent compared with 68–77 percent for those with a high school education or less. Relatively speaking, ethnicity has not created as big a divide as income, age, and education have when comparison is made between different categories. The variation in percent of internet users between Whites (Non-Hispanic) and Blacks (Non-Hispanic) was about 10 percent in 2012. Such a gap has been narrowed to 4 percent in 2014. The difference in use between Whites and Hispanics had narrowed from 10 percent in 2012 to 2 percent in 2014.

Internet use rate is a moving target. In the case of the United States, the internet use rate saw a significant jump from 18 percent to 70 percent from 1995 to 2005. During the period of 2005–10, internet use rate had been relatively stable in the 70–5 percent range according to surveys conducted by the Pew Research Center. However, there was a significant increase during the four-year period from 2010 to 2014: a 10 percent increase to 87 percent according to the results of an internet use survey conducted in January 2014 (Pew Research Center 2015b). This growth can be attributed to fast development and use of smart phones with data services that provide anytime, anywhere connectivity to the internet. More significant is the growing popularity of internet use for social networking purposes. The percentage of internet users utilizing social media moved from 8 percent in 2005 to more than 60 percent in 2010. The percentage continued to rise to 73 percent at the end of 2013 (Pew Research Center 2016).

In contrast, for many countries around the world, the rate of growth has been faster over the last decade. For example, China, with the fastest economic growth rate for the last decade, has seen its internet population grow from 4.6 percent of its population in 2002 to 50.3 percent in 2015 (see Table 3.2) based on the official statistics published by the China Internet Network Information Center (CNNIC). This is more than a ten-fold increase over a 13-year period. More significantly, the total number of the internet population in China surpassed that of the United States in 2008.

Table 3.1 Demographics of Internet Users (Statistics for 2012 and 2014 Surveys)

	2012	2014
	% of American adults within each group who use the internet	% of American adults within each group who use the internet
Total Internet Users	81%	87%
Gender		
Male	81	87
Female	81	86
Race/Ethnicity		
White, non-Hispanic	83	85
Black, non-Hispanic	74	81
Hispanic	73	83
Age		
18–29	95	97
30–49	89	93
50–64	77	88
65+	52	57
Education Level		
Less than high school	47	N/A
High school graduate	72	76 (high school grad or less)
Some college	90	91
College+	96	97
Annual Household Income		
Less than $30,000	68	77
$30,000–$49,999	86	85
$50,000–$74,999	95	93
$75,000 or more	97	99

Sources: 2012 data (accessed 2/1/2013): Pew Internet Summer Tracking Survey, August 7–September 6, 2012. N = 3,014 adults age 18+. Interviews were conducted in English and Spanish and on landlines and cellphones. Margin of error is +/− 2 percentage points; 2014 data (accessed 9/4/2016): Pew Research Center Internet Project Survey, January 9–12, 2014. N = 1,006 adults.

As of 2015, approximately 688 million people have internet access in China, which is twice as many as the total population in the United States.

The advent of Web 2.0, with the exponential growth of Facebook and other social media sites starting in 2006, has brought both opportunities and challenges for digital divide. Among internet users, a divide exists between those who use social media and those who do not. As of August 2012, 69 percent of online adults used social networking sites. The percentage rose to 74 percent based on the 2014 survey (Pew Internet and American Life Project 2015). This means that approximately a quarter of internet users were not involved in social networking afforded by Web 2.0 technologies (Duggan and Brenner 2013). More details on the use of social networking sites are reported in Table 3.3.

Table 3.2 Netizens[a] (Internet Users) in China

Year	Total number of netizens (millions)	Percentage of total population
2002	59.1	4.6%
2003	79.5	6.2%
2004	94.0	7.2%
2005	110.0	8.5%
2006	137.0	10.5%
2007	210.0	16.0%
2008	298.0	22.6%
2009	384.0	28.9%
2010	457.3	34.3%
2011	513.1	38.3%
2012	564.0	42.1%
2013	618.0	45.8%
2014	649.0	47.9%
2015	688.0	50.3%

Note

a Netizens: Chinese residents who are six years or older.

Sources: For data for 2002–12, China Internet Network Information Center, www.cnnic.cn/hlwfzyj/hlwxzbg/hlwtjbg/, accessed July 3, 2013. For 2013 data, 33rd Statistical Report. For 2014 data, 35th Statistical Report. For 2015 data, 37th Statistical Report.

When comparing two kinds of divide some interesting findings emerge: (a) between those who use and who do not use the internet; and (b) between internet users who use social media and those who do not. The comparison below is based on the national surveys conducted by the Pew Internet and American Life Project: one is on internet use (See Table 3.1), and the other is on the use of social networking sites (See Table 3.3). For race, income, and education levels, the differences in percentages of internet users utilizing social media are much less compared with the differences between those who have and those who do not have internet access. For instance, according to the 2014 survey data, for the difference seen in two extreme categories of education level, social media use is about 1 percent, while internet use is about 20 percent. Similarly, for the differences in the two extreme categories in income level, social media use is about 1 percent, whereas internet use is about 22 percent. Interestingly, unlike the divide in internet use, there are more divides in social media use between age groups and also more in gender, as evident in the 2012 and 2014 survey data. This could be related to the nature of social media that serves more of the social networking needs of internet users.

Nature and Sources of Digital Divide

An enhanced understanding of the nature of digital divide will assist in public managers' efforts to address it for better digital governance. Mossberger,

Table 3.3 Who Uses Social Networking Sites Among Internet Users (2012 and 2014 Surveys)

	2012*	2014**
	% of internet users within each group who use social networking sites	% of internet users within each group who use social networking sites
All Internet Users	69%	74%
Men	63	72
Women	75	76
Age		
18–29	92	89
30–49	73	82
50–64	57	65
65+	38	49
Race/Ethnicity		
White, Non-Hispanic	68	71
Black, Non-Hispanic	68	67
Hispanic	72	73
Annual Household Income		
Less than $30,000/yr	73	79
$30,000–$49,999	66	73
$50,000–$74,999	66	70
$75,000+	74	78
Education Level		
No high school diploma	65	N/A
High school grad	65	72 (high school grad or less)
Some college	73*	78
College+	72**	73

Sources: 2012 Data: Pew Internet Civic Engagement Tracking Survey, July 16–August 7, 2012. N = 2,253 adults age 18+. Interviews were conducted in English and Spanish and on landlines and cellphones. Margin of error is +/− 3 percentage points. pewinternet.org/Commentary/2012/March/Pew-Internet-Social-Networking-full-detail.aspx, accessed March 20, 2013. 2014 Data: Pew Internet and American Life Project Report: Social Media Update 2014.

Tolbert, and Stansbury (2003) have examined the nature of virtual inequality. They argue that digital divide extends beyond simple internet access to include skills, economic opportunities, and democratic participation (Mossberger, Tolbert, and Stansbury 2003). The skill divide concerns the ability to learn and is most pronounced among the poor and elderly along with minorities. The divide in economic opportunities is the result of lacking computer and/or math skills to gain from an economy that depends more on information technology (IT). The divide in democratic participation is about the under-representation in democratic governance of various groups such as the young and minorities.

The underlying factors are socio-economic in nature. Education, income, and race all play important roles in digital divide in a variety of formats.

Specific to digital citizenship, Shelley and his colleagues (2004) have argued that educational and racial factors play an important role in shaping attitudes toward technology and that this attitude, in turn, shapes the ability to participate in democratic governance via digital means.

Additional evidence on the relevance of socio-economic factors has been presented in the study of digital citizenship, mostly for the period of the first five years of the 2000s (Mossberger, Tolbert, and McNeal 2008). The digitally disadvantaged groups are less educated, lower income, older, and African-American or Latino, even after controlling for other factors (Mossberger, Tolbert, and McNeal 2008, 120). Less educated people experience difficulty in using the internet and getting the relevant online government information and services because of the lack of relevant skills in computer use as well as literacy. Income is also relevant in owning or getting access to information and communication technologies. These digital inequalities in terms of race and ethnicity are more enduring among the poor and less educated. Such inequalities could be explained by the concentration of these groups living in communities laden with barriers to education and technology, and problems of poverty and crime.

The rise of social media has tended to provide a more equalizing force along racial and income lines among internet users in the United States. As shown by participation in social networking sites (see Table 3.3), the racial divide is not significant and the income gap has only minimal effect on the use of social networking sites. Nonetheless, it should be noted that the rise of social media does not fully address the fundamental question of whether various aspects of digital divide have been bridged for people with different racial and financial backgrounds.

For public managers, it is important to know how various stakeholders contact government online and access government information and services online. The ultimate goal of digital inclusion includes both the supply and demand sides of e-government. On the supply side, inclusion means the provision of government information and services online, known as e-government. If government information and service is not made available online, even the most technologically savvy citizens will not be able to access and use the information. On the demand (use) side, digital inclusion for e-government requires an understanding of citizens engaging with government online. As a result, the next section will discuss the divide in e-government (supply) and in e-citizens (demand).

Divide in E-Government and E-Citizens

Divide in E-Government

A federal/central government agency, as a general rule, tends to have more sophisticated e-government services than a government at a lower level. In the United States, the federal government has the most sophisticated and greatest adoption rate of special-purpose websites as well as social media use. The sophistication of the sites can be measured by their usability, such as support for people with various challenges (visual impairment) and channel preferences (social media vs. websites). An example of a special-purpose site is data.gov, which provides one-stop, user-friendly access to high-value government data sets from various federal agencies. At the state level, websites are inclusive with online information and services, but the scope and scale are smaller compared with those of the federal government as a whole. Local government websites, on average, are much more limited in scope and scale than state government websites. All these differences could be the function of the extent of the responsibilities held by various levels of governments and the size of operation entailed.

The electronic government divide is also seen across national governments. The United Nations' e-government surveys have provided rankings on e-government based on various criteria (United Nations 2008, 2012, 2016). For instance, the 2008 e-government survey focused on readiness—including web presence for e-government, telecommunication infrastructure, human capital, and e-participation. In terms of regional differences, Europe leads the way, America ranks second, and Asia and then Africa follow (United Nations 2008, 19). For the top ten countries in 2008, three of five Nordic countries were among the top five, with the United States ranked fourth. As the only Asian country in the top ten, the Republic of Korea ranked number six. The Netherlands, the United Kingdom, and France were the three European countries in the top ten. In contrast, e-government in 2016 puts more emphasis on encouraging e-participation and supporting sustainable development. The United States fell out of the top ten both in terms of e-government and e-participation. The Republic of Korea remained in the top five after four years of being ranked number one in e-government. The United Kingdom won the number one ranking in e-government development and e-participation (United Nations 2016).

Government use of social media is another interesting dimension to explore in the world of the e-government divide. Given the newness of this phenomenon for government, statistics are difficult to find. The 2011 International City/County Management Association (ICMA) e-government survey for U.S. local governments serving communities of 10,000 or more people suggests that about two-thirds of the governments use social media (including Twitter, YouTube, blogs, Flickr, etc.), while 97 percent have a website (ICMA 2011; Norris and Reddick 2013). A closer look at a sample of local governments in the state of Illinois (half of them serving a population of less than 1,000) reveals that less than 50 percent have any kind of social media presence (Foster and Chen 2013). These two preliminary statistics suggest that although the majority of local governments with 10,000 people or more have a social media presence, we must recognize that about one-quarter of them have not utilized this tool. When considering smaller local governments, the rate of social media utilization is less than half.

Studies of e-government have identified a number of factors that explain the difference in e-government performance measured by the sophistication of government websites. The surveys of local governments in the United States suggest that lack of financial resources and shortage of technical staff are the two main barriers to e-government (ICMA 2002, 2004, 2011). This has consistently been the case for the last ten years. The most recent 2011 survey suggested that lack of financial resources is the number one factor. One plausible explanation is that local governments in the United States are still feeling the effects of the financial crisis in 2008, and e-government has been affected by it.

The size and capability of IT staff and their management constitute another important factor for successful e-government. A single-person operation usually only allows for basic computer and telecommunication services at the local government level (Wood 2012). In contrast, a full IT department can provide much more sophisticated 311 services that cover most services a local government provides to the entire community. Moreover, management capacity also matters (Melitski 2003; Garson 2006). This includes strategic orientation, project and performance management, and contract management for IT outsourcing projects, among other functions.

Top management commitment and a customer/citizen service orientation are enablers for a high-performing e-government. Top management commitment can come in the form of political support of elected officials who have been shown to make a difference in e-government adoption (Ho and Ni 2004; Ahn and Bretschneider 2011). An innovative and/or customer/citizen service orientation is also important in driving e-government performance. Moon and Norris (2005) have shown that a more innovative management helps create a more sophisticated e-government presence. Chen (2010) also documents the importance of customer service orientation in the context of citizen-service information systems.

Divide in E-Citizens

Divide in e-citizens refers to the divide among internet users between those who interact with government via digital channels and those who do not. Citizens contact governments for information and/or services. Examples of government information include contact and service information of government offices, availability of government services, various procedures and forms for permits and licenses, etc. Citizens can also access government services online. Examples of such services in the United States would include paying taxes, paying bills/fines, obtaining permits, obtaining certified government documents, applying for jobs, etc. Citizens can also be business owners or managers of non-profit organizations. Serving in these roles, citizens can contact governments to register businesses, obtain business licenses, query criminal record databases for background checks, etc.

Moreover, citizens are not merely recipients of government information and services, but they are also participants in setting policy priorities as well as in the production and delivery of public services (Denhardt and Denhardt 2000; Thomas 2012). Such a notion of citizenry extends to the interactions between citizens and governments in the digital realm (Milakovich 2012; Mossberger, Tolbert, and McNeal 2008). On some government websites in the United States, citizens can find information about city council meeting agendas and announcements of public meetings. The availability of budget documents online also provides citizens some basic information about how taxpayer dollars are spent. Moreover, digital town hall meetings provide technology-enabled opportunities for deliberation and aggregation of individual preferences to community guiding values. For instance, America Speaks organized a town hall style meeting to discuss policy priorities to rebuild downtown New York City after September 11.[3] Moreover, the advancement of Web 2.0 technologies and the growing prevalence of mobile devices offer a collection of low-cost options for online citizen participation. For instance, citizens can upload information about a garbage problem in the community to the city-wide service information system via apps on their smart phones or participate in expressing preferences for bike routes via a geographic information system (GIS)-enabled map system.

A 2002 national survey conducted by the Pew Internet and American Life Project suggests that a majority (58 percent) of adult internet users have visited a government website. That translates into 68 million American adults in 2002 as opposed to 40 million American adults who visited government websites in 2000, a more than 50 percent increase in a two-year period. Government website users tend to be male, in the age group of 30–49, and in the highest income category ($75,000 or more) (Larsen 2002). Education does not seem to play as important a role as that of internet use. This could be explained in part by the need for interacting with government in general and online as a convenient way of doing so. For instance, the middle-aged adult population is more likely to interact with governments for basic government information, services, taxes, and others as opposed to younger people (18–29). In the State of Georgia in the early 2000s, a substantial minority, though not majority, of internet users actually visited government websites (Thomas and Streib 2003). Based on a state-wide study, visitors to government websites tended to have higher incomes, consist of a lower proportion of minorities, live in urban areas, and be middle-aged (Thomas and Streib 2003).

A more recent national survey in 2009 suggests a significant increase in the percentage of internet users utilizing government websites, less divide among internet users along demographics, and a shift to a more participatory form of engaging governments and public affairs online (Smith 2010). The percentage of internet users who utilize government websites for transactions and information had risen from 58 percent in 2002 to 82 percent in 2009.

Table 3.4 2010 Use of Government Websites for Transactions and Information[a]

Total Internet Users (n = 1,676)	82%
Gender	
Male (n = 748)	83
Female (n = 928)	81
Race/Ethnicity	
White, non-Hispanic (n = 1,273)	83
Black, non-Hispanic (n = 158)	72
Hispanic (n = 135)	78
Age	
18–29 (n = 318)	83
30–49 (n = 560)	83
50–64 (n = 505)	80
65+ (n = 259)	74
Education Level	
Less than high school (n = 80)	68
High school graduate (n = 435)	71
Some college (n = 438)	83
College+ (n = 711)	93
Annual Household Income	
Less than $30,000 (n = 338)	70
$30,000–$49,999 (n = 313)	85
$50,000–$74,999 (n = 261)	90
$75,000 or more (n = 510)	91

Note

a The proportion of internet users within each group that has used a government website in the last 12 months to conduct a specific transaction or get information.

Source: Pew Research Center's Internet and American Life Project, November 30–December 27, 2009 Tracking Survey. N = 2,258 adults age 18 and older, including 1,676 internet users. Please see the methodology section for margin of error calculation.

This constitutes a more than 60 percent increase from 2002, and, more importantly, more than four in five adult internet users in the United States utilizing government websites. Moreover, there is less divide along demographic lines, including age, education attainment, and race. For instance, according to the same 2010 report, the percentages of age groups utilizing government websites were 83 percent for the 18–29 group, 83 percent for the 30–49 group, 80 percent for the 50–64 group, and 74 percent for the 65+ group (for details see Table 3.4). Another important trend is growing citizen participation (nearly one-quarter of internet users) in sharing their views on the business of government (Smith 2010, 2). Interestingly, American adults have a similar level of online contact, information-searching, and engagement for all three levels of government (federal, state, and local) (Pew Research Center 2015a, 14).

There are several factors identified as influencing citizens' use of e-government. Utilization of information channels, interpersonal influence, and civic-mindedness are three additional important factors for citizens' interaction with government online (Dimitrova and Chen 2006). Controlling for demographics (i.e. age, education), Dimitrova and Chen (2006) found that a higher level of information channel utilization to learn about e-government makes a difference, as does the influence from family and friends about the use of e-government. The interpersonal influence is a significant factor in determining whether an individual uses e-government information and services. In addition, what is less explored, but significant, in the e-government literature is the notion of civic-mindedness. The utilization of e-government, controlling for other factors, is influenced by how engaged a citizen is with government (Dimitrova and Chen 2006). This being the case, the use of online services is probably an extension of civic engagement traditionally conducted off-line.

The rapid growth of social media is likely to bring a different dynamic to the determining factors for digital divide in utilization of government information and services online. As opposed to internet users, social media users tend to be younger, and income and education are less important factors (see Table 3.3). Some initial evidence suggests that demographics played a less divisive role in the use of government websites for transactions and information in 2009 (Smith 2010) than was found in 2002 (Larsen 2002). With the increasing popularity of mobile devices and affordability of internet access, the socio-economic divide in access is likely to be lessened.

Nonetheless, the extent to which such a divide can be lessened will depend on the extent to which governments develop mobile versions of their websites and utilize social media. Public managers need to carefully monitor how social media have impacted citizens' use of government information and services online. As innovators, the 75 largest cities in the United States have seen the adoption rate of Facebook increase from 13 percent in 2009 to 87 percent in 2011 (Mossberger, Wu, and Crawford 2013). Attention should also be paid to the channels used to communicate with governments as well as the quality of such utilization. As of 2011 in some of the largest cities in the United States, information push has been the predominant way that governments used social media (Mossberger, Wu, and Crawford 2013).

Digital Inclusion and Opportunities

Management and Policy Challenges

The multiple dimensions of digital divide present significant management and policy challenges for public managers. First, the extent to which digital divide can be bridged depends on the available resources and competition with other public policy objectives. Governments around the world are facing financial challenges in providing even basic public services. Although the growth of internet and smart phones has made a compelling case for the economic necessity to bring connectivity to ordinary citizens, governments still face a real trade-off between providing basic services (i.e. transportation, public safety, and social services) and offering citizens connectivity to the internet economy.

Moreover, the evolving nature of digital divide as a result of fast technological advances makes it challenging for public managers to adapt. The availability of smart phones and the growth in the entire eco-system of applications for those phones create a new divide between those who have smart phones and those who do not. Public managers need to monitor the changing technological landscape and its implications for digital divide. Moreover, the larger management issue is the challenge of implementing consistent messaging across the growing array of communication channels offered by social media and mobile web that governments utilize for communication and engagement with stakeholders.

At the national level, the challenge for bridging e-government divide between various units of government is even greater. The studies of the development of e-government in the United States have shown that development is slow and incremental (Norris 2010; Norris and Reddick 2013). An earlier formulation of an e-government maturity model seems to assume that government will automatically move to the next stage of development (i.e. Layne and Lee 2001). However, later studies have called this linear notion of development into question (Coursey and Norris 2008; Brown 2007). Moreover, doubt has been cast on the hype over online civic engagement, when the primary focus of e-government on service delivery and interactivity is likely to be on the margin of delivering core public services (Norris and Reddick 2013). Recognizing the slow and incremental nature of e-government development, the challenge is for national/federal government (federal government in the United States) or other organizations to create incentives for accelerating the development of low-performing e-governments.

Inclusion Programs and Strategies

Governments have a selection of policy options and management strategies to help address digital divide. One is for government to provide financial assistance for the provision of internet services to particular populations that otherwise cannot afford these services. The second is for government to provide or help finance telecommunication infrastructure to remote or disadvantaged communities. Third is the promulgation and implementation of accessibility standards for online content to make it accessible for people with disabilities. The last strategy is the creation or facilitation of community-based programs to take a more holistic and customized approach to digital divide. These will be discussed in greater detail later.

In the United States, the E-rate program is considered one of the most important federal government efforts to bridge digital divide (Garson 2006). First authorized by the Telecommunication Act of 1996, the E-rate program is formally known as the Schools and Libraries Universal Service Support Mechanism. This program collects a fee from telecommunication services for the purpose of addressing digital divide. It then distributes money to pay for internet connection services for public libraries, Indian reservations, schools, and other groups in need of bridging the divide. This program is in the magnitude of billions of dollars (Garson 2006, 110). It is a main policy tool for providing free internet access to underprivileged populations that otherwise could not afford such access. Moreover, these public libraries usually provide some basic training on computer use for information-searching to further bridge the skill divide.

For remote and economically deprived communities, the building of telecommunication infrastructure is the first and most important task to bridge the digital divide. In the United States, telecommunication services are predominantly provided by private companies. Such a business model requires a sizable market and future payoff for private companies to invest in telecommunication infrastructure such as fiber optics, cables, and cellular/digital towers. As a result, telecommunication/internet services are limited or unavailable for small rural communities or Indian reservations with a small economic base. The U.S. Department of Agriculture has provided grants and loans to rural communities for building such telecommunication infrastructures.[4] A more recent policy tool in the United States are the American Reinvestment and Recovery Act (ARRA) grants to lay the telecommunication infrastructure for small rural communities (such as one in Northern Illinois) to lay fiber optics and link up small communities, schools, governments, and universities to provide broadband services. The goal is to first provide broadband and fast internet connection to the main (anchor) institutions that provide public services and education. Then these institutions can serve as main centers for providing low-cost or free internet services to the entire community.

Another management and policy tool for bridging digital divide is to require compliance with accessibility standards for websites. Section 508 of the Rehabilitation Act, especially §1194.22, provides specific instructions for federal government websites to be accessible for people with disabilities. For instance, one basic instruction for content on federal government websites is to provide options of font size to help the elderly; another one is to provide alternate texts for images to allow text reader software to read the online content to the blind. To keep pace with the development of internet technologies, the assistance Section 508 mandates for people with disabilities has extended to web-based intranet and internet information.[5]

For instance, training materials using video should have open or closed captions for people who are hearing impaired.

Moreover, a more sophisticated way of bridging the divide is to make sure the content is written in a way that is comprehensible for people with basic education and to offer the option of translating the content to a different language for accessibility purposes. Public managers can help bridge these digital divides by requiring a wide range of accessibility measures detailed in Section 508, including the ones on web-based content and those for telecommunication as well as other video/audio interfaces and content.

Community-based user-centric programs can also be helpful for addressing the unique digital divide in a community in a holistic and targeted manner. For instance, partnering high school students with the elderly at a senior center is a way to help senior citizens improve their computer skills and, at the same time, enhance these high school students' understanding of the challenges faced by the elderly population (Shelley et al. 2004). These community-based programs can be more responsive to the needs of the community. In some cases, for a certain community, programs could be more about making free WiFi accessible in open public spaces such as train stations, city squares, parks, and central business districts. Or it could be a computer skill program geared toward the Spanish-speaking population in a community when the lack of such computer skills is the main source of digital divide. Another advantage of these community-based programs is the ability to draw funding from public, private, and non-profit organizations. The diversity of revenue sources and flexibility in personnel also improve the speed in which such a program is delivered.

For bridging digital divide among governments, there is a need for a strategy distinct from that of bridging divide in internet access and e-citizens. Such a strategy should be based on establishing shared infrastructure/services, collaboration, and common standards for various units of governments. Establishing shared infrastructure/services is an important way of leveraging the economy of scale in increasing the capacity of government to deliver high-quality e-government services (White House 2012). These shared services could take the form of the central government paying for the establishment of infrastructure, such as the financing of the telecommunication backbone and central systems in the case of the National Health Service in Britain. Alternatively, it could be a public–private partnership model such as the partnership between Kansas City and Google for the Google Fiber Project in Kansas City that will bring gigabyte connectivity to more than 140,000 homes (*The Economist* 2013). Additional partnerships with Google were expanded to 18 cities in the Southeast at the beginning of 2015.[6] As a result, governments, regardless of size and capacity, can utilize the same state-of-the-art system to provide quality e-government services.

Collaboration among governments in key e-government areas is a complementary approach to address e-government divide. Resource-sharing and information-sharing in the areas of cybersecurity, GIS, data centers, software services, etc., is already in place. For instance, the Multi-state Information Sharing and Analysis Center was established to meet the need for secured information-sharing and coordination of cybersecurity issues.[7] Moreover, the promulgation and implementation of common technology and data standards are other methods of bridging the divide. A minimum standard for online accessibility ensures that no government is left behind in providing basic e-government services online. In addition, common technology and data standards create a larger pool of information resources that small governments can tap into to narrow the divide and lower the cost of development and implementation of e-government services.

An Innovative Approach

An innovative approach to bridging digital divide brings our focus back to humans. The rise of Apple products and smart phones—as well as the entire ecosystem of applications—is a return to usability for humans. With the assistance of these devices, the approach to bridging the last mile or to reaching the populations most inaccessible for e-government services is to introduce human agents rather than forcing these internet non-users to adopt and/or pay for internet services or a new piece of technology. For instance, in the case of Seoul, Korea, they have a 120 Dasan Call Center (the equivalent of 311 in the United States) that allows people with phone access to ask questions about government and obtain services 24 hours a day, 365 days a year. Such a call center is backed by a robust citizen service information system that integrates information across various departments and units of government with a staff of over 350 people and a call volume of over five million a year just for the first two years.[8] Such an approach bridges the digital divide in access to the internet when the phone penetration rate is over 99 percent. Moreover, Seoul's 120 Dasan Call Center is staffed with sign language interpreters for the hearing impaired, translation for foreign visitors and residents, and other services to increase accessibility. Overall, the use of phones helps bridge sources of digital divide such as education, income, and cultural and other barriers, by empowering citizens with a human agent at their service.

The effort to bridge the last mile in Taiwan also underscores the human-centered approach to bridging digital divide. When helping the elderly and people with disabilities, it is the responsibility of the human agent rather than these citizens to utilize technology and e-government services. The human agent can be a government official, a community volunteer, or a family member. Such an approach requires investment in human capital for these agents, low-cost internet access for agents, and the availability of high-quality e-government services for their utilization. The Taiwanese government's efforts to provide digital opportunities for all citizens is a case in point.

More broadly, the provision of digital opportunities for the citizens in Taiwan has several main components. First, the i-Taiwan Government

58 *Digital Divide and Inclusion*

Agency launched a Public Area Free WiFi Access Project to install more than 5,000 free WiFi hot spots in selected government offices, tourist attractions, and transportation nodes, as well as cultural and educational facilities.[9] Next, the Ministry of Education in Taiwan established 173 digital opportunity centers in rural areas to provide courses and training. Lastly, a Digital Outreach Project in 2012 targeted senior citizens, low-income households, indigenous people, and women. Consequently, the project has generated significant improvement in internet use by indigenous people (from 39.9 percent to 63.5 percent).

The future of digital inclusion relies on an innovation-focused strategy to provide digital opportunities for all (Bertot, Estevez, and Janowski 2016). Such a strategy is firmly founded on the advancement of public values such as transparency, accountability, and open collaboration. Governments can adopt strategies such as digitization, transformation, engagement, and contextualization. Moreover, digital inclusion can leverage digital co-production opportunities for governments, non-profit organizations, corporations, and individuals to create digital service. These approaches can help move digital government from emergent, enhanced, and transactional, to connected, bringing digital inclusion to various areas of public service and the entire range of population groups.

Conclusion

Digital inclusion is an imperative for digital governance because one of the core values in public administration is to provide public services to all. The purpose of digital inclusion is to bridge digital divide between people who have access and those who do not, as well as to address the divide between governments that have information technologies and those that do not. Therefore, an examination of digital divide and its sources is foundational for devising strategies for digital inclusion.

In the United States, digital divide is found in varying socio-economic factors and demographics such as income, education, ethnicity, and age. People with higher income and more education, those who belong to the major ethnic group (white), and the younger population group are more likely to be online. The results of a more in-depth analysis of digital divide suggest that skills and cultural issues are the likely root causes (Mossberger, Tolbert, and Stansbury 2003). In general, there is a consensus that digital divide goes beyond access, and the root causes include these long-standing socio-economic and even cultural divides. Social media, to a certain extent, has made the internet more accessible to previously disadvantaged socio-economic groups (Duggan and Brenner 2013). However, concerns have been raised about a new form of divide between those who have and those who do not have broadband access and whether social media use brings users any tangible economic benefits.

Another important line of digital divide for digital governance is between internet users who use government websites and those who do not. In the United States, internet users who are middle-aged, white, with more income and high educational attainment tend to use government websites more. It is worth noting that the divide in age is less pronounced than that of internet users vs. non-users. Educational attainment seems to be the main distinguishing factor for being an e-citizen, as seen in Table 3.4. In the effort to engage internet users in government websites or other official online presences, governments need to pay attention to these lines of divide by finding ways to reach out to those users who do not utilize e-government. Diverse capabilities of governments to provide electronic services (e-government) are typically the functions of level of government, financial resources, size of IT personnel, and management commitment. The sources of these challenges also suggest plausible strategies such as IT investment, scale of economy, and political will.

There are several established strategies to bridge digital divides to provide digital opportunities for all. The most basic one is to provide internet service to disadvantaged populations in rural, remote, and poverty-stricken areas. This can be done via a financial assistance program such as the E-rate program in the United States or via major infrastructure grants/investment that bring the telecommunication infrastructure to these communities. Another strategy is to develop and implement standards for government websites to accommodate people with disabilities. Moreover, online government content should be easy to use and easy to understand instead of being difficult to navigate and full of technical jargon. Community-based programs provided by a partnership between governments and non-profit organizations can meet the specific needs and challenges of digital divide in the community. The most recent innovation is to deploy human agents powered by high quality e-government services to provide personalized services to people who are disadvantaged by digital divide. These human agents are able to bridge all types of digital divide.

The discussion in this chapter focuses attention on the fundamental issue of digital divide to advance public values as the guiding principles presented in the framework in Chapter 2. Moreover, digital inclusion involves expanding the reach of e-government services to benefit the entire population. Knowing the sources of digital divides is the first step in developing appropriate strategies for bridging them. A successful implementation of these strategies focused on innovations will broaden the reach of digital government service to everyone (Bertot, Estevez, and Janowski 2016).

Digital inclusion addresses the underlying issues for enabling interactions between governments and stakeholders in conducting digital governance, as shown in the framework presented in Chapter 2. Bridging digital divide fundamentally shapes interactions with stakeholders. It first reaches citizens and other groups that do not use the internet to benefit from e-government services. Second, such bridging has the potential to be more interactive with stakeholders to learn more about the wants and needs of various stakeholder groups for better allocation of public money. Bridging digital divide is also about enhancing cross-boundary collaboration both in terms of working with organizations in all three sectors (public, private, and non-profit) and in terms of working with other units of government. As previously mentioned, bridging digital divide requires a concerted effort that leverages resources from public, private, and non-profit sectors. For instance, a community-based approach to digital inclusion needs to mobilize organizations in all three sectors. Collaborating with other units of government helps lower the cost of services and addresses public service issues that are cross-boundary in nature (i.e. transportation and public safety).

Digital inclusion is also about addressing fundamental issues in online civic engagement. One of the main criticisms of online civic engagement is the exclusion of people who are not online. Providing digital opportunities (such as Dasan 120 in Seoul and the last-mile initiative in Taiwan) should be the core strategy to offer more convenient channels for civic engagement. Digital opportunities such as broadband infrastructure and community-based programs could bring accessibility to e-government information and services. In the process of information and service delivery, governments can engage citizens and other stakeholders for feedback or even deliberation on main issues confronting the community. The introduction of human agents empowered by IT to bridge the last mile provides opportunities for civic engagement—although this strategy does not conform with the traditional sense of online engagement when citizens interact directly with computers and other digital devices. It is citizen/user-centric civic engagement enhanced by the use of information and communication technology. Such engagement allows government to reach under-served populations and presents opportunities to generate data and information for providing better services to them.

Notes

1 For more details, see www.itu.int/ITU-D/ict/statistics/ict/, accessed February 16, 2013.
2 This is based on the statistics produced by the Pew Internet and American Life Project. For more details, see www.pewinternet.org/data-trend/internet-use/internet-use-over-time/, accessed September 1, 2016.
3 For more details, see americaspeaks.org/projects/topics/disaster-recovery/listening-to-the-city/, accessed March 10, 2013.
4 For more details and a list of the variety of programs in this area, visit www.rd.usda.gov/programs-services/all-programs/telecom-programs, accessed September 5, 2016.
5 See www.access-board.gov/sec508/standards.htm, accessed July 25, 2015. Please note, the website link is for information only and no longer works.

6 Source: www.govtech.com/dc/articles/Google-Fiber-Expands-to-18-Cities-in-American-Southeast.html, accessed September 1, 2016.
7 For more details and current service, visit msisac.cisecurity.org/, accessed September 5, 2016.
8 Source: www.visitkorea.or.kr/enu/FU/FU_EN_15.jsp?cid=880985, accessed March 20, 2013.
9 For more details, visit taiwan.gov.tw/en/faq_service.php, accessed September 5, 2016.

References

Ahn, Michael J., and Stuart Bretschneider. 2011. "Politics of E-Government: E-Government and the Political Control of Bureaucracy." *Public Administration Review* 71 (3):414–24.
Bertot, John Carlo, Elsa Estevez, and Tomasz Janowski. 2016. "Universal and Contextualized Public Services: Digital Public Service Innovation Framework." *Government Information Quarterly* 33 (2):211–22.
Brown, Mary Maureen. 2007. "Understanding E-Government Benefits." *American Review of Public Administration* 37 (2):178–97.
Chen, Yu-Che. 2010. "Citizen-Centric E-Government Services: Understanding Integrated Citizen Service Information Systems." *Social Science Computer Review* 28 (4):427–42.
Coursey, David, and Donald Norris. 2008. "Models of E-Government: Are They Correct? An Empirical Assessment." *Public Administration Review* 48 (3): 523–36.
Denhardt, Robert B., and Janet Vinzant Denhardt. 2000. "The New Public Service: Serving Rather than Steering." *Public Administration Review* 60 (6):549–59.
Dimitrova, Daniela, and Yu-Che Chen. 2006. "Profiling the Adopters of E-Government Information and Services: The Influence of Psychological Characteristics, Civic Mindedness, and Information Channels." *Social Science Computer Review* 24 (2):172–88.
Duggan, Maeve, and Joanna Brenner. 2013. The Demographics of Social Media Users—2012. Washington, DC: Pew Internet and American Life Project.
Foster, Melissa, and Yu-Che Chen. 2013. "Municipal Social Media Policy: A Best Practice Model." In *Human Centered System Design for E-Governance*, edited by Saqib Saeed and Christopher Reddick, 15–36. Hershey, PA: IGI Global.
Garson, David. 2006. *Public Information Technology and E-Governance: Managing the Virtual State*. Sudbury, MA: Jones and Bartlett Publishers, Inc.
Helsper, Ellen Johanna. 2012. "A Corresponding Fields Model of Digital Inclusion." *Communication Theory* 22 (4):403–26.
Ho, Alfred Tat-Kei, and Anna Ya Ni. 2004. "Explaining the Adoption of E-Government Features: A Case Study of Iowa County Treasurers' Offices." *American Review of Public Administration* 34 (2):164–80.
International City/County Management Association (ICMA). 2002. Electronic Government 2002. Washington, DC: International City/County Management Association.
International City/County Management Association (ICMA). 2004. 2004 E-Government Survey. Washington, DC: International City/County Management Association.

International City/County Management Association (ICMA). 2011. Electronic Government 2011. Washington, DC : International City/County Management Association.

Larsen, Elena Rainie Lee. 2002. *The Rise of the E-Citizen: How People Use Government Agencies' Web Site*. Washington, DC: Pew Internet and American Life Project, Pew Charitable Trust.

Layne, Karen, and Jungwoo Lee. 2001. "Developing Fully Functional E-Government: A Four Stage Model." *Government Information Quarterly* 18 (2):122–36.

Melitski, James. 2003. "Capacity and E-Government Performance: An Analysis Based on Early Adopters of Internet Technologies in New Jersey." *Public Performance and Management Review* 26 (4):376–90.

Milakovich, Michael E. 2012. *Digital Governance: New Technologies for Improving Public Service and Participation*. New York and London: Routledge, Taylor and Francis Group.

Moon, Jae, and Donald Norris. 2005. "Does Managerial Orientation Matter? The Adoption of Reinventing Government and E-Government at the Municipal Level." *Information Systems Journal* 15 (1):43–60.

Mossberger, Karen, Caroline Tolbert, and Mary Stansbury. 2003. *Virtual Inequality: Beyond the Digital Divide*. Washington, DC: Georgetown University Press.

Mossberger, Karen, Caroline J. Tolbert, and Ramona S. McNeal. 2008. *Digital Citizenship: The Internet, Society, and Participation*. Cambridge, MA: Massachusetts Institute of Technology.

Mossberger, Karen, Yonghong Wu, and Jared Crawford. 2013. "Connecting Citizens and Local Governments? Social Media and Interactivity in Major U.S. Cities." *Government Information Quarterly* 30 (4):351–58.

Norris, Donald. 2010. "E-Government 2010: Plus ca change, plus c'est la meme chose." *Public Administration Review* 70 (Supplement):S180–S181.

Norris, Donald, and Christopher Reddick. 2013. "Local E-Government in the United States: Transformation or Incremental Change?" *Public Administration Review* 73 (1):165–75.

Pew Internet and American Life Project. 2015. Social Media Update 2014. Washington, DC: Pew Research Center.

Pew Research Center. 2015a. Americans' Views on Open Government Data. Washington, DC: Pew Research Center.

Pew Research Center. 2015b. "Internet Use Demographics." Pew Research Center. Available at: www.pewinternet.org/data-trend/internet-use/latest-stats/ (accessed September 3).

Pew Research Center. 2016. "Social Networking Fact Sheet." Available at: www.pewinternet.org/fact-sheets/social-networking-fact-sheet/ (accessed June 23, 2016).

Shelley, Mack, Lisa Thrane, Stuart Shulman, Evette Lang, Sally Beiser, Teresa Larson, and James Mutti. 2004. "Digital Citizenship: Parameters of the Digital Divide." *Social Science Computer Review* 22 (2):256–69.

Smith, Aaron. 2010. Government Online: The Internet Gives Citizens New Paths to Government Services and Information. Washington, DC: Pew Internet and American Life Project.

The Economist. 2013. "Google Fiber: We're Not (Just) in Kansas Anymore." *The Economist*, April 13, 64.

Thomas, John Clayton. 2012. *Citizen, Customer, Partner: Engaging the Public in Public Management*. Almond, NY; London, UK: M.E. Sharpe.

Thomas, John Clayton, and Gregory Streib. 2003. "The New Face of Government: Citizen-Initiated Contact in the Era of E-Government." *Journal of Public Administration Research and Theory* 13 (1):83–102.

United Nations. 2008. United Nations E-Government Survey 2008: From E-Government to Connected Governance. New York: United Nations.

United Nations. 2012. United Nations E-Government Survey 2012: E-Government for the People. New York: United Nations.

United Nations. 2016. United Nations E-Government Survey 2016: E-Government in Support of Sustainable Development. New York: Department of Economic and Social Affairs, United Nations.

White House. 2012. "Digital Government: Building 21st Century Platform to Better Serve the American People." Washington, DC: White House.

Wood, Colin. 2012. "Lone Stars." *Government Technology* 10 (3):8–11.

Zickuhr, Kathryn, and Aaron Smith. 2012. *Digital Difference*. Washington, DC: Pew Internet and American Life Project.

4 Open Government in the Era of Digital Governance

Introduction

Open government online must engage with earning public trust in an era of innovative information and communication technologies (ICTs). According to a survey distributed in 2015 to city and county chief information officers (CIOs) in the United States, open government/data has been ranked as one of the survey respondents' top five priorities (*Government Technology* 2015). From the citizen perspective, about two-thirds of Americans use the internet to interact with government online (Pew Research Center 2015). Slightly over 40 percent of Americans consider that current government data-sharing efforts are at least somewhat effective (Pew Research Center 2015).

Advances in ICTs like social media (for example, the use of a government Facebook page) and mobile devices afford low-cost opportunities for governments to inform and engage citizens online. Social media and other Web 2.0 tools make it convenient for citizens to report public service issues and offer innovative policy ideas. A landmark legislative effort in the United States (the passage of the Data Accountability and Transparency Act of 2014 (DATA Act)) has ushered in machine-readable federal government spending data for advancing accountability and transparency. The rapid development of big, open, and linked data provides opportunities for new online public services, citizen engagement, and digital collaboration among stakeholders (Janssen, Matheus, and Zuiderwijk 2015). Online transparency also has the potential to strengthen citizens' trust in government; with open government, citizens can be active participants in public policy-making and public services provision rather than mere customers of governmental services. Governments can provide information about how tax dollars are spent, so citizens can monitor governments as well as help shape policy priorities.

At the same time, there are challenges associated with open government concerning the goal of earning citizen trust. The protection of privacy and security becomes more complex when more online channels and services are deployed since such proliferation increases the need for coordination across platforms to ensure consistent messages and also heightens demands on technical and management staff. Opening government data may have unintended consequences that do not match the intent of promoting transparency (Bannister and Connolly 2011). Moreover, ensuring meaningful participation is an enduring issue as citizen expectations continue to rise with the increasing amount of information available and the sophistication of online venues for engagement.

This chapter provides an overview of the concepts and issues related to open government. Such an overview covers the three pillars of open government as proposed by the Obama Administration in the United States and the institutions that support it. Moreover, this chapter introduces a strategy to achieve the goal of open government amid the challenges identified. Lastly, an integrated practical implementation approach is introduced to guide public administrators in taking advantage of online opportunities for open government.

Open Government

The advancement of ICT, coupled with the increasing use of social media, provides opportunities for governments to be more open. Such openness, as articulated by the Obama Administration in the United States, has three pillars: transparency, participation, and collaboration (Orszag 2009) (see Figure 4.1). This chapter has adopted the open government ideal advocated by the Obama Administration because it is encompassing and forward-looking but, more importantly, it is relevant to public managers/administrators—as has been shown in the adoption of similar open government concepts by innovative governments around the world. Therefore, the following discussion will be organized around the three pillars mentioned above: online transparency, electronic participation (e-participation), and online collaboration.

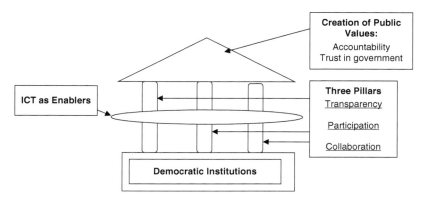

Figure 4.1 A Framework for Open Government

Transparency

Transparent digital governance makes information about governments readily available online. Studies have shown transparency helps reduce corruption and makes governments more professional and accountable (Bertot, Jaeger, and Grimes 2010). Online transparency also empowers citizens and provides policy-watch organizations with the needed information to monitor government actions. Such monitoring helps create and support public pressure to fight corruption. Moreover, online transparency helps even out the balance of power between government and citizens since governments usually have a monopoly on public sector information. With better information on government operation and performance, citizens can be more informed participants in governance. A likely consequence of such participation is trust in government, which public administrators strive to achieve.

Because the type of government information made available online matters in managing online transparency, public administrators must make decisions about what kinds of information should be made available online in relation to the level of transparency. Categorization of online transparency aids in making a better decision on what information should be made available online for transparency purposes. Grimmelikhuijsen and Welch (2012)—adapted from Heald (2006) and Drew and Nyerges (2004)—discuss three kinds of government transparency: (a) decision-making transparency; (b) policy information transparency; and (c) policy outcome transparency. This chapter further extends public policy to public service information to maximize relevancy for public administrators and public managers as reflected in the following headings.

Decision-making Transparency

Decision-making transparency entails both openness in the step-by-step process to reach a public policy/service decision and deliberation with rationales to reach such a decision (Grimmelikhuijsen and Welch 2012, 563). Transcripts or videotapes of major policy deliberation, supporting background documents, and vote counts are examples of this type of transparency. Local governments are pioneers in such decision-making transparency. For instance, some local governments in the United States have gone beyond the public notice requirement for public meetings to make the entire city council agenda available online. Moreover, some local governments even stream their city council meetings online for citizens to watch in real-time or on demand.[1] Offering city council meetings online provides a high level of decision-making transparency. An even higher level of decision-making transparency is to stream senior staff meetings online for citizens to watch. Doing so provides citizens with access to discussions about decisions on how policy is implemented.

For instance, an experiment initiated by a Korean local government allowed citizens to watch senior staff meetings online (Ahn and Bretschneider 2011).

Public Policy and Service Information Transparency

Policy content information is about public policies with a focus on objectives, rationales, and plans. One type of policy content information frequently disclosed online by governments in the United States is budget information. For instance, the entire U.S. federal budget is made available to the public. An app was developed for the general public to navigate over $4 trillion of U.S. federal budget for 2016.[2] Such availability of documents represents policy priorities as captured in resource allocation and specific plans to achieve public policy objectives. A government's strategic plan is another example of a policy document. Such a strategic document includes sections on policy goals, priorities, and master implementation plans to guide the entire organization.

An equally important kind of information covers public services. Citizens need to know what public services are available and where and how to obtain those services. Most government websites place their emphasis on making information regarding services for residents, visitors, and businesses available as a way to promote online transparency of public service information. For instance, they often have specific drop-down menus that feature frequently used online services by citizens in the community.

Policy and Service Outcome Information Transparency

The decision to release policy and service outcome information online represents another dimension of transparency. Government expenditure can be considered policy outcome information as it is the execution of policy priorities as captured in actual spending. The 2014 DATA Act has gradually made U.S. Federal Government expenditure information available in a machine-readable format.[3] Online air quality information is an example of releasing information on the results of clean air policies, and unemployment statistics show the outcome of employment policies. For instance, information on the number of jobs created as the result of the American Recovery and Reinvestment Act (ARRA) of 2009 was available online on the Recovery.gov website. As a result, citizens could utilize such information to hold government accountable for spending under ARRA. Such public service outcome information is particularly relevant for accountability. Some progressive local governments have posted citizen satisfaction scores with public services, such as police and fire, on their websites. Such information also constitutes service outcome information as measured by satisfaction.

Participation

Citizen participation is an essential component of democratic governance. Transparency deals with governments making information (including decision-making, content, and outcomes) available, focusing on one-way communication from government to citizens. Participation, on the other hand, is more concentrated on citizens communicating with and engaging government online. Transparency and participation together complete the two-way communication needed for constructive democratic governance. The advancement of ICTs, notably the internet and social networking services/platforms, has lowered the cost and increased the speed of citizen participation for providing input on public policy and public services decisions. When quality information is presented and the input process is organized, the quality of citizen participation can also be improved (Holzer et al. 2004; Leighninger 2011). The two main types of e-participation discussed below fit the open government framework.

E-consultation

E-consultation occurs when citizens provide their input on public policy or public service issues electronically via an official channel or forum to advance public values such as democratic governance, sustainability, and inclusion (United Nations 2008, 2016). In practice, most e-consultation involves the generation of policy ideas. One example is the IdeaScale project launched by the U.S. Federal Government. Participating citizens provided the best policy ideas for different governmental agencies to use through a voting process to rank those ideas. Another example is the city of Omaha, Nebraska, which had a website that allowed citizens to provide ideas, such as cleaning up graffiti.[4] A much smaller portion of e-consultation is about discussing or even ranking already formulated policy proposals. Generation of policy ideas does not significantly raise the issue of representation, as it is a brainstorming exercise. In contrast, voting or ranking policy proposals may raise the issue of restricted representativeness as the result of digital divide. This reduction of representativeness likely explains the limited use of e-consultation for ranking existing policy proposals.

E-policymaking

The general notion of e-policy-making relates to citizens providing input into public policy-making (United Nations 2008, 2016). One prominent example is e-rulemaking in the United States, a process in which citizens can electronically provide their comments on proposed federal rules and regulations. E-policy-making also includes the availability of e-petitioning (United Nations 2005, 102). It is important for citizens to be able to petition or file a complaint online. For instance, the United States has an e-petition website called "We the People," and the UK also has a similar site for electronic submission of petitions. Citizen input is received and then incorporated into the decision-making process, another important measure of success for e-policy-making (United Nations 2005, 102). A higher level of e-policy-making takes a more integrated approach. For instance, the Republic of Korea has a more integrated web portal (e-People) that unifies complaints, proposals, and policy discussions by government in one place.[5]

Collaboration

Online collaboration deepens the two-way online communication between government and citizens and expands to organizations and various sectors of a society. In the context of open government, collaboration extends to various stakeholders in e-governance, including businesses, non-profit organizations, citizens, and others. For example, a family policy advocacy group can leverage publicly available government information to conduct independent research. Such research serves as collaboration between government and non-profit organizations in providing enhanced understanding of relevant policy issues. The advent of social media and social networking platforms provides tools and avenues for such online collaboration. Online collaboration is still emerging and mostly experimental in nature, but there are at least two emerging types of online collaboration based on the objectives for advancing public interests as discussed below.

Online Collaboration for Generating, Deliberating, and Ranking Policy Ideas

Online collaboration utilizes several features commonly available in electronic forums and social media for citizens to post ideas, comment on them, and rate them appropriately. More importantly, citizens can collaborate with one another by providing feedback to each other and by using the aggregated results for reference. The IdeaScale project sequenced this process into three phases: idea generation, idea commenting, and then idea ranking (by vote). Such online collaboration occurs mostly among citizens on government-sponsored websites.

Another example is a call from the White House in December 2011 for generation of the best and brightest policy ideas, namely the "Startup America Policy Challenge." The Public Affairs School at Arizona State University mobilized concerned citizens, students, scholars, and practitioners to answer the call.[6] This event is an example of online collaboration going beyond individual citizens to involve multiple groups and organizations in a society. Another example of engaging individual citizens, non-governmental organizations, and government agencies is an online forum discussing how the Australian Government Consultation Blog should work.[7]

Online Collaboration for Producing Public Policy/Service Applications

A typical arrangement for online collaboration involves governments making raw data available in the public domain along with data and technical standards/tools on accessing the data (i.e. application programming interface (API)). Then, individuals, non-profit organizations, or companies take on the task of developing value-added applications or websites for the public to use. For instance, government makes traffic data available, and then individual software developers can develop applications for people to download to monitor traffic. Both New York City, USA, and the City of Shanghai, China, have annual competitions that allow teams to develop apps or websites that provide valuable public information and service to address a societal need. Furthermore, making detailed technical information available is critical. For instance, the U.S. Federal Government provides common resource description framework documents for data sets available on data.gov to enlist citizens and other groups in developing software applications. One example on the data.gov website is a software application that allows citizens to check ozone levels across the United States.[8]

Institutions for Open Government

Democratic Institutions for Open Government

Democratic institutions as exhibited in executive orders, laws, and regulations are foundational for open government to utilize ICTs (Ahn and Bretschneider 2011). ICTs serve as enablers. But the enactment of e-government is influenced by political will (Ahn and Bretschneider 2011; Ahn 2010), institutions (Fountain 2001; Tolbert, Mossberger, and McNeal 2008), citizen-centric orientation (Chen 2010), and innovativeness (Moon and Norris 2005) among others. Open government as an extension of e-government is likely to rely on the same institutional arrangements for success. For instance, the public notice and commenting requirement for federal rule-making in the United States is foundational for extension to electronic rule-making by utilizing ICTs to allow for the addition of an electronic channel. What follows is a discussion of democratic theories that are likely to shape the policies and orientation of open-government initiatives.

Open government is rooted in the notion of democracy, and a fundamental issue of democracy is information asymmetry between government and citizens. Such asymmetry needs to be addressed to foster a vibrant and productive society where members of the society are informed about government actions and have meaningful dialogue and participation in good governance. The nature of information that government shares with citizens should be meaningful for public governance. For instance, budget proposals instead of lists of street names are meaningful documents for broad policy priority discussions for a government. The need to address information asymmetry provides justification for transparency as one of the three pillars in open government as well as the need for transparency in policy-making, policy/service content, and policy/service outcomes. All three aspects of transparency aid in addressing any asymmetry of information and enable meaningful participation.

Moreover, increasing usability (understandability) and disseminating information about government are both important aspects of addressing such asymmetry. One of the earlier initiatives on making content available for public use on government websites was developed to ensure that the content targets readers at the 8th-grade reading level, which is the average reading level of American adults. Doing so makes the content understandable without too much use of jargon and/or technical language. The ease of information dissemination from civic groups to individual citizens also helps in information-sharing.

Citizen participation is central to democracy. The goal of electronic democracy is to "enhance the degree and quality of public participation in government" via the use of ICTs (Kakabadse, Kakabadse, and Kouzmin 2003, 47). Such participation can be direct, via representatives, or deliberative in nature (Kakabadse, Kakabadse, and Kouzmin 2003). Public managers can explore any of the three modes of participation or a certain combination of them in online participation. For instance, direct participation could take the form of a virtual town hall meeting that allows citizens to participate electronically. A public policy forum allows the exchange of various viewpoints and comments (and even votes) on policy ideas, a form of participation that is more deliberative in nature.

Collaboration online with citizens and other groups in a society is consistent with the key notion of new public service—citizens should be involved in the production and delivery of public services and participate in democratic governance (Denhardt and Denhardt 2007). In addition to being citizens and customers, people can also play the role of partners in working with government to improve public service (Thomas 2012). The role of citizens and citizen participation are highlighted in the study of collaborative public management as areas of critical importance (O'Leary and Bingham 2009). As part of open-government strategies, the new public-service notion of citizen engagement can help guide the efforts of engaging citizens online.

Public administrators need to approach collaboration by understanding the structures, shared goals, trust, resources, and risks when working across organizational boundaries (O'Leary and Bingham 2009). These are the issues that public managers need to consider when initiating online collaboration with other individuals and organizations. Moreover, collaboration should extend beyond government and citizens to include the non-profit and private sectors. Intersector collaboration has become more prevalent, especially in the areas of human services and emergency management (Berry and Brower 2005; Berry et al. 2008). Public managers need to examine a broad spectrum of potential partners for collaboration in the design and implementation of online platforms for improving public policy and services.

Laws and Policy Documents for Open Government

In the United States, the basic principle underlying open government is the citizens' right to know. The most significant legislation for open government is the 1966 Freedom of Information Act (FOIA), which allows citizens to request information from governments about their actions. The Federal Government is obligated to disclose information as requested. Exceptions can only be made on the basis of nine specific exemptions stipulated in the FOIA. This act was later extended to require federal agencies to publish FOIA guides on their websites, known as E-FOIA (Electronic Freedom of Information Act Amendments of 1996).[9] Moreover, the E-Government Act of 2002 has provided the impetus for making government data available in an electronic format. More recently, the passage of the DATA Act in 2014 in the United States has provided the legal mandate to make government financial data available in machine-readable format as a legislative act addressing open government.

At the state level in the United States, state legislations such as the Open Records Acts in the States of Pennsylvania, New Jersey, and Georgia mandate that state agencies make public records available to the public via regular postings and requests. In the case of the State of Georgia, public records include any documents (including maps, photographs, and computer-generated information) that are produced "in the course of the operation of a public office or agency" (Open Records Act, State of Georgia). When a request is received, a public agency has a specific timeframe in which to respond. Such a response needs to inform citizens about the kind of information that will be released, any information that will fall under an exemption, and the cost associated with fulfilling the information request. A typical exemption is one that removes confidential personal information such as home address, phone number, and social security number of a public employee. Trade secrets are also protected under the State of Georgia's Open Records Act.

The move to building open government institutions has gained momentum around the world. Legislative efforts have been launched to make government information more available to the public both online and through the publication of government documents in countries like China and India. After years of development, the Regulations of the People's Republic of China on Open Government Information were adopted in 2007 and went into effect on May 1, 2008. In the case of India, its Right to Information Act was adopted in 2005 and went into effect the same year (Puddephatt 2009, 24–6).

Main Policy Documents for Open Government in the United States

The Open Government Directive as a policy document is instructional in understanding the institutional components of open government (Orszag 2009). This directive outlines the steps towards open government, including online publication of government information, improvement of government information quality, cultivation of an open-government culture, and creation of an enabling policy framework. This directive also contains specific action items and deadlines. Noteworthy is that within 45 days each federal agency shall have three high-value data sets published online in an open format, and within 60 days agencies shall create Open Government Webpages that have online public input mechanisms. Moreover, within 120 days, a review of Office of Management and Budget (OMB) policies is due to clarify or modify existing policies/guidance and to formulate new policies to promote open government.

One leading open-government effort is "prizes and challenges," which emphasizes engaging citizens and non-profit organizations to further innovate the business of government. The main policy document delineates the policy goals, related policy issues, prize authority, and partnership authority (Zients 2010). For instance, this document identifies the specific statute that allows the Department of Energy to select a third party to administer a prize competition (Zients 2010, 5). Moreover, this document also addresses legal issues such as intellectual property, procurement, and federal endorsement of products or services. For example, this document cites the Bayh-Dole Act, which allows non-profit organizations to retain title to and profit from inventions funded by the Federal Government while the government has a royalty-free license to utilize these inventions. Such a policy document enables the wide use and adoption of the Challenge.gov platform by federal agencies to seek innovative ideas and products to solve complex public problems.

Managing Open Government

Trends

With the advances of technologies in the internet, mobile applications, and social media, open government has gone online. The general trend is for governments to be open to citizens and society as a whole via the utilization of both established and emerging technologies. Even for local governments in the United States, 97 percent of them have an official website based on a 2011 survey (International City/County Management Association (ICMA) 2011). China, which, since 2008, has had the largest internet population, has also seen its governments launching websites. By the end of 2008, over 96 percent of central agencies and all provincial governments, and around

99 percent of local governments, had established websites (Ministry of Industry and Information Technology 2009). In addition, a survey reported that 76 percent of Chinese government CIOs pointed to websites/web portals as the most common and most frequently used e-government application (Wu and Sun 2009). Websites have mostly been used as platforms for the provision of information with an emphasis on policy and public-service information, followed by outcomes and decision-making. The overall trend is to continue the effort to increase the depth and relevance of information and services available on the official websites and to integrate social media into the portfolio of online communication and engagement.

The increasing popularity of social media and mobile devices such as smart phones and sensors has ushered in an era of innovation for open government, fostering an active engagement paradigm. Such a paradigm can be characterized by governments engaging citizens in their online social spaces (Chang and Kannan 2008). Based on a 2011 survey of local governments in the United States, 67 percent use social media (ICMA 2011). Among these social media platforms, Facebook is the primary social media tool, followed by Twitter and YouTube. In China, there has been an exponential growth by governments in the use of microblogs to engage citizens. By the end of 2011, the number of government microblogs reached 50,561, an increase of over 700 percent compared to 2010. These Chinese government microblogs can be run by government agencies (32,358) or by individual government officials (18,203), mainly hosted on Sina.com followed by Tencent (Chinese Academy of Governance 2012).

The increasing use of mobile devices also calls for government to move to the next level of connectivity and engagement with citizens. In the United States, 98 percent of 18–29-year-old Americans own a cell phone based on the information released by the Pew Internet and American Life Project in 2015.[10] Statistics by the Pew Internet and American Life Project show that over half of mobile phone users get online with their phones, and Americans have become increasingly accustomed to using mobile phones (including smart phones) to register for text messages/SMS, to purchase tickets, and to share photos and videos via digital or cellular networks.[11] In response to the widespread use of mobile devices, the U.S. Federal Government initiated the Making Mobile Government Project.[12] For internet-ready mobile devices, governments are increasingly looking at making mobile-device-friendly versions of their existing websites. With the growth in the use of smart phones, an increasing array of mobile government applications have sprung up that allow citizens to report public-service issues, get updates on traffic information, and much more.

Another important trend is the move toward more openness. Making raw data collected by government available is an important dimension to such openness. Raw data allow citizens to ask the questions that interest them and conduct their own analyses. For example, the raw data on toxic waste sites combined with census data allow environmental groups to conduct their own analysis while linking other socio-economic conditions such as investigating the issue of environmental justice. A related trend is to provide online analytical tools with the raw data to make data analysis user friendly, even for ordinary citizens. For instance, on the Recovery.gov website, the U.S. Federal Government made the expenditure information on the over US$750bn authorized for the ARRA available to citizens and all stakeholders online. Citizens and organizations can examine how much money is being spent on the level of individual projects and aggregated to a specific jurisdiction or geographic area through a user-friendly interface with a map of the states and drop-down boxes of filtering criteria.

The last dimension is the kind of information made available to citizens. Some government officials are publishing their reimbursed expenses online for people to see. Some communities provide video on-demand for their city council meetings. There seems to be a move toward releasing more policy/service outcome information as well as decision-making process information.

Challenges

The move to open government is not without some major challenges. The U.S. Federal Government recognizes the resource issue (General Service Administration 2008). Making government open requires human and technical resources such as staff time, web servers, and data management. Engaging citizens via a variety of online channels (such as traditional websites, social media sites, and mobile devices) requires a significant number of resources. A related complication is possible fragmentation as the result of juggling multiple online outlets from websites to social media alike. The multiplicity of types of online presence is prone to error and results in a lack of consistent message.

Another consistent challenge of opening government data for accountability and transparency is the quality and completeness of government data coming from a variety of government agencies (Government Accountability Office (GAO) 2014). The fundamental issue is the difference in data standards and quality assurance among different agencies. The effort to integrate data from different sources needs to confront the challenge of disparity in data quality, that some data may cause more confusion rather than enhance accountability. The other issue is the lack of comparability when data are defined and collected differently in various agencies.

Other challenges include privacy, security, and management of public records. These are concerns for official government websites. Americans have also expressed privacy concerns with opening government data including personal information such as mortgages, real-estate transactions, and property information (Pew Research Center 2015). It may take hours for governments to go through the content of an elaborate website to remove personal identifiable information and any other privacy concerns. The rise of social media further exacerbates these problems (General Service Administration 2008). Social media presence is facilitated via third-party organizations, so governments do not have a contractual relationship for ensuring privacy and security. An added complication is the public records requirement. The question is whether the information published on social media sites managed by a particular government agency will be subject to the same regulations for freedom of information requests and related archiving requirements.

The early experience of opening government data also faced the challenge of unintended use of government data (Bannister and Connolly 2011; Worthy 2015). Opening government data is premised on using available government data to improve public service and create public value. In some instances, newly available government data were used to jeopardize government decision-making to advance the interests of a few. The availability of machine-readable data has the complication of disproportionally benefiting the powerful interest groups that have the resources to conduct data analytics over individuals. The use of government data can become highly political.

The last challenge is the ability to promote meaningful citizen participation, which requires that citizens are informed and make their choices accordingly. Governments need to make sure that relevant policy information is provided for ordinary citizens in an understandable way. The advances of geographic information systems (GIS) help communicate the implications of government decisions, especially those that can be illustrated on a map (Ganapati 2011). Moreover, the kind of decision-making in which citizens can get involved is also relevant. Most online citizen participation in public policy/service centers on generation of ideas. Much less has been developed for voting, such as referenda on particular policies. Another dimension of meaningful participation is representation. Questions about the issue of representation are typically raised on any online citizen-participation mechanism, as about 20 percent of the adult population does not use the internet on a regular basis.

Strategy for Digital Open Government

The best way to manage digital open government is to have a strategy. As a public executive, the lead question is how to use open government to advance public values. A sound strategy should be grounded in the scholarship of transparency, citizen participation, and collaborative governance. Moreover, such a strategy should leverage advances in ICTs and correspond to how citizens use them. ICTs are enablers for open government initiatives. The open-government strategy of the City of Boston has highlighted the advancement of public values as captured in Box 4.1.

Box 4.1 City of Boston's Open Government Strategy

Open Government Strategy for the City of Boston, U.S.A.

This document highlights the public benefits of open government such as citizen engagement, improving policy, and improved management. Then it details the City's strategy with regard to transparency, participation, and collaboration (three pillars of open government). This strategy discusses transparency in terms of types, access, and prioritization of data along with the engagement of data users. The section on participation outlines opportunities, emergency response, and fraud reporting as areas of online citizen participation. Collaboration as discussed focuses on innovation, online analysis, visualization, and software applications. The section on collaboration also contains a specific discussion on research collaboration with various academic disciplines. Moreover, this strategy goes into guiding theories and principles for open government such as theories of democratic governance and targeted transparency (Goodspeed, August 2010, Open Government Strategy for the City of Boston, a policy planning document).

As the first step, a government needs to define the overarching goal of its open-government initiative. Is it to provide citizens with basic government operation information for transparency? Or is it to engage citizens in making public-policy decisions and collaboration? Such a decision is probably contingent on citizen demand as well as the current level of openness. For instance, in response to citizen demand on city expenditure and program performance information, a government will probably focus on transparency of policy content and outcome information. This overarching goal should be followed by a mixture of components (pillars) of open government, namely transparency, participation, and collaboration. For example, a progressive community or political leader that has improving deliberative democracy as the overarching goal for the creation of public values would place emphasis on "participation" and "collaboration" as the two main components of the open-government strategy supplemented with transparency on decision-making.

Policy

A general strategy needs to incorporate a set of policies to provide a framework for implementation. A comprehensive open-government policy will have specific requirements for online transparency, participation, and collaboration. For instance, the Obama Administration's Executive Order on Open Government Initiative has specific requirements for the number of government data sets available to citizens and the deadlines for doing so (Orszag 2009). This executive order also sets the general policy guideline to err on the side of openness. Governments should develop a comprehensive policy for all online communication and interaction with citizens that includes social media, official websites, e-mail, and electronic newsletters, among others, to promote integration and consistency across online channels.

For citizen participation, governments should formulate and implement policy governing the purposes and types of online citizen participation as well as the ultimate use of the products as the result of such participation. For instance, a government needs to articulate whether the input from online citizen participation is advisory in nature or constitutes a policy mandate. The U.S. Federal Government's "Challenges and Prizes" program takes input from such online citizen participation under advisories for government agencies seeking innovative policy ideas. In the event that an application (software program) is the product of citizen participation, a policy for participation is needed to delineate the kind of incentives that can be offered and the ownership of the application. Moreover, online participation should be part of an overall strategy of civic engagement that includes multiple channels of inputs (online, off-line, etc.). A policy document is needed to articulate such linkages.

Policy governing online collaboration needs to be clear about the responsibilities of government. Typically, it involves government making raw data available that has potential for transparency, policy analysis, and development of software applications. The DATA Act of 2014 requires various federal government agencies to ensure data quality and completeness while making spending data available to the public (GAO 2014). The City of Chicago, USA, has a data portal that publishes information on various areas of public service such as crime, traffic, and public health (i.e. food service inspection results).[13] The availability of raw data in various formats empowers citizens and non-profit organizations alike to actively engage in monitoring and policy-making in an informed way. Another example is the publication of XBRL-format financial information by the Securities and Exchange Commission (SEC) in the United States. The availability of machine-readable data sets will allow citizens, businesses, and various organizations to monitor the behavior of publicly traded companies. At minimum, government bears the responsibility for data quality, timely release, and the protection of privacy.

Moreover, an open government policy needs to include a specific section on security and privacy that cuts across various channels of online interaction with citizens to achieve transparency, participation, and collaboration. The proliferation of social media offers significant new channels and opportunities for advancing open government (Mergel 2013). At the same time, such proliferation also introduces concerns about digital privacy and security. At minimum, the protection of privacy should ensure confidentiality of individual citizens providing information in the course of interacting with government. It should cover text message services, electronic forums, posting and commenting on social media sites, online business transactions with government, etc. A digital security policy should ensure integrity, confidentiality, and availability of stored and transmitted government information. More details are discussed in the chapter on digital security and privacy.

Another overarching policy requirement is the definition and treatment of public records. An open-government policy needs to properly define public records in accordance with legal requirements. In areas where the existing laws and regulations offer little guidance, the definition and treatment of public records should be consistent with the goal of open government. The general policy intent should empower citizens with access to the records of their interactions with governments, such as their postings on social media and other people's responses to the postings.

Implementation Approach

Executive support is foundational to the successful implementation of open government, which also requires a coordinated effort to integrate other components as listed in Table 4.1. A high level of transparency in decision-making, such as broadcasting senior staff meetings, requires the commitment of elected officials and the chief executive (Ahn and

Table 4.1 Components of an Open Government Implementation Approach

Components	Specifics
Executive support	Garner executive support for opening government data; provide additional resources for open-government projects
Portfolio management	Manage the collection of online communication channels utilized as a coherent portfolio of online open-government communication and interactions
Targeted effort	Target open-government efforts by focusing on a particular type of information and defining the goal for a given period of time
Careful planning and execution	Focus on strategic alignment between the open-government initiative and the public values that it aims to create, and carry it out accordingly
Sustainability promotion	Engage citizens with their preferred tools and platforms, and sustain their attention with incentives and fresh design
Incremental implementation	Initiate small steps in government efforts while learning and adapting quickly to scale up
Enhancement with ICT	Take advantage of emerging technologies and capabilities such as open geographic information systems (GIS) and semantic web

Bretschneider 2011). Even just making government data available requires the commitment of the governing boards and management because it goes beyond the standard operation of government and is considered as e-government innovation. Moreover, implementation of e-government projects, especially those required for a higher level of integration, requires management support to be successful. The experience of citizen service information systems highlights such a need (Chen 2010). Such executive support for additional allocation of resources is critical for supporting open data efforts and is typically in addition to a government's existing responsibilities (Dawes and Helbig 2010).

Implementation of an open-government initiative should take a portfolio approach to managing various online communication and interaction outlets. These outlets include websites, e-mails, Twitter, social media presence, text-messaging services, mobile apps, etc., and should be treated as a portfolio of communication tools available to government. Public administrators need to be cognizant of the cross-fertilization of contents and the relative strengths and weaknesses of tools. For instance, a downtown annual parade would require communication and promotion beforehand. Such promotion can be done via websites, Facebook, Twitter, and a community e-mail blast with one consistent message catering to various outlets. At the same time, each outlet has its strengths and weaknesses. Compared with event description on a website, a tweet does not provide all the details, but provides a more timely information push to interested citizens. There is often a trade-off between the depth of the message and the timeliness of the message. Interactivity is another element for consideration. Facebook is more social and interactive, while websites or text messages are much less so. Integration also means implementation of open-government policies as discussed earlier. A consistent set of policies should be applied to various online outlets for consistency.

At the same time, open-government efforts need to be targeted and specific to manage expectations as well as minimize unintended damaging use of open data (Worthy 2015). For transparency to work, it needs to be targeted (Fung, Graham, and Weil 2007). Targeted transparency focuses on a defined set of information and presents it in a way that empowers citizens to make informed choices. The lessons for public administrators are to provide citizens with well-defined, easy-to-understand online policy information that allows them to make an informed choice on public services and policy issues. Online citizen participation and collaboration should be done in a meaningful way. A registration process is important to provide legitimacy to the input, so there is accountability in online exchanges both on the side of citizens and governments too. Moreover, citizens should be informed about the issues and relevant facts for meaningful participation. For instance, online participation can be designed to ensure a thoughtful review of relevant information before citizens can make a comment or cast a vote on a public policy issue.

Successful online citizen participation requires careful planning and execution (Holzer et al. 2004; Leighninger 2011). In planning for online citizen participation, a government needs to first articulate its goals and appropriate strategies to publicize the participation forum. At the implementation stage, a government needs to make sure that clear guidelines, as well as assistance, are provided to citizens for participation and input. Special attention needs to be paid to facilitation of discussions by clearly framing the issue and by doing so in a responsive manner (Holzer et al. 2004). Moreover, it is important to organize and present information in a way that does not overwhelm citizens while promoting a clear understanding of the issue at hand (Holzer et al. 2004). Recent advances in the usability of presented information have aided in this effort. A glance at the cases of utilizing citizen online participation forums on the Mysidewalk website suggests an extensive use of icons for concepts or ideas, and a real-time tally of votes and comments.[14] A user/citizen can easily follow a stream of relevant comments or even respond to them as part of an online dialogue. In addition, a GIS with collaborative features can be used for meaningful online citizen participation (Ganapati 2010). For instance, Portland provided a "Build-a-System" tool online on top of the Google Maps platform for citizens to conduct their own assessment of cost, ridership, and environmental impact of various proposed scenarios for a transportation system. Then citizens were allowed to fill out an online questionnaire as part of the public input process (Ganapati 2010, 23).

Sustainable implementation of open government is about capturing citizens' attention online and demonstrating the relevance of their input. With the competition between various types of information and services online, governments must make any online civic engagement convenient and attractive. This requires governments to engage citizens online where they congregate, such as the use of Facebook and social media to get citizens' attention (Mergel 2013; Zavattaro and Bryer 2016). Making websites mobile-device friendly is another constructive way of attracting citizens online. Sustainability also involves government implementing top-ranked policy ideas that citizens help generate. As knowledge management studies (i.e. Wagner 2003; McNabb 2007; Gottschalk 2007) have argued, a major incentive for people to contribute is to see whether their ideas have actually made a difference.

Implementation should take a more incremental and experimental approach. A study examining local government efforts in open government underscores the relevance of an incremental approach to understanding and managing data release (Conradie and Choenni 2014). The same discipline of project management also applies to online open-government initiatives. It is better to start small with a pilot project and then draw lessons from that pilot project before expanding to a more comprehensive online presence and engagement. For instance, a government can start with a Facebook page as an extension of its website with a single author and a consistent message. This will trigger discussion about issues such as privacy, security, and public records as well as the level of online engagement with citizens. At the same time, governments should be innovative and experimental, even in small ways. For instance, the City of River Forest in Illinois, USA, worked with a company to offer apps for citizens to find local city services and business information. This application also allows citizens to submit service requests via their smart phones.

Moreover, an open-government implementation needs to be forward-looking in adapting and leveraging the ever-changing landscape of ICTs. The rise of smart mobile devices, including phones, tablets, and GPS, offers ample opportunities for government to connect with citizens on a more timely and personal basis. An open GIS platform to advance transparency, participation, and collaboration has significant potential in allowing people to share information on a map and collaborate through a GIS platform (Sui 2014). The advent of semantic web, the web that serves not only as text or information but also as database, will also have implications for transparency, participation, and collaboration. An appropriate institutional mechanism is to have joint meetings between an open government committee (one in the State of New York) and a technology committee to identify trends and be an innovator.

Conclusion

Overall, technology is an enabler for transparency, participation, and collaboration, the three pillars for open government. As illustrated in Figure 4.1, technology enactment builds on relevant institutions that provide citizens with government information, allowing them to participate in policy-making, and fostering collaboration between citizens and government for solving challenging public problems. In the past, collecting and sharing citizen input for the entire community, state, or national government was cost prohibitive and time-consuming. However, the advances of ICTs significantly lower the cost of coordination and transactions for governments, citizens, and other groups as they work together. With websites and Web 2.0 technologies, citizen comments can now be collected electronically and can be shared instantly. The essence of Web 2.0 is a participatory platform (O'Reilly 2005; Lytras, Damiani, and de Pablos 2009), an environment that also allows a process of electronic deliberation through posts and comments. Moreover, open government represents a paradigm shift from treating citizens as customers to regarding them as people who have obligations and duties for making sound public policy and co-producing public services.

The realization of the full potential of ICT-enabled open government faces management challenges. One is to build the appropriate institutions and muster the political will to meet the intensive resource requirements for open government. There are emerging issues such as the application of open records laws to records generated via social media and other emerging electronic communication. Moreover, concerns have surfaced about privacy and security along with the proliferation of online forums and mobile devices. Sustaining citizen engagement, as some social media experiments have discovered, takes sustained attention, creativity, and commitment to responsiveness.

This chapter offers public administrators/managers a comprehensive strategy for addressing the challenges of open government. This strategy lays an institutional foundation and focuses on developing a policy framework for online citizen engagement. Such a framework addresses issues such as the level of transparency, meaningful online engagement, collaboration requirements, and digital privacy and security. Moreover, it offers an implementation approach with several policy considerations for public managers to consider in regard to the goal of customizing their implementation to fit their unique needs and circumstances. Such an approach needs to garner executive support, increase integration across online engagement platforms, conduct targeted transparency, sustain meaningful engagement, and practice incremental implementation. Lastly, an innovative and forward-looking culture will help governments leverage the innovations in ICT to deliver values to citizens.

Notes

1. For example, the City of Jacksonville, Florida, has streamed their city council meetings online: www.coj.net/city-council.aspx, accessed June 28, 2013.
2. This app provides interactive visualization of the U.S. Federal Government budget: www.govtech.com/data/Open-Data-App-Visualizes-US-Budget-for-2016.html, accessed September 15, 2016.
3. For more details, visit www.govtech.com/data/The-DATA-Act-Passes-3-Takeaways-and-Interactive-Timeline.html, accessed September 20, 2015.
4. Such participation was made available via its EngageOmaha.com website (www.engageomaha.com/, accessed June 20, 2012; please note, the website no longer exists and is here for information only).
5. The website is www.epeople.go.kr, accessed March 15, 2013.
6. The website used by the university is policychallenge.asu.edu/, accessed July 1, 2012.
7. www.finance.gov.au/e-government/service-improvement-and-delivery/australian-government-consultation-blog.html, accessed June 20, 2012 (please note, the website no longer exists and is here for information only).
8. For more information, visit www.data.gov/communities/node/116/apps/124, accessed January 20, 2012.
9. For more details, visit www.justice.gov/oip/foia_updates/Vol_XVII_4/page2.htm, accessed December 2, 2011.
10. For additional information, visit www.pewinternet.org/2015/10/29/the-demographics-of-device-ownership/, accessed September 15, 2016.
11. For more details, visit pewinternet.org/Infographics/2012/Our-Smartphone-Habits.aspx, accessed September 1, 2013.
12. See www.gsa.gov/portal/content/288141, accessed July 30, 2016.
13. For more details, visit data.cityofchicago.org/, accessed June 30, 2012.
14. For more examples, visit www.mysidewalk.com, accessed September 16, 2016.

References

Ahn, Michael. 2010. "Adoption of E-Communication Applications in U.S. Municipalities: The Role of Political Environment, Bureaucratic Structure, and the Nature of Applications." *American Review of Public Administration* 71 (4):428–52.
Ahn, Michael J., and Stuart Bretschneider. 2011. "Politics of E-Government: E-Government and the Political Control of Bureaucracy." *Public Administration Review* 71 (3):414–24.
Bannister, Frank, and Regina Connolly. 2011. "The Trouble with Transparency: A Critical Review of Openness in e-Government." *Policy & Internet* 3 (1):1–30.
Berry, Carolyn, Glen Krutz, Barbara Langner, and Peter Budetti. 2008. "Jump-Starting Collaboration: The ABCD Initiative and the Provision of Child Development Services through Medicaid and Collaborators." *Public Administration Review* 48 (3):480–90.
Berry, Frances, and Ralph Brower. 2005. "Intergovernmental and Intersectoral Management: Weaving Networking, Contracting Out, and Management Roles into Third Party Management." *Public Performance and Management Review* 29 (1):7–17.
Bertot, John C., Paul T. Jaeger, and Justin M. Grimes. 2010. "Using ICTs to Create a Culture of Transparency: E-Government and Social Media as Openness and Anti-Corruption Tools for Societies." *Government Information Quarterly* 27 (3):264–71.
Chang, Ai-Mei, and P. K. Kannan. 2008. "Leveraging Web 2.0 in Government." Washington, DC: IBM Center for the Business of Government.
Chen, Yu-Che. 2010. "Citizen-Centric E-Government Services: Understanding Integrated Citizen Service Information Systems." *Social Science Computer Review* 28 (4):427–42.
Chinese Academy of Governance. 2012. "Evaluation Report on Chinese Government Microblogs in 2011" (in Chinese) (2011 nian zhongguo zhengwu weibo pinggu baogao). Beijing, China: Electronic Government Research Center, Chinese Academy of Governance.
Conradie, Peter, and Sunil Choenni. 2014. "On the Barriers for Local Government Releasing Open Data." *Government Information Quarterly* 31 (Supplement 1): S10–S17.
Dawes, Sharon, and Natalie Helbig. 2010. "Information Strategies for Open Government: Challenges and Prospects for Deriving Public Value from Government Transparency." In *E-Government: Lecture Notes in Computer Science*, edited by M.A. Wimmer, J.-L. Chappelet, M. Janssen and H.J. Scholl, 50–60. IFIP: EGov 2010.
Denhardt, Janet, and Robert Denhardt. 2007. *The New Public Service: Serving, Not Steering* (Expanded Edition). Armonk, New York: M.E. Sharpe.
Drew, Christina H., and Timothy L. Nyerges. 2004. "Transparency of Environmental Decision Making." *Journal of Risk Research* 77 (1):33–71.
Fountain, Jane. 2001. *Building the Virtual State: Information Technology and Institutional Change*. Washington, DC: Brookings Institution Press.
Fung, Archon, Mary Graham, and David Weil. 2007. *Full Disclosure: The Perils and Promise of Transparency*. Cambridge, NY: Cambridge University Press.
Ganapati, Sukumar. 2010. "Using Geographic Information Systems to Increase Citizen Engagement." Washington, DC: IBM Center for the Business of Government.

Ganapati, Sukumar. 2011. "Uses of Public Participation Geographic Information Systems Applications in E-Government." *Public Administration Review* 71 (3): 425–34.
General Service Administration. 2008. *Government and Social Media*. Washington, DC: Office of Citizen Services, General Service Administration.
Gottschalk, Petter. 2007. "Information Systems in Police Knowledge Management." *Electronic Government: An International Journal* 4 (2):191–203.
Government Accountability Office (GAO). 2014. *Federal Data Transparency: Effective Implementation of the DATA Act Would Help Address Government-wide Management Challenges and Improve Oversight*. Washington, DC: Government Accountability Office.
Government Technology. 2015. "Year in Data: CIO Priorities." *Government Technology* 28 (8):13.
Grimmelikhuijsen, Stephan, and Eric W. Welch. 2012. "Developing and Testing a Theoretical Framework for Computer-Mediated Transparency of Local Governments." *Public Administration Review* 72 (4):562–71.
Heald, David. 2006. "Varieties of Transparency." In *Transparency: The Key to Better Government?*, edited by Christopher Hood and David Heald, 25–43. Oxford, UK: Oxford University Press.
Holzer, Marc, James Melitski, Seung-Yong Rho, and Richard Schwester. 2004. *Restoring Trust in Government: The Potential of Digital Citizen Participation*. Washington, DC: IBM Center for the Business of Government.
International City/County Management Association (ICMA). 2011. Electronic Government 2011. Washington, DC: International City/County Management Association.
Janssen, Marijn, Ricardo Matheus, and Anneke Zuiderwijk. 2015. "Big and Open Linked Data (BOLD) to Create Smart Cities and Citizens: Insights from Smart Energy and Mobility Cases." In *EGov 2015*, edited by Efthimios Tambouris, 79–90. Switzerland: Springer.
Kakabadse, Andrew, K. Nada Kakabadse, and Alexander Kouzmin. 2003. "Reinventing the Democratic Governance Project through Information Technology? A Growing Agenda for Debate." *Public Administration Review* 63 (1): 44–60.
Leighninger, Matt. 2011. "Using Online Tools to Engage—and be Engaged by—The Public." Washington, DC: IBM Center for the Business of Government.
Lytras, Miltiadis, Ernesto Damiani, and Patricia Ordónez de Pablos, eds. 2009. *Web 2.0: The Business Model*. New York: Springer.
McNabb, David E. 2007. *Knowledge Management in the Public Sector: A Blueprint for Innovation in Government*. Armonk, NY; London, UK: M.E. Sharpe.
Mergel, Ines. 2013. *Social Media in the Public Sector: A Guide to Participation, Collaboration and Transparency in the Networked World*. San Francisco, CA: John Wiley & Sons.
Ministry of Industry and Information Technology. 2009. The Publicity of the 7th (2008) Chinese Government Website Performance Review. Beijing, China: Ministry of Industry and Information Technology.
Moon, Jae, and Donald Norris. 2005. "Does Managerial Orientation Matter? The Adoption of Reinventing Government and E-Government at the Municipal Level." *Information Systems Journal* 15 (1):43–60.

O'Leary, Rosemary, and Lisa Blomgren Bingham, eds. 2009. "The Collaborative Public Manager: New Ideas for the Twenty-first Century." In *Public Management and Change Series*, edited by Beryl Radin. Washington, DC: Georgetown University Press.

O'Reilly, Tim. 2005. "What is Web 2.0? Design Patterns and Business Models for the Next Generation of Software." Available at: oreilly.com/pub/a/web2/archive/what-is-web-20.html?page=1 (accessed April 29, 2014).

Orszag, Peter R. 2009. Open Government Directive, Memorandum for the Heads of Executive Departments and Agencies, edited by Executive Office of the President Office of Management and Budget: Office of Management and Budget.

Pew Research Center. 2015. *Americans' Views on Open Government Data*. Washington, DC: Pew Research Center.

Puddephatt, Andrew. 2009. *Exploring the Role of Civil Society in the Formulation and Adoption of Access to Information Laws: The Cases of Bulgaria, India, Mexico, South Africa and the United Kingdom*. Washington, DC: World Bank.

Sui, Daniel. 2014. "Opportunities and Impediments for Open GIS." *Transactions in GIS* 18 (1):1–24.

Thomas, John Clayton. 2012. *Citizen, Customer, Partner: Engaging the Public in Public Management*. Almond, NY; London, UK: M.E. Sharpe.

Tolbert, Caroline, Karen Mossberger, and Ramona S. McNeal. 2008. "Institutions, Policy Innovation, and E-Government in the American States." *Public Administration Review* 68 (3):549–63.

United Nations. 2005. Global E-Government Readiness Report 2005: From E-Government to E-Inclusion. New York: United Nations.

United Nations. 2008. UN E-Government Survey 2008: From E-Government to Connected Governance. New York: United Nations.

United Nations. 2016. United Nations E-Government Survey 2016: E-Government in Support of Sustainable Development. New York: Department of Economic and Social Affairs, United Nations.

Wagner, Christian. 2003. "Knowledge Management in E-Government." *Proceedings of the Ninth American Information Systems Conference*: 845–50.

Worthy, Ben. 2015. "The Impact of Open Data in UK: Complex, Unpredictable, and Political." *Public Administration* 93 (3):788–805.

Wu, H., and B. Sun. 2009. "An Empirical Study on the Status Quo, Challenges and Countermeasures of Contemporary Chinese E-government (in Chinese)." *Journal of Chinese Academy of Governance* 5:123–7.

Zavattaro, Staci M., and Thomas A. Bryer, eds. 2016. *Social Media for Government: Theory and Practice*. New York: Routledge.

Zients, Jeffrey. 2010. Guidance on the Use of Challenges and Prizes to Promote Open Government, edited by Executive Office of the President Office of Management and Budget: Office of Management and Budget.

5 Citizen-centric Digital Governance

Introduction

The advances in information and communication technologies (ICTs) have provided the technical foundation for providing citizen-centric online experiences with public information and services. One prominent example in this area is the citizen-service hotline (usually referred to as 311 in the U.S.) that is supported by customer service representatives as well as a sophisticated citizen service information system connected with phone and other communication devices. Such citizen service information portals have increasingly been made available via multiple platforms such as social networking platforms, websites, smart phones, and others.

One of the aspirations of citizen-centric digital government service is the notion of personalized and responsive service (Goldsmith and Crawford 2014). Citizens receive customized public information and services from government delivered right to them. South Korea, a leading nation in e-government (United Nations 2010, 2012, 2014), has touted Government 3.0 that embodies this exact idea (Creative Government Planning Division 2013). For instance, a disabled citizen has his/her own portal of information and benefits individualized to the government's assistance to him/her. The United Kingdom won the top ranking in 2016 with the provision of full transactional capability and whole-of-government integration to better serve users (United Nations 2016, 83). The responsibility rests with the government to fully integrate its information and services with needs from the customer/citizen perspective.

The realization of the promise of a personalized citizen service requires standardization of government information, sharing of information across agencies, design of appropriate interfaces (i.e. voice command or live assistance for visually impaired), etc. (White House 2012). The real challenges are more about policies, management, and governance and less about technology as suggested by studies of e-government (Ahn and Bretschneider 2011; Dawes, Cresswell, and Pardo 2009). For instance, for an integrated citizen service information system (a sophisticated form of 311), city departments need to agree to use the same information system and standard ways of codifying and routing services. The investment of resources both in terms of time and money, which is essential for a citizen service information system, is a key political and managerial decision.

To convert the promise of citizen-centric digital government into a reality, this chapter will focus on the challenges facing public managers in providing citizen-centric digital services as well as management strategies to address them. It will begin with a definition of citizen-centric digital governance. Next, it will articulate management challenges associated with conducting citizen-centric digital governance. Then, the chapter will present management strategies and techniques to further improve digital governance.

Citizen-centric Digital Governance: Public Values, Roles of Citizens, and Illustration

Citizen-centric digital governance is the ICT-enabled attainment of public values such as efficiency, effectiveness, equity, transparency, democracy, and accountability.[1] Efficiency could manifest as the time saved as the result of renewing a driver's license electronically rather than waiting in line for hours for such a renewal. Effectiveness could involve making real-time bus arrival information available on smart phones to enable people to optimize their schedules and plan activities. Transparency might take the form of making health inspection information on restaurants available online, allowing customers to make more informed individual decisions about what establishments to patronize. City governments can stream their city council meetings for transparency and accountability. Democratic principles are served when citizens can engage government via various means convenient to them. It is important to note, however, that when governments seek to pursue multiple values, it may imply trade-offs (Brown 2007; Bretschneider and Wittmer 1993). For instance, the procedural justice that prioritizes thoroughness and participation above speed can sometimes come into conflict with efficiency.

Three Roles: Citizens, Customers, and Partners

Citizen-centric is about recognizing and incorporating various roles that citizens play in the community as they interact with government. The three main roles that citizens play are citizens, customers, and partners (Thomas 2012). Citizens embody the notion of rights such as basic human rights as well as the freedom of assembly and freedom to petition. In the United States, the "We the People" federal government website allows citizens to exercise their right to petition as protected under the First Amendment to the Constitution. The South Korean government has even gone one step further to develop a one-stop portal for all citizen complaints.[2] This portal will allow citizens to offer their thoughts and feedback directly to the South

Korean government, and the government is then tasked to direct the complaints to the appropriate agency. This design pays more attention to ensuring it to be citizen-centric (customer-centric).

At the same time, citizenship implies a responsibility to uphold the constitution and perform civic duties to sustain governance and government. One way of sustaining governance is to actively participate in the development of rules and regulations that affect citizens' lives and communities. ICTs can also facilitate citizens' ability to govern via established mechanisms. One prominent example in the United States is e-rulemaking, which allows citizens to provide their comments electronically on proposed federal regulations. In the past, such comments were only allowed by hard copy. E-rulemaking lowers the cost and barrier to commenting for those who have access to a computer and the internet.

Citizens can serve as partners in improving public services via the use of ICTs. One of the main ways for citizens to serve as partners is for them to capture and share information about their community with government and other residents in that community. The City of Boston, for example, has a "Citizens Connect" smart phone application that allows citizens to be reporters on community issues. Partnering involves the co-production of public services. The use of social media for public safety has shown promise and potential cost-savings for building a network of citizens working with the police department to co-produce 24/7 public safety information (Meijer 2014). A long-standing example is community policing: when people in the community join with the government to improve public safety. Some local police departments in the United States utilize Facebook pages for receiving alerts and information on disruptive or even criminal activities from members of their communities.

More recently, the growth of open data allows citizens to serve as partners. These volunteer programmers can serve the role of information aggregators and make information available in a user-friendly format. Another way for citizens to act as partners (co-producers) is for them to develop applications by utilizing large public data sets. One such example is the development of a software program that expedites the process of getting a permit to get into the carpool lane. This software program was later purchased by government for wide adoption. Moreover, the U.S. Federal Government has a challenge.gov website to crowdsource solutions to policy problems. Through the use of ICTs, citizens can be co-producers (partners) with government to solve complex public problems.

Among the three roles, the role of citizens as customers is the most prominent in the studies of e-government. This could be the result of governments adopting customer-relationship management strategies and supporting information systems for serving citizens. A customer-oriented e-government makes finding government information easy by incorporating elements such as search engines. This strategy is evident in the most recent award-winning state government websites, such as the State of Utah, which prominently feature search boxes. Moreover, customer-friendly means integrating various services into a one-stop, all-inclusive service portal. A sophisticated citizen service information system (311 in some large cities) empowers government employees to answer all the questions that a customer citizen has on the spot and initiate a service request right away.

The role of customers is beyond individual residents in the community simply receiving government services such as public safety and emergency services, transportation, utilities, etc. A citizen can also be a business owner. A significant portion of e-government services serves businesses in accomplishing regulatory policy objectives. These include business registration, health inspection, etc. In addition, a citizen might be a manager of a local non-profit organization. These non-profits may receive government grants or work with governmental agencies for providing human services. A customer-oriented digital governance needs to consider all aspects of citizen customers because these individuals could be business owners or non-profit managers.

An Illustrative Case: New York City 311

The 311 system in New York City illustrates the citizen-centric notion of digital governance. It is citizen-centric by considering the issues of equity and accessibility as core public values. Using a phone number as the main way of communicating with government addresses one of the main concerns of providing information and services solely online—digital divide. The 311 system is available to anyone with access to a phone, which addresses the issue of access provided that the penetration rate of phones is over 99 percent. Such penetration is better than the internet use rate of approximately 87 percent according to the January 2014 survey conducted by the Pew Internet and American Life Project. The NYC 311 system is supported by telecommunication agreements between telecommunication service providers (landline and mobile) that enable individuals to just dial 311 on their mobile phones to access a customer service representative (as long as they are inside the city boundary).

NYC's 311 system exists to put customers/users first in terms of how government information and services are provided. For instance, one feature of the system is the ability to communicate with people in the city in their native languages. Combined, the customer representatives speak more than 170 languages, indicative of the diverse array of languages spoken in the city. The highlights of NYC's 311 system are presented in Box 5.1. This system embodies the basic principle of personalized public services. Moreover, the NYC 311 system supports multiple platforms for accessing information and services that are convenient for users. People can access NYC 311 via their smart phones, i-Pads, and other mobile devices. In addition, the channels of communication include websites, social media,

> **Box 5.1 Highlights of NYC's 311**
>
> *Customer Contact*: 28 million in 2014; peak is more than 200,000 a day
> *Services Provided*: City service information; service request submission and tracking
> *Channels Supported*: Phone, website, apps for smart phones and mobile devices, Skype
> *Languages Supported*: More than 170 spoken languages and 50 written languages
> *Population Served*: over eight million (2010 Census data)
> *Budget*: US$58m (2008 data)
>
> Sources: NYC's 311 website (www1.nyc.gov/311/about-311.page, accessed February 15, 2015); NYC Independent Budget Office.

Twitter, text messaging, etc. This perspective induces the city to support such services in ways that users (citizens, residents, and visitors) prefer rather than what the city government prefers. In the past, citizens have borne the burden of navigating complex bureaucratic structures to identify the right office to contact and of preparing the correct information for various types of paperwork. In contrast, the current NYC 311 allows citizens to track their service requests. They can get status updates on their phones. They can determine when service tickets are open in response to their requests and when tickets are closed. Such a 311 system provides a personalized service by integrating information and services from various city departments.

The NYC 311 system also positions citizens as partners. It allows citizens to make a complaint via the website or by using 311 applications. This partnership extends to giving citizens voices as community members by reporting issues in the community. Collectively, these citizen complaints/reports can help the city discover the nature and extent of problems more easily, without the time and manpower required for city employees to patrol city blocks. Moreover, the NYC government has made 311 content an application programming interface (API) for volunteer application developers to add value to 311 city service data, as well as hosted a "BigApps" annual apps development competition to motivate citizens to develop applications using open city data to provide better public service.

Regarding the role of citizens in governance, the NYC 311 citizen service information system takes an indirect approach. This is probably by design because the goal and purpose of the 311 system is to provide city information and services as opposed to "e-rulemaking" or "e-petition"

("We the People") systems that allow for direct commenting on a proposed regulation or policy initiation. The NYC government treats 311 as a rich source of service information for good governance as indicated in its statement on using such information for improving city services.

Cross-boundary Collaboration

Citizen-centric is also about working across sectors (public, private, and non-profit) for the purpose of placing citizens rather than government at the center of public service. ICTs, when properly deployed, help facilitate the exchange and dissemination of information as illustrated in the use of social media for providing up-to-date disaster and rescue information. Improving financial transparency via the use of a standard semantic web language is another case in point (Chen 2012). Governments (especially financial regulators), reporting corporations, software vendors, and non-profit organizations (i.e. professional associations representing accountants) need to follow a uniform standard for coding their information to make this information comparable, accessible, and understandable by citizens.

Another example of cross-boundary collaboration for public service is the need to create a people-centered approach to social services, which requires information sharing among government, non-profits, and private companies. A non-profit organization in the state of Illinois provides a cloud-based application to offer an integrated view of the clients that receive social services from government and other entities.[3] A case worker can review all the services that his/her client received for the last year, which helps to identify problems and avoid duplication of services. A more recent example is the community platform established for residents in North Florida that provides access to information on various types of services and related access and transportation information.[4]

Management and Governance Challenges of Citizen-centric Digital Government

The most fundamental challenges for adopting citizen-centric digital governance are institutional and managerial in nature. The technology for integrating databases to create citizen-centric views and functionalities is available, as it has been developed in the private sector to serve corporations. In the public sector, the real issues are usually ones of institutions and competing goals. The discussion that follows is organized around two main institutional and organizational configurations to illustrate the challenges involved. The first institutional arrangement exists inside a single unit of government such as a city or state government. The second one involves citizen-centric digital governance via cross-boundary collaboration that could involve other governments, non-profit organizations, and even businesses.

Integration Challenges Inside a Unit of Government

The challenge of providing citizen-centric e-government services lies in the supporting institution/rules for integration of information and systems, even among departments of a local or state government. Traditionally, there has been a lack of coordination or standardization in either data standard or information systems. Each department selects an information system and accompanying data standards that are optimized for its respective service area, such as finance, human resources, or public safety. Additionally, there is a lack of incentives for coordination and/or data sharing if the logic of public administration calls for citizens to figure things out by themselves in terms of navigating through governmental structure by going to various government departments for service.

The current reality of government websites reflects the well-established practice of department or service-specific logic of government information organization and information system specification. Each department provides its information and online services on the relevant pages of the website. To a large extent, e-government websites simply organize information in a way that is easier for citizens to find. The dominant mode of operation is still department-driven, with little data sharing or implementation of common standards for information interoperability. Although the search engine option on many government websites greatly reduces the time and effort to find information, it does not integrate information and services to offer citizen-centric services. Citizens may, after searching information, realize that they still need to travel to multiple departments and wait in line to complete the entire process of getting services (i.e. obtaining a building permit or driver's license). They may even encounter conflicting information that adds to the confusion.

The integration challenge is significant even inside unitary governments such as local governments. A local government needs to forge agreements between city departments, and sometimes independently elected offices/commissions, to provide citizen-centric online public services. A case in point is the 311 system for Minneapolis, Minnesota. Such a system, in its full implementation, requires cooperation between all 18 governmental units, but only half of them report to the city coordinator (Fleming 2008). As mentioned before, each department has its own priorities and tends to put department interests above the interests of the collective. An added complication is the potential tension between the elected offices inside a local government and those under the direction of a city manager's office.

In addition to the potential disparities in policy priorities and resources, the coordination and data standardization process is simply time consuming. An integrated 311 system requires the ability to query various information systems in various departments and bring the data together to present a citizen-centric view. Such a system requires a clear definition of key terms and a classification system that works in tandem with public works systems, among others. What adds to the analytical power of an integrated 311 is the ability to geo-code service information. However, the effort involved to take advantage of geo-coded service information, often under-appreciated, is the digitizing of maps and overlaying service orders onto these maps as typically seen in a geographic information system (GIS) (Ganapati 2011). To create a citizen-centric view, a city needs to have all its service records identify with individuals. At minimum, it is necessary to use the same ID for the same individual across various information systems. As a result, government agencies can pull any service requests tied to one individual with precision by using the same ID number. Such standardization for information interoperability is time consuming, especially when there is disagreement about which department's ID should be the standard and other departments need to invest resources to conform with the new standard.

Cross-boundary Integration Challenges for Citizen-centric Digital Government Service

Cross-boundary or cross-jurisdiction citizen-centric information systems have added another layer of complexity to the integration of information and systems to provide citizen-centric services. Cross-boundary or cross-jurisdiction integration faces more severe challenges on several fronts. First, the issue of different jurisdictional priorities has become a dominant factor in comparison with inter-departmental collaboration inside a city hall or state capitol. The source of conflicts could be as foundational as the basic values brought in by various organizations. For instance, a recent study of a Swedish healthcare information sharing initiative indicates some fundamental value conflicts in what is legal and desirable (Hellberg and Grönlund 2013). Some of the fundamental conflicts are rooted in value differences, especially when new legislations are required for interoperability.

Another challenge associated with information-sharing and/or information system integration across organizational boundaries is difference in incentive structures among participating organizations. The basic question of who is going to bear the cost and who is going to reap the benefit can determine whether, and the extent to which, organizations are willing to participate in a collaborative project (Agranoff 2007; Agranoff and McGuire 2003). Even when a shared value exists for providing a citizen-centric service at the local level, city and county governments can get entangled in negotiations on whose data standards to follow and who is going to bear the responsibility of providing needed support and resources, as there are cost implications. For instance, it is much more challenging for a county government to justify the provision of GIS services to nearby cities if there is no cost-sharing among these government entities. This speaks to a larger point: the need for a robust incentive structure (network management) ensuring that the payoff (political, managerial, or financial) for each participating organization should exceed their investment, at least in the long run.

Even on an operational level, the logistics of harmonizing a multitude of data definitions, standards, and information policies is a challenge (Dawes, Cresswell, and Pardo 2009). Information interoperability starts with a shared taxonomy of terms and definitions. Given that these definitions are developed in the context of the specific information needs of individual organizations, it is not surprising that a variety of terms are developed. For example, in an effort to standardize business reporting to government, the Dutch government found that there are over nine definitions of businesses across various government agencies (Bharosa et al. 2011). In addition, there are a variety of information policies and regulations that various participating organizations need to follow. A challenge is created when information coming from various organizations is centralized in one place for these organizations to share but differential standards are applied to that information. For instance, creating a holistic point of view for individuals receiving government assistance requires information sharing among government agencies and service providers (non-profit or for-profit) that centers around these clients. However, medical and health service information, as required by the Health Insurance Portability and Accountability Act (HIPAA), needs to meet a different standard than criminal records or information on the receipt of government services. Such disparity adds complexity to information management and stewardship in terms of negotiating and implementing an acceptable information-sharing protocol and information system development.

Cross-sector information-sharing for personalized public services adds another layer of complexity due to the different goals and values that separate one sector from another. The profit motivation of private corporations is different from the motivation of government to advance public values (Rocheleau 2006; Bretschneider and Wittmer 1993; Bozeman and Bretschneider 1986). For instance, the ideal world of financial transparency would require governments and corporations to share financial information to help understand and manage risks involved in investing and the financial market as a whole. However, private corporations do not have the incentives to make their financial report transparent and, at minimum, to convert it into a format (i.e. XBRL) for the ease of analysis for regulators. In addition, some of the firms specializing in providing financial information services are concerned about a growing government role in making such information services available directly to investors. Such availability can result in a loss of business for these financial information service firms.

The challenge of cross-sector participation is present even in the event of a compelling shared interest. Taking the example of an emergency response system, a study of the response to the September 11 terrorist attack has shown that some of the utility companies and cell phone service providers affected were not even in any agreement prior to the attack to share information (Kapucu 2006). This was the case even when all of them were willing to share information to cope with disasters. Another example is information security. Although it is beneficial for public, private, and non-profit organizations to share information about any issues they have experienced with information security, there is a lack of established mechanisms and incentives for doing so. This is particularly challenging when these organizations are concerned about the bad publicity that goes with admitting any security breaches in their information systems.

Management Strategies for Citizen-centric Digital Governance

General Guidelines for an Integrated Strategy

The ultimate success of citizen-centric digital governance is rooted in a citizen-centric culture that permeates not only various sub-units (i.e. departments) of a single government (state or local) but also organizations that participate in any collaborative to provide citizen-centric digital government services. As articulated earlier in this chapter, the fundamental challenge for integrated e-government services is one of policy and institution. The culture of many governments is dominated by bureaucratic structure. Although such structure is helpful for efficiency and accountability, it can also create problems of inertia and rigidity (Merton 1957). One way of countering the problems associated with traditional bureaucratic culture is exemplified by customer services demonstrated by the National Performance Review in the United States in the 1990s and the New Public Management movement around the world. Such customer-service orientations help counter the turf battles that are evident among departments and governments over jurisdiction issues and resource competition (Barzelay and Armajani 1992).

The importance of addressing such a basic issue as instilling a citizen-centric organizational culture is also seen in various e-government studies. A study of the modernization in the Department of Revenue in the state of Colorado with electronic services has pointed to the challenge that can occur when an institution initially encounters major resistance to implementation (Bhattacherjee 2000). Once the citizen-centric culture and the incentive structure was in place, the implementation went smoothly. A survey of local governments that have adopted such systems shows that the sophistication of those systems is less the function of technical capacity than the function of a customer-service orientation (Chen 2010).

A system perspective is productive for designing and implementing an integrated strategy for citizen-centric digital governance. Governments need to join up and work together to provide citizen-centric services (6 et al. 2002). A system perspective shifts focus back to the service and delineates various components of the system that need to work together to provide that service. Such a system perspective is more inclusive than a government-centric perspective. For instance, healthcare services in the United States are a system that includes governments, non-profit hospitals and health services, for-profit healthcare service providers, insurance companies, healthcare professionals, and patients. A system-perspective can put citizens in the center and map out how various components of the system work together to make it truly citizen-centric. Such a perspective should guide design and implementation.

Moreover, such a system perspective recognizes and includes various sub-systems and their interdependence in a large system of citizen-centric public service. A vibrant urban community requires that various sub-systems of public services such as environment, economy, healthcare, energy, resources, education, transportation, social services and more work together. Interdependence between sub-systems is an important feature of such a system perspective (Falconer and Mitchell 2012). For instance, air pollution would exert pressure on the healthcare system when people have respiratory problems. Poor education is likely to hamper economic development as companies making location decisions would seek to gain access to a skilled workforce. The lack of social services such as care for the homeless population can create problems for the healthcare sub-system. The inherent interdependence of various public service areas demands system thinking.

Another important guideline for pursuing a citizen-centric digital governance solution is the ability to work with the dominant mode of the administrative system for public service delivery in question. A citizen-centric digital governance project resting on the assumption that technological change will automatically drive wholesale administrative reform is likely to fail. The examination of e-government development at the local level has shown incremental rather than transformational development (Norris and Reddick 2013). In government, institutional and organizational factors are the dominant factors determining the adoption of technology (Fountain 2001). Therefore, a more practical and achievable approach strives to recognize and work with the dominant mode of the administrative system in question (Lindblom 1979).

An illustrative example of applying this guideline is the adoption of relevant ICTs to healthcare. The British system is a centralized one with government as the single payer for healthcare services and the biggest healthcare service provider. In this type of case, a national electronic patient record information system is fitting to provide a citizen-centric healthcare service. Citizens have access to all the medical services received and their health information when visiting any clinic or hospital in Britain. In contrast, such a national and centralized approach is simply not feasible in the United States due to the important role that private and non-profit organizations play in the payment for (i.e. health insurance companies) and delivery of healthcare services (i.e. the role of non-profit hospitals and

98 *Citizen-centric Digital Governance*

Table 5.1 Strategies for Citizen-centric Digital Governance

Main strategies	Specifics
Elevation of citizen-centric digital governance inside a government	Building political and administrative support for an enterprise perspective
	Building supportive governance structure and rules for enterprise information technology
Cross-boundary collaboration for citizen-centric digital government service	Stakeholders' identification and activation
	Information and policy mapping
	Building governance structures for citizen-centric cross-boundary information sharing and system integration
	Institutionalization and implementation
Citizen–government collaboration for citizen-centric service	Citizens as reporters and partners for public service production
	Leading and managing citizen–government collaboration

systems), and the resulting fragmented nature of patient-centered health information exchange. As a result, a more successful digital governance approach to improve a patient- (citizen-) centric service tends to be regional in nature and governed by a federated system of information-sharing.

There are three general strategies that a government can pursue to improve its citizen-centric digital governance as summarized in Table 5.1. The first strategy emphasizes a government's internal concerns by elevating political and administrative support as well as building a governance structure for an enterprise citizen-centric administrative system. The second strategy embodies an external orientation, focusing on collaboration with a variety of stakeholders outside a particular government. The last strategy engages citizens as partners and collaborators for citizen-centric service with a support structure. The specifics on these strategies follow below.

Elevation of Citizen-centric Digital Governance Inside a Government

Build Political and Administrative Support for an Enterprise Perspective

One of the first steps in ensuring citizen-centric digital governance is to garner the political and administrative support to lay the foundation for a citizen-centric organization. The case for political and administrative support is grounded in achieving public values to which citizens subscribe. For instance, elected officials and policy makers can see the value of pushing for a more citizen-centric approach to public services as a way to serve their constituents and, consequentially, secure their offices. Such political support has been recognized as one of the main factors for pushing major investment and progress in e-government services (Ahn and Bretschneider 2011). To gain support from public administrators and employees, an appeal to the spirit of public services can be effective. Such an appeal is about showing how government employees can deliver a high level of public services to benefit citizens with the help of ICTs. In general, an appeal to public service is one of the ways to gain support from career public administrators.

Building such political and administrative support is also about growing the organizational culture for citizen-centric enterprise thinking. The citizen-centric culture typically challenges the status quo. As a result, instilling this type of culture implies organizational changes that would require the support of leadership and the commitment of organizational members (Khademian 2002). Organizational change inevitably faces resistance on both the basic operational level and on the tactical level, as government reform has demonstrated. Political and administrative support is the capital that is needed to propel the growth of a citizen-centric culture. The goal is to have such citizen-centric culture permeate the entire government and its services to citizens.

Build Supportive Governance Structure and Rules for Enterprise Information Technology

Building supportive governance structure translates the initial administrative and political momentum into a sustainable structure for effective implementation. A focus on governance is critical in order to ensure a lasting impact. Such a governance structure needs to provide alignment and coordination on both strategic and operational levels. For most governments, the challenges associated with providing citizen-centric e-government services arise from: (a) the lack of representation of information and technology concerns at the enterprise strategic level; and (b) a department-driven, rather than government-wide, approach to information technology (IT) purchase. One way to create supportive governance structure is to institute a chief information officer (CIO), as required by the Clinger-Cohen Act, at the top-level of the organizational structure to direct all the information and technology projects for enterprise alignment. From the process point of view, this Act also requires treating information as a resource like other resources such as human and financial ones. Such a strategic perspective is crucial for increasing the impact of information and technology resources management.

Another supporting governance structure for integrated and personalized digital governance is to institute a CIO council with government-wide rules on information and technology. A CIO council is the main institution at the federal level for coordination and collective decision-making. Moreover, it is also suitable for U.S. state governments with a diverse array of departments and offices that have their own unique missions and lines of accountability. The federalist structure of the government in the United States makes individual state departments (i.e. transportation and education) relatively independent from other state departments due to its reliance on federal rather than state funding. A CIO council is an established governance mechanism to align the interests of individual departments to those of the government as a whole (enterprise perspective).

On an operational level, the governance structure needs supporting rules and regulations for an integrated digital governance. For instance, the United States federal government mandates a set of rules on architecture (infrastructure) in terms of the design and implementation of information and technology infrastructure (standards). It also provides rules for purchasing IT equipment and services in terms of process and interoperability requirements. These rules help save costs and promote interoperability. In addition, there are information access and security requirements that all information technologies and systems need to follow. For example, the Federal Information Security Management Act (FISMA) dictates the information security standards for federal information systems. Section 508 standards need to be followed by federal agencies to ensure access to IT and information.[5] For instance, there should be an easy way of changing fonts on federal government websites, and alternative texts need to be provided for images on websites for the visually impaired.

It is noteworthy that the focus of a governance strategy for citizen-centric digital governance inside a government is somewhat different for a centralized administrative system. In contrast to a federalist government, a government with a centralized administrative system can achieve a high level of integration by having a single information system and/or technology standard for all governmental agencies at the cabinet levels, and sometimes even down to state/province or to local levels. As a result, there is less need for a council form of governance structure for alignment and coordination or any other federated system of governance. For instance, the government of South Korea provides a case in point when all cabinet offices need to use the same information system for budget preparation and accounting. In that case, there is less need to rely on a CIO council for collaborative decision-making and aligning interests. The decision-making structure could more closely resemble that of corporations without the need for buy-in from various departments.

For a centralized form of government, the focus is more on translating institutions and rules to the design and implementation of a centralized citizen-centric information system. As opposed to the need for monitoring compliance via reporting or inspection, the use of a single information system/platform allows for such implementation (with the goal of integration of government services to provide citizen-centric services) to be coded into the system as early as its design. In South Korea, there is a single platform for the entire national government in its budget and accounting. It has integrated the budget and finance processes of 51 governmental agencies into one system that allows a holistic view of the entire process.[6]

Cross-boundary Collaboration for Citizen-centric Digital Government Service

A citizen-centric digital governance across jurisdiction, levels of government, sectors, and even countries requires qualitatively different governance structures and processes than the ones associated with integration within a single governmental unit. As mentioned earlier, there are significant challenges in dealing with a pronounced tension between jurisdictions and levels of governments as well as goal alignments among organizations in different sectors. Given the practical relevance and the rich literature that already exists, this section focuses on cross-boundary government information-sharing and process integration.

Stakeholders Identification and Activation

One of the first steps in cross-boundary information sharing and system integration for citizen-centric services is the identification and activation of key stakeholders while articulating shared goals. The experience of the Standard Business Reporting (SBR) effort in the Netherlands is instructive (Bharosa et al. 2011). The identification of key stakeholders is part of the essential first step to ensure successful implementation for building common standards and integrated systems for cross-boundary business information sharing. The goal is to reduce the redundancy and inconsistency among cabinet-level offices that require compliance information from businesses. On the government side, the stakeholders in the SBR include all cabinet-level agencies that require businesses to report any aspects of their activities. On the business side, the stakeholders include businesses of all sizes. A distinction is made between small- and medium-sized businesses and large corporations. In addition, intermediaries provide services to corporations to meet government reporting requirements.

Furthermore, activation is as important as identification. The literature on network management emphasizes the role of public network managers to activate some key stakeholders (McGuire 2002). The study of the response to the September 11 terrorist attack reveals the deficiencies of a failure to activate some of the key communication companies in dealing with a large-scale attack (Kapucu 2006). These communication companies' active involvement in governance from the beginning will ensure that governments address their concerns when these companies' cooperation is required for success. Such activation requires the network manager to articulate these companies' stake in the outcome of citizen-centric government services. In addition, the manager needs to articulate the interdependence in the framework of shared goals and benefits (Lundin 2007; Bryson, Crosby, and Stone 2006).

Information and Policy Mapping

At the same time, it is important to gain better knowledge of citizen-centric information and information policy surrounding the information. This type of approach should center on the public service in question to identify valuable data for this service as opposed to a government-centric one. For instance, if the goal is to understand homeless people and provide them with appropriate services, the search for pertinent information should center on the basic knowledge about homeless people and the strategy to assist them with breaking the cycle of homelessness. Consequently, such a search would reach out to all organizations that have interacted with these individuals and have information on them, including social service agencies, law enforcement agencies, healthcare providers, and local non-profit organizations.

In addition, there is a need for compiling an inventory of information policy, privacy requirements, and disclosure policy for both the participating organizations and for information-sharing across organizational boundaries. The privacy and disclosure aspects of information policy are salient in cross-boundary information-sharing efforts. One of the main obstacles to cross-boundary information sharing is the need to protect individuals' privacy (Hellberg and Grönlund 2013; Pardo et al. 2009). Another concern is about meeting the demand of information disclosure as dictated by the Freedom of Information Act (FOIA) in the United States. A cross-boundary information-sharing effort needs to map and navigate varying information disclosure requirements and privacy safeguards. Consequently, one of the most influential factors in such an effort is the ability to design rules and systems to accommodate different information disclosure and privacy policies across participating organizations.

Building Governance Structures for Citizen-centric Cross-boundary Information Sharing and System Integration

There are two main models of governance structures for cross-boundary information-sharing and system integration for citizen-centric public service. One is more centralized in its governance, and the other is more federated in nature. The centralized model incorporates a network administrative organization to implement a single information system for the integration of information. For instance, the Taiwanese government has a single business/commerce information system that is used by all government agencies, from central to local, for business registration and license information. This type of governance structure is effective when there is one dominant governmental unit that has both the authority and resources to implement such a system. It is particularly useful when other participating governmental units have limited technological resources but existing information exchange and service responsibility working with a central service agency. Such a governance model, when coupled with major improvement in workflow, can provide a citizen-centric experience. For instance, a citizen as a building contractor can obtain a building permit in a matter of days rather than weeks when all the departments responsible for issuing the permit are using the same system for review and approval with supporting accountability measures in place.

The other governance model utilizes a federation that focuses on forging agreements between all participating organizations. These agreements are made between organizations to form an information exchange mechanism that specifies what information to share as well as the identification number to use for querying information across various information systems. For instance, there is an agreement to support a law enforcement agencies data system called "LEADS" to share law enforcement information across all public safety agencies at local, state, and federal levels in the United States. Due to the federated governance structure, each agency has the final say on what it wishes to share and how it shares the information. The Federal Bureau of Investigation, for example, can decide how many details it wishes to share on a particular individual with local law enforcement authorities. The agreement, however, provides the binding commitment that for an agency to receive information from other agencies, it needs to reciprocate.

The appropriateness, in terms of the emphasis, of the model lies in its fit with the dominant administrative structure for the integration task in question. In the preceding example of law enforcement, the long-standing tradition of independent jurisdictions in the United States makes it more conducive to a federated arrangement. In contrast, in the case of food safety in China, a more centralized model is probably more desirable to provide a single monitoring and reporting system with a common standard. A governance structure that builds on the existing institution and the mainstream political logic is more likely to garner sustained support and commitment.

Institutionalization and Implementation

Implementation of these information-sharing initiatives requires formalizing and institutionalizing governance structure and respective information policies on information exchange, disclosure, and privacy protection. Such institutionalization can take various forms. For a more centralized administrative system, institutionalization can be a mandatory requirement for all participating organizations to adopt the same information system and follow the same set of information disclosure and privacy-protection rules. For instance, in dealing with food safety information reporting issues, the Chinese government could establish a national reporting and information sharing system for all governmental and business units. For a more decentralized system, information and privacy-policy compliance can be addressed with the access and information-sharing protocol as incorporated in the information system. Such institutionalization can be accomplished by a federated agreement that provides policy and procedure for information exchange. It is preferable to automate information exchange so that it is conducted in a way that conforms to the stipulations of the agreement for cross-boundary information exchange.

The long-term sustainability and success of the citizen-centric cross-boundary effort rest on the ability of the collective to govern and regulate behavior. The most challenging issues facing the initiative for citizen-centric information integration involve policies and competing values/interests. For instance, in the case of an international smart disclosure of food safety regime, the examples of policy and governance issues include the following: what is the process for handling the appeal of a company on the certification result of a third-party certifier?; who should sit on the appeal board?; and how will the board make sure the appeal decision is legitimate and binding? An established mechanism to resolve conflicts is vital for the success of cross-boundary collaboration. Conflicts, although less frequently mentioned in the literature, are facts of collaborative endeavors (O'Leary and Bingham 2009). The establishment of a governance board for conflict resolution is critical.

A related governance effort is monitoring and sanctioning behavior of the participating organizations. This is important for cross-boundary collaboration, especially when there is the lack of a single jurisdiction that has the final authority and resources for enforcement. The collective nature of governance and enforcement underscore the need for monitoring and sanctioning (Ostrom 2010). The cross-boundary agreement needs to establish the capability of the central governance board to collect information on policy compliance and sanction non-compliance.

Moreover, there need to be incentives for participating organizations to share information to facilitate the creation of a citizen-centric view of public service information. In the case of a federated public safety information network, the most important incentives for participating police departments around the country are access to the public safety information residing in the federal database and the ability to request information from other local jurisdictions. Doing so will allow participating departments to obtain timely access to critical information when fighting crime or responding to public safety issues that know no jurisdictional boundary. In the case of food certification and inspection information exchange, the incentives for independent certifiers to participate and share information are to gain access to food information from private producers and to be recognized as one of the legitimate certifiers.

Citizen–Government Collaboration for Citizen-centric Service

Citizens as Reporters and Partners for Public Service Production

Citizen-centric digital governance also incorporates a strong component of citizen participation. This is made possible by the proliferation of mobile devices connected to the internet. Progressive and technology-savvy governments also make efforts to ensure that information systems and applications are available to enable citizens to act as partners for improving citizen-centric services. The city of Boston has made an award-winning effort to engage citizens. Its "Citizens Connect" application (see Figure 5.1) empowers citizens to be the "eyes and ears" of the city by giving them tools to report any issues or problems that they have seen in the city. These

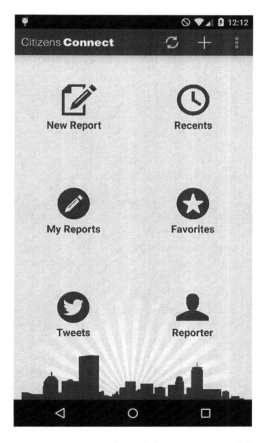

Figure 5.1 Screen Shot of the Homepage of the "Citizens Connect" App

problems could be potholes, damaged signs, graffiti, or any other issue. The application provides easy operations for citizens to tag a location and attach photos to the report. Another channel of communication and reporting is via Twitter. The city offers a convenient tool for communicating directly with the city by providing the option of tweeting the report directly to the city. More importantly, the results of such reports are shared via a website and are accessible via smart phone apps. This is an important improvement when governments host a platform for citizens to share information to benefit both government and fellow citizens.

The involvement of citizens goes beyond problem reporting or community information-sharing. In the area of citizen-centric e-government services, cities partner with civic groups such as Code for America, a volunteer organization for people with programming skills to contribute to the society by writing computer codes, to provide applications that interact with a city's 311 system to make city services even more citizen-oriented. For instance, the Smart Chicago Collaborative is a civic group that brings together the city, leading city community foundations, and a national foundation to make city-service information more personalized and user friendly.[7] These civic groups such as Code for America and Smart Chicago Collaborative are involved in developing applications for citizens to track their service requests by working with the city to get the data needed for these citizen service applications. Such effort reflects a larger international initiative on Open 311 that has a partnership with Code for America.[8] Similar volunteer groups have emerged outside the United States to serve the same needs, such as BetaCityYEG in Edmonton, Alberta, Canada.[9]

Leading and Managing Citizen–Government Collaboration

The task of public managers is one of designing effective governance structures and ensuring successful implementation. There are several components that enable citizens and civic groups to act as partners in providing more citizen-centric digital governance experiences. For gathering citizen input, the governance issue centers around who can make decisions on how the input is gathered, disseminated, and acted upon. For a city government, this may involve the CIO or an advisory committee to make policy decisions. There should be a policy in place for how the input is to be gathered and who can submit reports to a city on community problems such as potholes via their smart phones. The completion of a user registration is typically required for citizens to serve as reporters and submit their reports via smart phones. For content management, the city usually reserves the right to delete a report when the report is in violation of city information and communication policy (Mergel 2012).

In addition, there is debate about whether these types of reports from citizens on community issues should become public records that could be requested under the FOIA. In terms of dissemination, this is a question of whether these reports will be made available to the public as well as various service departments. Moreover, there is debate over whether these reports should be acted upon in terms of whether a service ticket will be generated that is tied to a specific report. These are salient policy and management issues that public managers need to address.

In response to these issues of citizen-generated community and service information, public managers need to develop policies that fit their jurisdictions' technological capabilities and overall policies on the information generated by citizens for public service. In the United States, governments at all levels need to have a clear understanding of the FOIA and its application to electronic records (E-FOIA). The FOIA dictates the kind of records that governments are responsible for stewarding and making available following requests by citizens. Variations of open-records legislation are the norm at the state and local levels in the United States. Therefore, it is important for public managers to tailor their information policies and management strategies to fit the unique legislative and policy contexts.

Successful implementation would require public managers to tailor their strategies to the type and integration level of citizen–government collaboration. The higher the level of integration of citizen input to government information systems and processes, the more stringent and rigorous the policy and process should be. An example of low-level involvement and integration would be the hosting of an electronic forum for community issue identification and reporting by a non-profit organization. Both citizens and government officials act as participants and contributors to the electronic forum. All the online comments and postings are not subject to the same level of scrutiny and disclosure requirements as government records. On the other extreme is a high level of integration and citizen involvement. At this extreme, citizen reporting of community problems is recorded by the designated government information system and reviewed by respective government offices for proper response and action. In addition, citizens are directly involved in the creation of computer or smartphone applications that are linked directly to government databases. This direct access and interfacing with official government information systems and the demand of government actions, as well as open records requirements for public records, would require careful deliberation and planning for electronic information and service generated by citizens.

Conclusion

Citizen-centric digital governance allows governments to provide citizens with personalized services rather than asking citizens to navigate potentially burdensome and confusing government procedures and processes. ICTs offer possibilities for information-sharing and system integration that were simply not realistic and feasible before. Powered by a citizen service information system (311 or others), government employees can provide timely and professional services that are relevant to individual citizens.

Citizen-centric is both about being responsive to multiple roles that citizens play and about working across organizational and sectoral boundaries. From a customer point of view, citizens could be business owners, directors/managers of non-profit organizations, and community members. Therefore, a citizen-centric digital governance service also implies online services to businesses and non-profit organizations in order to meet their regulatory requirements. Citizens can also play the role of active partners in the production and delivery of public services. With the use of IT, being a partner could be as simple as uploading a picture and location of a community problem (i.e. pothole) or as extensive as developing a smart-phone application for tracking city buses. Moreover, the focus on citizens and particular service areas requires coordination and collaboration among organizations that cross levels of governments and sectors. Two prominent examples are public safety and environmental protection as neither one of them recognizes jurisdictional boundaries.

Connecting to the digital governance framework for public managers mentioned in Chapter 2, citizen-centric digital governance emphasizes creating public values such as effectiveness, efficiency, accountability, transparency, citizen participation, and good governance. It utilizes some of the framework features to realize the potential of ICTs including multi-stakeholder perspectives, cross-boundary collaboration, and open collaboration with citizens. Citizen-centric digital governance focuses on the interactions between individual government units or organizations in various sectors and citizens.

The main challenge facing citizen-centric digital governance is systematic in nature. The bureaucratic structure of most governments takes a department-specific orientation. Over time, such a department-centric approach creates rules and information systems that could be optimal for a single department or one segment of the business process. However, this type of approach makes it cumbersome for individual citizens to navigate various government departments and separate sets of rules to complete the entire business process by themselves. Any attempt to integrate information and systems runs into the resistance of well-established bureaucratic culture and inertia, sometimes known as silo mentality. The challenge is further intensified when the need for aligning interests, not only across governmental agencies but also organizations in different sectors (public, private, and non-profit), increases with the complexity of alignment and coordination.

This chapter recommends three guiding principles in advancing citizen-centric digital governance. First is to establish a citizen-centric organizational culture. Such a culture is fundamental to further advances in the provision of online government services. Second is to take a system perspective in the development and implementation of citizen-centric information and service. This requires addressing the challenge of existing department-focused approaches and finding opportunities to integrate the relevant main components and develop common standards. Lastly is working with and leveraging the established administrative structure. This is the adoption of a pragmatic and incremental approach that has a better chance of success.

The applicable strategy depends on the type of citizen-centric digital governance. For digital governance inside a unit of government in a federalist administrative system, it is important to build political and administrative support for an enterprise perspective. Such a perspective will help shift the focus from department-based decision-making to an enterprise one (government-as-a-whole). Meanwhile, public managers need to build the supportive governance structures and rules (such as a CIO council and enterprise technology purchase policy) to enable citizen-centric digital governance. For a centralized administrative system, the emphasis should be placed on customer-service orientation and implementation.

For cross-boundary collaboration for citizen-centric digital governance, identifying and activating relevant stakeholders is an important first step. In conjunction with this step, information for the relevant public service (such as public safety) needs to be identified and policy on information use and dissemination (i.e. privacy and use) needs to be mapped. This is especially critical for information-sharing across organizations. After initial fact-finding, the next major task is to build a governance structure that will allow stakeholders a voice in expressing their needs and concerns for the collaborative to address. To ensure long-term sustainability of cross-boundary collaboration, institutionalization of these governance structures and rules will help with implementation.

Citizen–government collaboration for citizen-centric governance takes on a different dimension. Leading and managing such collaboration depends on the level of engagement and integration. For low levels of engagement, governments can utilize community organizations for getting citizens' input on community problems. These types of open forums do not have to be bound by layers of regulations on government purchase and information disclosure. High levels of integration will allow citizen inputs to be loaded directly into citizen service information systems (i.e. 311) via a variety of smart devices. The integration of applications developed by citizen volunteers with existing government information systems is another example of a highly integrated approach. A prudent approach is to assess the political will, organizational readiness, and technological capability when deciding the level of integration that is appropriate to long-term growth in advancing public values via citizen-centric services.

Notes

1 See Chapter 1 for a fuller discussion.
2 The information is from www.epeople.go.kr, accessed March 10, 2013.

3 More details on the application were available on: www.mpowr.com/Default.aspx, accessed August 5, 2013. Please note, the website no longer exists so the link is for information only.
4 For more details, visit the "Community Platform" website: www.thenonprofitlink.org/communityplatform/nefl, accessed September 25, 2015.
5 For more details, see: www.access-board.gov/guidelines-and-standards/communications-and-it/about-the-section-508-standards, accessed October 1, 2015.
6 For more details, see: unpan3.un.org/egovkb/en-us/Data/Country-Information/id/138-Republic-of-Korea, accessed November 15, 2015.
7 More information can be found at www.smartchicagocollaborative.org/, accessed February 20, 2016.
8 Open 311 has a wealth of information on the cities with an open 311 initiative. For more details, see: www.open311.org/, accessed January 5, 2016.
9 For more details, visit www.govtech.com/civic/Edmonton-Alberta-Pushes-Boundaries-for-Cheap-Civic-Tech.html, accessed September 1, 2016.

References

6, Perri, Diana Leat, Kimberly Seltzer, and Gerry Stoker. 2002. *Toward Holistic Governance: The New Reform Agenda*. New York: Palgrave.
Agranoff, Robert. 2007. *Managing Within Networks: Adding Value to Public Organizations*. In *Public Management and Change Series*, edited by Beryl Radin. Washington, DC: Georgetown University Press.
Agranoff, Robert, and Michael McGuire. 2003. *Collaborative Public Management: New Strategies for Local Governments*. Washington, DC: Georgetown University Press.
Ahn, Michael J., and Stuart Bretschneider. 2011. "Politics of E-Government: E-Government and the Political Control of Bureaucracy." *Public Administration Review* 71 (3):414–24.
Barzelay, Michael, and Babak Armajani. 1992. *Breaking Through Bureaucracy*. Oakland, CA: University of California Press.
Bharosa, Nitesh, Remco van Wijk, Marijn Janssen, Niels de Winne, and Joris Hulstijn. 2011. "Managing the Transformation to Standard Business Reporting: Principles and Lessons Learn from the Netherlands." Dg.o'11, the 12th Annual International Conference on Digital Government Research, College Park, MD, USA, June 12–15.
Bhattacherjee, Anol. 2000. "Customer-Centric Reengineering at the Colorado Department of Revenue." *Communications of the Association for Information Systems* 3 (16):1–43.
Bozeman, Barry, and Stuart Bretschneider. 1986. "Public Management Information Systems: Theory and Prescription." *Public Administration Review* 46 (Special Issue):475–87.
Bretschneider, Stuart, and Dennis Wittmer. 1993. "Organizational Adoption of Microcomputer Technology: The Role of Sector." *Information Systems Research* 4 (1):88–108.
Brown, Mary Maureen. 2007. "Understanding E-Government Benefits." *American Review of Public Administration* 37 (2):178–97.
Bryson, John, Barabra Crosby, and Melissa Middleton Stone. 2006. "The Design and Implementation of Cross-Sector Collaborations: Propositions from the

Literature." *Public Administration Review* 66 (Supplement to Issue 6 (Special Issue)):44–55.
Chen, Yu-Che. 2010. "Citizen-Centric E-Government Services: Understanding Integrated Citizen Service Information Systems." *Social Science Computer Review* 28 (4):427–42.
Chen, Yu-Che. 2012. "A Comparative Study of E-Government XBRL Implementations: The Potential of Improving Information Transparency and Efficiency." *Government Information Quarterly* 29 (4):553–63.
Creative Government Planning Division. 2013. Government 3.0: Openness, Sharing, Communication, and Collaboration. Seoul: Ministry of Security and Public Administration.
Dawes, Sharon, Anthony Cresswell, and Theresa Pardo. 2009. "From 'Need to Know' to 'Need to Share': Tangled Problems, Information Boundaries, and the Building of Public Sector Knowledge Networks." *Public Administration Review* 69 (3):392–402.
Falconer, Gordon, and Shane Mitchell. 2012. "Smart City Framework: A Systematic Process for Enabling Smart+Connected Communities." CISCO Internet Business Solutions Group.
Fleming, Cory. 2008. Call 311: Connecting Citizens to Local Government Case Study Series: Minneapolis 311 System. Washington, DC.
Fountain, Jane. 2001. *Building the Virtual State: Information Technology and Institutional Change*. Washington, DC: Brookings Institution Press.
Ganapati, Sukumar. 2011. "Uses of Public Participation Geographic Information Systems Applications in E-Government." *Public Administration Review* 71 (3):425–34.
Goldsmith, Stephen, and Susan Crawford. 2014. *The Responsive City: Engaging Communities Through Data-Smart Governance*. San Francisco, CA: Jossey-Bass.
Hellberg, Ann-Sofie, and Åke Grönlund. 2013. "Conflicts in Implementing Interoperability: Re-Operationalizing Basic Values." *Government Information Quarterly* 30 (2):154–62.
Kapucu, Naim. 2006. "Interagency Communication Networks During Emergencies: Boundary Spanners in Multiagency Coordination." *American Review of Public Administration* 36 (2):207–25.
Khademian, Anne. 2002. *Working with Culture: The Way The Job Gets Done in Public Programs*. Washington, DC: CQ Press.
Lindblom, Charles E. 1979. "Still Muddling, Not Yet Through." *Public Administration Review* 39 (6; November/December):517–26.
Lundin, Martin. 2007. "Explaining Cooperation: How Resource Interdependence, Goal Congruence, and Trust Affect Joint Actions in Policy Implementation." *Journal of Public Administration Research and Theory* 17 (4):651–72.
McGuire, Michael. 2002. "Managing Networks: Propositions on What Managers Do and Why They Do It." *Public Administration Review* 62 (5):599–609.
Meijer, Albert Jacob. 2014. "New Media and the Coproduction of Safety: An Empirical Analysis of Dutch Practices." *American Review of Public Administration* 44 (1):17–34.
Mergel, Ines. 2012. "A Manager's Guide to Designing a Social Media Strategy." Washington, DC: IBM Center for the Business of Government.
Merton, Robert K. 1957. *Social Theory and Social Structure*. New York: The Free Press.

Norris, Donald, and Christopher Reddick. 2013. "Local E-Government in the United States: Transformation or Incremental Change?" *Public Administration Review* 73 (1):165–75.

O'Leary, Rosemary, and Lisa Blomgren Bingham, eds. 2009. *The Collaborative Public Manager: New Ideas for the Twenty-first Century*. In *Public Management and Change Series*, edited by Beryl Radin. Washington, DC: Georgetown University Press.

Ostrom, Elinor. 2010. "Institutional Analysis and Development: Elements of the Framework in Historical Perspective." In *Historical Developments and Theoretical Approaches in Sociology*, edited by C. Crothers. UK: EOLSS (Encyclopedia of Life Support Systems).

Pardo, Theresa, J. Ramon Gil-Garcia, G. Brian Burke, and Ahmet Guler. 2009. "Factors Influencing Government Cross-Boundary Information Sharing: Preliminary Analysis of a National Survey." Albany: Center for Technology in Government, University at Albany, SUNY.

Rocheleau, Bruce. 2006. *Public Management Information Systems*. Hershey, PA: Idea Group Publishing.

Thomas, John Clayton. 2012. *Citizen, Customer, Partner: Engaging the Public in Public Management*. Almond, NY; London, UK: M.E. Sharpe.

United Nations. 2010. United Nations 2010 Global E-Government Survey: Leveraging E-government at a Time of Financial and Economic Crisis. New York: United Nations.

United Nations. 2012. United Nations E-Government Survey 2012: E-Government for the People. New York: United Nations.

United Nations. 2014. United Nations E-Government Survey 2014: E-Government for the Future We Want. New York: United Nations.

United Nations. 2016. United Nations E-Government Survey 2016: E-Government in Support of Sustainable Development. New York: Department of Economic and Social Affairs, United Nations.

White House. 2012. "Digital Government: Building 21st Century Platform to Better Serve the American People." Washington, DC: White House.

6 Information and Knowledge Management for Digital Governance

Introduction

One of the defining trends in the 21st century is the growth of data and information that are created, stored, and disseminated digitally (*The Economist* 2010). This trend is fueled by the confluence of technological advances and service needs. First is the growing availability of smart devices empowering individuals to create gigabytes of data with photos and videos. Second is the internet connectivity that allows quick dissemination of digital information. Lastly is that governments, along with large corporations, routinely collect and analyze digital information to offer services. For instance, national governments around the world conduct surveillance over cyberspace, telecommunication, and human activities for national security and public safety. Such rapid growth of data and information is also evident in the private sector. For instance, Facebook claimed over 1.6 billion active users, all contributing photos, posts, and/or Likes with one billion of these users logging on every day (*The Economist* 2016), and Google also has massive amounts of information stored and available to process for internet searches as well as e-mail services.

As a result, governments around the world face the significant challenge of managing fast-growing digital information along with their existing responsibilities of information stewardship with paper-based and/or other forms of information. To remain responsive and accountable, governments need to keep pace with the expectations of citizens, who are accustomed to the online services available via e-commerce websites and apps on their smart phones. Businesses and non-profit organizations also exert rising expectations about the quality of government online services as these organizations' own online services have become more sophisticated over time. Moreover, the unique challenge of government is to serve as a last-resort information steward. Such a role demands that a government keep paper documents, as well as information in digital format, while dealing with a wide variety of document types and data formats.

The current proliferation of data also presents an opportunity for governments to provide better services and involve citizens in digital governance.

A citizen service information system that supports 311 can be a source of information and knowledge about both the needs and concerns of citizens (Goldsmith and Crawford 2014). Moreover, such a system helps track public-service performance and devise ways of providing better services; one example is the use of 311 information for performance management in Kansas City, MO. The large amount of data available from the Healthcare Exchange in American states presents an opportunity for government to learn about potential waste as well as abuse and to also reduce health care costs while improving health—an opportunity exemplified by the effort by the State of Maryland.[1] In addition, opening government data empowers citizens and civic groups to understand and share information about government services and provide citizens with a way to make governments more accountable for their actions.

Additionally, government can leverage the deluge of information to propel innovation. For instance, the publication of geographic information system (GIS) information in the United States has been credited with providing a foundation for innovation because a slew of devices and applications have been taking advantage of geo-coded information for transportation, agriculture, telecommunication services, and more. The Census Bureau publishes census data to aid in data-driven decision-making for governments to allocate resources in order to advance public services and address social issues such as poverty. Businesses also utilize census data for making decisions about office location and customer tastes and demands. More importantly, forward-looking governments develop their knowledge and build creative economies; they use information and knowledge strategically for research, development, and innovation (Research Office of Legislative Council Secretariat 2013; United Nations 2010).

In short, governments around the world are in a unique position to advance information and knowledge management for digital governance. In terms of responsibilities, they are the ultimate information stewards, responsible for providing safety and security for their citizens by performing tasks ranging from maintaining vital records and government benefit information to keeping track of air quality and safety information. They are trusted with preserving national archives to keep information and records about the history and development of a country as well as with being the ultimate guarantors of public information and services. In terms of opportunities, governments can be engines of growth and innovation by moving toward a knowledge-intensive economy. Governments can stimulate or provide broadband service (United States Department of Agriculture (USDA) programs), offer cyber-infrastructure to support collaboration in scientific innovation, and engage citizens to solve complex public problems such as the use of challenge.gov.

This chapter will first introduce information and knowledge as a strategic resource and outline the principles of managing such a resource. Next, it introduces the importance, as well as the principles and processes, of knowledge management in the public sector. Then, the discussion turns to recent developments in the creation and leveraging of information and knowledge resources such as big data, crowdsourcing, and data visualization. Finally, this chapter provides practical leadership and management strategies for advancing information and knowledge management for public service.

Data, Information, and Knowledge as Strategic Resources of Government

Definitions of Data, Information, and Knowledge

The discussion about information and knowledge management begins with appropriate definitions. Data are bits and bytes of raw facts such as words and numbers (Laudon and Laudon 2006, 13). For governments, data are typically stored either in an electronic file or in paper form to serve a specific regulatory or service purpose. A spreadsheet of budget data, for instance, can help a government understand a proposed resource allocation down to precise dollar amounts. A collection of those files forms a database (Hoffer, Prescott and McFadden 2002). For instance, a government could maintain a business registration database for enforcing applicable rules and regulations on these businesses. The size of database ranges from hundreds of records to hundreds of millions of records. Although people tend to loosely equate data with information, it is instructive to highlight the distinction.

In concise terms, information is data plus meaning. With meanings, human beings can begin to relate to the data and use them for specific purposes. For instance, XXX-XX-XXXX is the typical format of a nine-digit social security number for an individual living in the United States. The meaning of this number is its function as the primary identifier for obtaining social security benefits. Moreover, a social security number is used by many organizations as an identifier for tax and record-keeping purposes. Such context gives meaning to the number. Once given meaning, such as social security benefits or tax ID, data can be useful for serving a specific purpose.

The increasing amount and variety of information (A) demands that a system (B) make information manageable, accessible, and useful. An information system is a system for collecting, storing, and disseminating information. It constitutes technical components such as data, hardware, and software. More importantly, it also includes people and processes to give meaning to the data and to ensure the desirable qualities of information (Laudon and Laudon 2012). Therefore, the depiction of a government information system, such as a citizen service information system, should go beyond the description of the data and information stored and shared to include the users who interact with the system, as well as the processes in which information is updated and used.

Information becomes knowledge when human experiences are added to it and/or additional connections to information/ideas are made (Polanyi 1962). The addition of human experiences is context-specific and draws from relevant experiences, expert insights, and values (Davenport and Prusak 2000, 5). There are two types of knowledge: explicit and tacit. Explicit knowledge is the type that can be codified and captured in documents, numbers, charts, and drawings. In the public sector, examples of explicit knowledge include rules in an operation manual, documented workflow, guidelines, and laws. Tacit knowledge is more holistic and situational, and therefore not amendable to codification. The transmission of tacit knowledge occurs through mentoring, dialogue, and/or deliberation. Both types of knowledge share a focus on the "skilled action of understanding" (Polanyi and Prosch 1975, 44; Tsoukas 2005, 158).

Policy Framework for Strategic Information Resource Management

Information should be treated as a government-wide strategic resource for federal government in the United States as mandated by the Clinger-Cohen Act (formally known as the Information Technology Management Reform Act of 1996). Government has long relied on information for enforcing regulatory policies and providing government services. However, before the Clinger-Cohen Act, a government-wide approach to information resources management was lacking. In general, information usually exists inside a single department within an agency for a single purpose. Such a department-specific focus creates a bureaucratic structure that leads to a fragmentation of information. As a result, it would require specific information policies and targeted implementation efforts to integrate information from various agencies.

The Clinger-Cohen Act of 1996 includes several components to support a government-wide information resource strategy. First, this Act requires federal government agencies to devise a plan for strategic use of its information to accomplish agency missions. This strategic thinking, connecting to the missions of governmental agencies, allows those agencies to modernize their operations by capitalizing on advancements in information technologies. Examples can be seen in the modernization of information systems in the Social Security Administration (SSA) and Securities and Exchange Commission (SEC) (U.S. Securities and Exchange Commission 2009); after modernization, both agencies became more efficient and effective in acquiring, storing, and analyzing relevant information to provide better service.

Second, this Act requires that each agency has a chief information officer (CIO) to oversee the development and use of information resources by leveraging appropriate information technology and systems. Having a CIO provides the supportive organizational structure that enables information to be treated at the top level of an organization, as financial and human resources have traditionally been treated. This organization-wide and high-level view facilitates leveraging information as a resource. Having an information officer position at the highest level of the organization addresses the problem of treating information as a low-level concern or simply as a technology issue.

Lastly, the Act specifically links capital and budget processes to the purchase of information technology to facilitate the strategic use of information and information technology for a specific agency. This is critical because of the need to infuse strategic consideration of information use into the development and/or purchase of supporting information systems. Moreover, such integration is necessary for implementing any strategic priority.

The tenets of the Clinger-Cohen Act are useful guiding principles to support leveraging government information as a strategic resource. State governments in the United States also have their respective CIOs to promote strategic uses of information as resources to improve government operation. At the local level, despite recognition of the importance of a high-level office to oversee information as a strategic resource, the practice varies due to the size of operation and maturity of information technology. However, these process guidelines, coupled with comprehensive government-wide information resource strategy, are particularly relevant as government operation has become more information-intensive with the accumulation of data and increased capability of data analytics for improving government service.

Principles of Government Information Resource Management

Governments are the stewards of information entrusted to them by generations of citizens. Stewardship is one important meta-principle for government information policies (Dawes 2010). Government is the ultimate repository of important records to serve the basic functions of government: birth records, property information, deeds, business registration, taxes, criminal records, etc. These records support fair and basic government services in benefits, identities, business transactions, public safety, and more. Governments are also the repositories of information on the state of our physical environment, information that includes such natural resources as water and air as well as physical infrastructure such as roads, sewers, etc. Furthermore, government is the repository of national history as well as institutional and human knowledge. For instance, the National Archives of the United States holds the drawings of the battleships used in World War One. Overall, the preservation of human knowledge, going back thousands of years, as well as critical government information is an important information stewardship role that government plays.

Information security, the safeguarding of information against unauthorized access and use, is a principle of information resource management related to stewardship. Using locked file cabinets and restricted areas have been long-standing practices to protect valuable information in paper form. As the world becomes more connected and more information is available in digital format, the nature and scale of information security have evolved and increased (Deloitte-NASCIO 2014). The amount of credit card numbers and social security information stolen or compromised has been on the scale of hundreds of thousands, or even millions, as databases get bigger and attacks become more sophisticated. Information security should be an integral part of information resource management strategy, especially when information has become more strategic and its value has increased as a result.

Another high-level guiding principle as articulated by Dawes (2010) is usefulness. Government information, like other resources, takes effort to acquire, store, and utilize. Therefore, it is important for governments to make sure that the information collected is useful; otherwise, it is a waste of taxpayers' money. From the perspective of performance management, the collection of performance information should not pursue every single possible piece of information. Rather, this collection should be a deliberate effort to identify the key performance indicators (KPIs) and minimize the number of information items collected. Another aspect of usefulness is to make the best use of information already collected by utilizing data analytics for data-driven decision-making. For instance, data-driven decision-making could be the use of geo-coded crime data for deployment of police forces or infrastructure information displayed on a map using GIS for zoning and planning purposes. Another example is the State of Iowa's use of big data analytics to identify fraud and abuse of any government programs such as Medicare.

Another principle of information resource management, especially from the information acquisition perspective, is to minimize the burden on citizens and businesses for complying with mandatory reporting to the government. The growing array of regulations and the need for tracking performance have resulted in a growing list of information items that governments collect from various entities. Such efforts, as shown in a Dutch study, could cost a significant portion of a country's economy (Bharosa et al. 2011). To reduce citizens' burden of meeting government information reporting requirements, the Paperwork Reduction Act, one of the information management legislations in the United States, aims to reduce the paperwork requirement for any federal government agencies. More specifically, federal government agencies need to make efforts to reduce the number of questions required, streamline forms, and provide an accounting of the time and effort involved for the regulated entities to fill out each form.

Interoperability, another principle of government information resource management, can provide better citizen-centric public information and service. Information that is collected for one single purpose can create new value when linked to and combined with other information collected for a different purpose (Janssen, Matheus, and Zuiderwijk 2015). Increasingly, government recognizes the importance of information interoperability and makes efforts to implement it (Scholl et al. 2012; Scholl and Klischewski 2007). For instance, better social service can be provided when a case manager can access information from law enforcement, financial institutions, health care facilities, and government agencies to create a complete profile of the client's struggle and help him/her accordingly. Information interoperability is particularly salient in disaster response when the central command center would require information feeds from healthcare facilities, police and fire departments of local governments, schools, businesses, and others in order to create an integrated picture of the disaster response (Comfort 2007; Kapucu 2006). Another example of information interoperability in government is the use of layers of geo-coded information for planning and public service decision-making. This overlay of information on infrastructure, businesses, transportation, environmental resources, and governmental facilities can help governments make informed decisions on urban development.

Another principle of information resource management is the balance between transparency and privacy. Transparency, among other values, should be a guiding value for government information resource management. Transparency has been associated with the ability to fight corruption and make government more accountable (Bertot, Jaeger, and Grimes 2010). Increasingly, as documented in the Open Government Partnership, governments around the world are launching open government initiatives that have information transparency as one of the key components of their open government efforts. For instance, the United States has the Open Government Initiative, and India has open government legislation. Privacy is another important value that should be embedded in the design of any government information resource plan. In the United States, regulations and rules exist for the protection of privacy such as the Health Insurance Portability and Accountability Act of 1996. The most important objective is to find ways to increase transparency and interoperability while minimizing the risk of losing privacy (Duncan and Roehrig 2003). The idea is that the utilization of government information should not come at the expense of individual privacy.

Knowledge Management for Digital Governance

Knowledge Management Imperative

Knowledge is crucial for the production and delivery of public services, making knowledge management critical for government operation. In the United States, the situation is particularly relevant with a wave of baby boomers retiring into the public sector. These individuals' knowledge about rules, procedures, and specifics of government assets, if not captured, will create a gap in public service and may cause major disruptions in public service. For instance, an engineer working for a small local government for over 30 years may have all the details on the age and condition of elements of the infrastructure such as water mains. If the specifics are not codified or transferred to the next employee, it is likely that some of the critical information about the infrastructure could be lost. Such loss could result in major service disruption. Since government is the most important organization in responding to major disasters, business continuity is an imperative.

For government agencies, knowledge should be elevated to the strategic level. For public service provision, governments need to know what services are needed. For instance, a citizen service information system (resembling a customer relationship management system in the private sector) can provide us with knowledge about the nature and frequency of service requests from citizens in the community. In addition, governments need to know about the resources and time that it would take to provide certain public services such as road construction, downtown redevelopment, etc. More importantly, knowledge is needed for assessing the quality of public service rendered. Knowledge about service needs, provision, and performance can assist with understanding government operations and assessing whether these activities help achieve the strategic priorities of the organization.

Knowledge can be put into strategic use in the competition for economic development opportunities. Local, state, and national governments are in competition with one another for attracting residents and businesses. Knowledge about government services can help make governments more efficient and competitive when offering desirable services to residents and businesses. Equipped with knowledge about its own operation as well as others in the marketplace, government can also decide what partnership opportunities are productive. One example in the telecommunication area is the local government partnership with Google to offer gigabyte internet connectivity via Google Fiber.

Knowledge management in government at the national level should be an integral part of supporting knowledge economy and innovation. National governments can serve as engines of innovation. According to the World Bank (The World Bank 2013), national governments can invest in information and communication infrastructure, create constructive regulations and institutions, provide education and training, and generate an innovation system to foster the knowledge economy. Uniquely positioned to be the largest repositories of information and human knowledge for their respective nations, national governments are in a position to design and implement relevant policies and to lead knowledge management. Supporting the development of the knowledge economy should be in the domain of governments.

Processes of Knowledge Management

Knowledge management is the integration of four processes: knowledge creation, knowledge acquisition/capturing, knowledge sharing, and knowledge use/evaluation (see Figure 6.1). Knowledge creation is a process in which new knowledge is created. Such creation provides a fresh source of relevant knowledge into a knowledge management system. The creation process can be internal and structured, such as a local government trying to find more cost-effective ways to provide public services during budget preparation. Such creation can also be achieved by open collaboration with people outside government—for example, through citizen/customer surveys that some local governments have done on a regular basis. With 311 or any city service applications on their smart phones, citizens (users) can provide user-generated knowledge. For instance, a local resident can upload a community problem or historical fact to a city service information system. Then, other residents in the community can add to that knowledge by describing the history behind the problem. This is consistent with one of the key features of Web 2.0: employing user-generated contents as a main source of information.

A productive knowledge management system captures new knowledge created within the system while leveraging knowledge from both internal and external sources. The capturing of knowledge should be a well-established process for the ease of generating evidence-based insight. For instance, a citizen service information system can capture the time when a service ticket is opened and the time when a service ticket is closed as well as the resources taken to render the service. A rigorous process of knowledge capturing will build the capturing of such knowledge into an

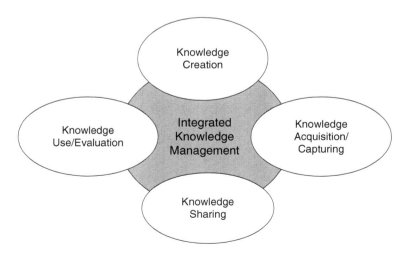

Figure 6.1 Four Integrative Processes of Knowledge Management

organization's business processes. More importantly, new insights as the result of data analysis will be linked to service improvement. Moreover, knowledge can be acquired from both internal and external sources. Internal sources of knowledge could be in the form of workflows for city services as contributed and documented by city employees as well as information systems that exist in law enforcement, public works, finance, human resources, and many other departments. Local governments routinely acquire knowledge from external sources. For instance, local governments can acquire knowledge about demographic information of local populations by accessing data from the U.S. Census. Government can also acquire geo-coded infrastructure information and aerial photos from external sources to update its GIS for planning and service purposes.

Knowledge sharing is an integral and important process of knowledge management. Sharing of knowledge gets knowledge to potential users. The process of sharing can be routine and structured such as the processes found in regular business meetings that share service insights. For a local government, knowledge about city services can be shared at weekly or monthly meetings. Alternatively, this knowledge can be shared through newsletters or communications within or across various departments. More ideally, such knowledge sharing can be on-demand. Many organizations have created knowledge bases ranging from simple frequently asked questions (FAQs) to more sophisticated instruction or process documents to guide employees through service processes. Moreover, knowledge sharing, especially knowledge that can be generated by government employees or citizens, can be done via collaborative platforms. Knowledge sharing can occur across organizations. One example is the collaborative effort of law enforcement agencies across levels of governments and agencies in the United States to share the information and knowledge that they collect on criminals or even persons of interest.

Knowledge use and evaluation is an essential but often ignored process of knowledge management. The majority of effort tends to go into knowledge generation and acquisition that resemble major organizational activity and purchases. Active use of knowledge and evaluation of its usefulness are typically less glamorous and sometimes require more discipline to perform. However, a rigorous evaluation of knowledge use is the source of major levers in improving the efficiency and effectiveness of knowledge management. Knowledge evaluation aligns knowledge management activities to the strategic priorities of an organization as stipulated in its strategic information resource management document. Information should be tracked on knowledge use, such as the number of times a specific document in the knowledge base has been accessed. More importantly, organizations need to track the impact of knowledge use. For some of the services impacted by knowledge use, organizations need to assess how much time is saved for information searches on average as opposed to searching for information in the absence of a knowledge management system. Such discipline guards against the general tendency to acquire and store knowledge for the sake of accumulation. Given the large amount of information and knowledge that an organization acquires and manages on a regular basis, it is important to have a sense of priority by conducting structured and periodic evaluations of knowledge use and its impacts.

Principles of Knowledge Management for Digital Public Governance

The first principle of effective knowledge management is to understand the nature of knowledge and to manage and design a knowledge management scheme accordingly. The two main types of knowledge are explicit (or codified) knowledge and tacit knowledge. Explicit knowledge is basically data, facts, and information for operation and services. A more advanced form of explicit knowledge is the building of step-by-step instructions, rules, workflows, and decision-making parameters to achieve public agency missions. Such explicit knowledge can be stored and managed in a structured format and environment. Automation can be implemented in business processes when facts and decision parameters are well-defined, such as in the provision of government benefits based on eligibility requirements. In contrast, tacit knowledge is rather unstructured and not amendable to a well-defined set of parameters. The creation, accumulation, and dissemination of such knowledge is best accomplished via human interactions (Tsoukas 2005). These interactions can be mentoring sessions, workshops, and conferences (Agranoff 2007). Such tacit knowledge requires bringing diverse and extensive experiences to bear in a specific situation and tapping into human interactions to stimulate insights.

Another principle of knowledge management is to focus on high value knowledge. Resources for governments are scarce. To be accountable, governments need to focus on knowledge that can directly advance public values such as transparency, efficiency, and effectiveness. For transparency and the promotion of efficiency and effectiveness, the U.S. Federal Government has asked federal agencies, under the Open Government Initiative, to identify high-value data sets to be made available via the federal government data portal. These include census data for data-driven decision-making by governments and businesses, and weather data for agriculture, transportation, safety, and more. Moreover, government can also focus on making use of knowledge that impacts the most people and affects the economy. For instance, automation of tax filing processes for many governments around the world utilizes tax filing regulations and process knowledge for major gains in efficiency and effectiveness.

The next principle is the strategic conversion of tacit to explicit knowledge. The strategic aspect of such conversion lies in a focus on understanding and codifying antiquated and cumbersome business processes for major process improvement to gain efficiency and effectiveness. Such conversion takes the process and procedural knowledge that is currently stored in individuals' heads and then captures this information in a workflow with roles, data, and decision parameters. An example of such practice is the management of the student loan application process in the UK (Dhillon, Weerakkody, and Dwivedi 2008). A use case was utilized to gather knowledge from individuals and documents about the steps of the application process, what information is needed for whom, and how information is shared or forwarded. Having such knowledge in an integrated format in one place is an example of such conversion from tacit and disparate knowledge to explicit knowledge. As a result of the use case, a recommendation was made to integrate process and information systems to significantly improve the UK student loan application process (Dhillon, Weerakkody, and Dwivedi 2008, 172). Mining natural language texts as expressed in social media is another way of converting seemingly tacit knowledge into explicit knowledge about what piece of advice might be particularly useful for recipients.

The last principle of effective knowledge management is the migration from paper-based to digital knowledge management as part of the strategic priorities of any organization. The growing amount of information and knowledge makes the migration from paper-based to digital knowledge management systems an imperative. As demonstrated by the internet, knowledge in digital format greatly lowers the cost of production, storage, dissemination, and search in comparison with knowledge and information stored in paper format. Once information and knowledge is digitized, it is quickly searchable, which significantly lowers the time and energy involved in information search. For instance, in terms of collaboration for the production and delivery of public service, a centralized information repository in the State of Iowa allows citizens to know which local government is working with whom for what service. Digitalization of healthcare records is another example of the need to go digital. The National Health Service in the UK has basic health information saved in the chips of the National Health Service cards. More importantly, it has a supporting integrated information system that stores and distributes all the healthcare information as related to a particular individual. As a result, hospitals and clinics around the country can have immediate access to all information about that patient rather than wait the hours and days that such access could take if the information were not in a digital format.

Data-Driven Decision-Making and Public Service: Big Data, Crowdsourcing, and Data Visualization

The overarching goal of managing data, information, and knowledge in government and other public-service organizations is to improve their ability to achieve their agency missions via data-driven decision-making, service production and delivery, and governance. Business analytics, a process particularly relevant to such efforts, has been around for a long time. It utilizes data on business processes and services by employing various tools such as text mining for social media posts, data mining for identifying new and emergent patterns of customer behavior, etc. Several recent developments in the world of information and knowledge management listed below deserve attention.

Big Data

Big data is typically characterized as having three Vs (see Box 6.1): volume, velocity, and variety (Soares 2012). Volume is about the size of data sets and/or databases. Size, however, is a relative term and usually refers to what standard database software or analytical tools can handle. For instance, a medium-size data set can have thousands of records with 50 or so fields for each. A "big" data set can have millions of records with hundreds of fields for each, such as the health insurance data handled by the Centers for Medicare and Medicaid Services (CMS) in the United States. In a practical sense, the definition of "big" is relative to the technical capability of an organization. For government, examples of big data are health insurance data managed by CMS and science data such as deep space exploration, weather data, bioinformatics, etc. The federal government's big data initiative, launched in 2012, has several such examples (National Science Foundation 2012).

Big data is also about the velocity of the data coming in and the dynamic ability of conducting data analysis to generate relevant results (McAfee and Brynjolfsson 2012). For most traditional databases, information comes in periodically with a predicable amount. In such a case, it is easier to plan the capacity and automate the process. The velocity implied in big data is quite different. For instance, in a manmade disaster such as a terrorist attack on the scale of September 11, cellular communication is considered big data, with millions of records coming in every hour. Social media traffic,

---

Box 6.1 The Defining Characteristics (Three "Vs") of Big Data

Volume: A big data set has millions of citizen service records, healthcare records, etc.

Variety: Big data typically have both structured and unstructured data as well as various types of data including images, videos (surveillance cameras), social media posts, telecommunication records (cell phone), location information, etc.

Velocity: Big data can be generated and collected in a dynamic fashion.

such as on Twitter and other microblogs, can also reach millions in a matter of minutes. Another aspect of velocity involves the ability to provide situational awareness and forecasting in the event of hurricanes, earthquakes, or tsunamis.

Variety poses another major challenge to big data in terms of storage, analysis, and dissemination. Traditional transactional databases predominantly deal with structured data such as numbers and well-defined categories. Big data tends to deal with other types of data such as images, videos, social media posts, cellular communication logs, and financial information contained in PDF reports. Variety is also about the disparity in the definitions embedded in a range of data sources. As a result of this disparity, combining data from a variety of sources to bring some uniformity and standardization of data to make it usable is challenging.

Big data can be a source of information and knowledge for better decision-making for public service (Desouza 2014). In the realm of science and innovation, big data can power new and fast discoveries of genomics, weather, earthquakes, and new materials. For instance, advances have been made in modeling earthquakes by employing big data (National Science Foundation 2012). The government databases capturing government service information, such as local government 311 data and e-government transactions data, can make government responsive to the needs of residents in the community and result in a better allocation of government resources (Goldsmith and Crawford 2014, 33). The potential is the ability to launch targeted efforts with increased returns on investment for high-impact public services.

Big data can also be useful in detecting abuse and waste in public service. For instance, the Iowa Workforce Development Agency has plans to utilize big data to understand potential abuse of its unemployment benefits program. Using big data, they can identify suspicious claim activities from out-of-state, large amount requested, etc. More importantly, when used appropriately, big data has the potential to help understand the impact of policy intervention and public problems down to the individual level and to aggregate to any geographical area and service priority. A recent health care example is the ability to access healthcare data for deciding on the best course of treatment, especially when there is no established literature to guide these decisions. Big data provided assistance in identifying the relevant cases to offer doctors some notion of the risks associated with various treatment options.[2]

The biggest challenge associated with big data in government is governance (Chen and Hsieh 2014). Active management and stewardship is fundamental to ensure the quality of data and, more importantly, to utilize data for the benefit of achieving the mission of a government. The State of Washington's P20W data warehouse illustrates the agreement needed among various stakeholders to integrate education data into big data useful for all stakeholders (Soares 2012). The guiding principles for big data governance should be that it is stakeholder-focused and performance-oriented (Chen and Hsieh 2014). Stakeholders of big data in government, which include public managers, elected officials, and residents, tend to have different goals and objectives with regard to big data. Residents are more concerned about privacy and data quality issues. Public managers tend to focus more on efficiency and effectiveness of service.

Crowdsourcing

Co-production of information and knowledge for public service is likely to be on the rise. The proliferation of social media platforms such as Facebook and Twitter, as well as the advancing availability of smart devices and computing resources, has allowed individuals and civic groups to be participants of information and knowledge production for enhancing public service and democratic governance. One of the formal government channels for integrating citizen-generated information and knowledge with existing government information systems is the citizen service information system (also known as the 311 system) for some innovative local governments (Goldsmith and Crawford 2014). Citizens can identify a community problem by taking a picture, describing the problem, and reporting it directly with a location marker. Governments can utilize social media posts to understand the spread of disease and pandemics. These posts provide dynamic clues and afford government timely information for dealing with problems. For digital governance, civic organizations that focus on government transparency and accountability can help create knowledge to hold government accountable for spending taxpayers' money. Online transparency is one of the tools to combat corruption (Bertot, Jaeger, and Grimes 2010). For instance, the publication of the meter-by-meter parking violation tickets in the City of Chicago allows software programmers to develop applications to identify any unusual patterns and spot any potential problems.

The website challenge.gov in the United States is a government online platform of knowledge creation via crowdsourcing. This involves government as a seeker of policy solutions to complex public service challenges and individuals or civic groups as solution providers. Such co-production of knowledge, as well as wide dissemination and utilization, is likely to gather more momentum when governments continue on the path of open data that makes complete government data sets available to the public and particularly available in a machine-readable format. As a result, such knowledge management gradually expands beyond the organizational boundaries of individual government agencies to the ecosystem of organizations and individuals who have a stake in the pertinent knowledge. For instance, the U.S. SEC's effort to make financial information publicly available and machine-readable can serve institutional and individual users (U.S. Securities and Exchange Commission 2010) and create an ecosystem of financial information service providers and online transparency civic and technology groups. Governments can also play a pivotal role in food and health information that leverages the entire civil society for management knowledge in this area.

Data Visualization

Another major area of development in information and knowledge management is the utilization of data visualization to inform decision-making. Human brains have a superior capability to recognize patterns and make new connections when presented with a picture, image, or video clip (Ward, Grinstein, and Keim 2015). Data visualization is a technique that aids in the creation of a picture or image that can be easily related to by a human being. This technique has the potential to stimulate new discoveries. In one of the classic examples, John Snow's drawing of the clusters of cholera cases in London in 1845 led to the discovery that these cases lived in London households that utilized the same well. A similar modern-day story is the mapping of people's locations when searching for flu information to predict and track the development and magnitude of flu outbreaks in various parts of the country.

The usefulness of data visualization rises with the growth of big data. For example, the Department of Homeland Security in the United States has a visualization and data analytics project using big data for first respondents (Executive Office of the President 2012). The variety and volume of big data render the traditional summary statistics with tables and charts less effective. A much more effective approach is to visualize the data for identification of any unusual patterns. For instance, software applications have been developed to spot unusual activity in Medicaid claims by integrating Google geospatial technology to visually display anomalies and clusters. These anomalies could be intensive billing activities, long-distance travel for getting services, unusual billing activities for a particular procedure or from a clinic, etc.[3] Another productive use of visualization is the analysis of connections in human and/or physical networks. Visualization of social networks of individuals and groups of people provides insights into the structure of the network and the role that certain individuals or organizations play in that specific network. For instance, the identification of a broker between two terrorist networks or the tracking of how people know one another with the visualization of social networks can provide insights into how such terrorist networks can be most effectively dismantled.

Moreover, such visualization can be a dynamic user-driven experience that provides on-demand answers to a question that is particularly relevant to a particular user (Ward, Grinstein, and Keim 2015). One of the more established examples in public administration is the forecasting of major weather events such as hurricanes, snow storms, and tornados.

Visualization of potential storm paths helps emergency response personnel understand and prepare for these major disasters. Overlaying the potential storm path with layers of maps such as terrains, medical facilities, shelters, roads, houses, and other assets helps with taking into account a large number of factors. In addition, such visualization has seen more use in the area of open government and online transparency. The United States had a discovery.gov website that provided project-level information about the projects funded by the American Recovery and Reinvestment Act (ARRA). It was an interactive website that allowed individuals to filter information based on a geographical area of interest (a state) and types of projects. At the local level, data visualization using heat maps can help people identify hot spots for public safety or other community issues.

Overall Leadership and Management Strategy for Data, Information, and Knowledge Management

Guiding Principles

The overarching guiding principle of information and knowledge management is to advance public service and governance. In terms of advancing public values, the goals are about improving efficiency and effectiveness of public services. Government can be responsive by utilizing information and knowledge to predict and prepare in order to meet a service need. For instance, the City of Pittsburgh launched a snowplow tracker application in 2015 that allows residents to see where the snowplow trucks are in response to resident information needs in the event of major snowfalls.[4] For public governance, information collection and disclosure can help achieve public policy objectives such as motor vehicle safety, public health, and food safety (Fung, Graham, and Weil 2007). Recent efforts to increase online financial transparency also serve the purpose of increasing transparency of government operation. One of the major shifts is the level of access to the government budget that has been made available in machine-readable format. In February 2015, Socrata launched an "Open Budget" app that allows people to decipher the US$4 trillion U.S. Federal Government budget.

Another guiding principle is to align the management of data, information, and knowledge to the strategic goals and objectives of government agencies. The highest level of maturity for data governance is the ability to align data governance to the strategic priorities of an organization, as is articulated in the CMMI's Data Management Maturity Model. Federal government in the United States, as well as the South Korean government, has elevated the level of information as a strategic resource. This strategic thinking and, more importantly, taking action to ensure strategic alignment of data and information use, is foundational for governments that are more information-intensive in their operation. Knowledge management should also be strategic in finding new ways of solving public problems and improving public service and governance.

Stewardship is a particularly important guiding principle for governments as opposed to non-profits and businesses (Dawes 2010). Such stewardship implies the assurance of quality, continuity, privacy, and security of government data and information. Governments are regarded as the ultimate steward of data and information that are the basis for providing services to the general public. As a result, the standard of care is higher. Moreover, stewardship implies the management of a large portfolio of data and information in various formats ranging from paper documents and maps, electronic records on old media (i.e. floppy disks), to digital footprints seen in social media. This ever-increasing portfolio makes stewardship a renewed challenge for government. Consequently, active management is critical.

Information and knowledge management should focus on items that provide high return on investment. The investment in information systems and applications for knowledge management should be evaluated on a regular basis. It is important to note that the accounting of investment should go beyond merely recording what investments government agencies are making. It should include, as articulated in the Paperwork Reduction Act, the accounting of the cost to society (individuals, businesses, and non-profits) as a whole in terms of preparing and submitting information for regulatory compliance. The benefits should outweigh the costs. More importantly, governments should not attempt to build knowledge management systems to be comprehensive in coverage. Rather, the focus should be on being strategic.

Leading and Managing Information and Knowledge Initiatives

Managers and executives need to elevate the discussion about information and knowledge to a strategic level, incorporating strategic planning processes and treating them as strategic priorities. The strategic relevance of information, as the Clinger-Cohen Act stipulates, should be part of the strategic planning process and is best advocated by a CIO who can oversee information and knowledge for the entire agency. Such strategic planning processes can involve various stakeholders both inside and outside government agencies to set priorities for the organization and identify ways in which government information can be useful. Moreover, the management of information and knowledge needs to be coordinated with the development and implementation of information systems, as well as information policies, as an integral part of managing resources, performance, and risks.

Managers can also cultivate a culture of valuing information as well as that of knowledge sharing. A culture of valuing information and knowledge is foundational for the success of information-intensive government. The drive for evidence-based decision-making and performance measurement has made the need for such a culture more salient. Managers should be information and knowledge champions in their organizations by demonstrating the value of information. Such demonstration can showcase how knowledge about community assets and various scenarios of long-term urban development (as shown in a series of maps) can help the community create a shared understanding of the future to make better collective decisions. Moreover, information and knowledge can have a multiplying effect when shared. It is up to the leaders and managers of government to create incentives for knowledge sharing because the provision of incentives is a critical success factor for knowledge management in government (Wagner 2003). An incentive could be in the form of an award and recognition of the knowledge champion for an organization. Alternatively, it could be a tangible financial reward in the form of payment or a favorable performance review.

Leaders and managers need to adopt an appropriate strategy for the creation and dissemination of tacit knowledge and to make a conscious effort to migrate from tacit to explicit. Tacit knowledge is best created and shared via social interactions. The use of communities of practice, forums, retreats, mentoring sessions, etc. are means in which tacit knowledge can be shared and created (McNabb 2007). The advances of information and communication technology as well as big data analytics can help to codify such knowledge. Coaching sessions can be tagged and videos can be created for capturing the essence of professional experiences tailored to address a specific problem.

Promoting interoperability of data and information is also in the domain of managers and leaders. Increasingly, data and information come from various sources and, frequently, include a variety of data definitions and data collection methodologies. Interoperability can be accomplished with a common set of data standards or a standard way of converting data to the same unit and definition. Such interoperability greatly increases the usefulness of information for decision-making purposes by allowing extensive data analysis, comparison, and pattern recognition. Another way to promote interoperability is the use of a semantic web language that can attach the meanings of data to numbers. When such embedding of meanings is done by following a taxonomy, then all these data can be machine-readable, and translation and comparison can be done via computer scripts.

Conclusion

Information is a strategic resource for governments along with human and financial resources. The growth of big data and advances in information and communication technology will further elevate strategic imperative for effective information and knowledge management. Such strategic use is relevant at all levels of government including local, state, and national governments. Some leading e-government countries have leveraged information resource management to advance their knowledge and creative economy as well as national competitiveness. Local government can use citizen service information strategically to identify the most fruitful areas for service improvement.

Effective government information resource management is distinctive in its guiding principles. The focus on public values such as transparency, effectiveness, accountability, and stewardship is paramount. A thoughtful information resource management program needs to consider the balance between privacy and transparency, information stewardship, relevance and usefulness of information, information interoperability, and minimization of the burden of regulatory reporting on citizens and businesses.

Knowledge management is an imperative for governments as they strive for continuous improvement of their performance. Knowledge management consists of four main integrated processes: knowledge creation, knowledge capturing/acquisition, knowledge sharing, and knowledge use and evaluation. An effective knowledge management program for governments will require developing an appropriate strategy to fit the type of knowledge being managed: explicit vs. tacit knowledge. Moreover, the focus of knowledge management should be on the high-value knowledge that can enable the accomplishment of a government's strategic priorities. With the advances in information-processing power and analytics, the migration from a paper-based system to digital-only is also important to enable all four processes of knowledge management. For well-defined business processes or procedures, the move from tacit knowledge to explicit knowledge will empower governments to provide better services with fewer resources.

The strategic use of information and knowledge by governments can support data-driven decision-making for improving public services. The growth of data in terms of volume, variety, and velocity will gradually, but fundamentally, shape how data-driven decision-making is conducted in the public sector. The increasing use of open collaboration for the production and delivery of public services through crowdsourcing and co-production will continue to provide new opportunities for engaging civil society in the production of information and knowledge for public service. The advances in data visualization techniques and technologies will continue to elevate the sophistication and usefulness of utilizing data for decision-making.

Leadership and management ultimately determine the success of strategic use of information and knowledge by governments. The overarching principle is to focus on the creation and advancement of public values such as efficiency, effectiveness, transparency and accountability. Then, the specifics of knowledge should support the strategic goals of a governmental agency. The value of knowledge should be evaluated against its contribution to the strategic priorities of the agency. Government leaders and managers also need to keep a long-term perspective with the focus on business continuity and stewardship.

Notes

1 For more details on how the State of Maryland is doing, visit www.govtech.com/data/States-Turn-to-GIS-Analytics-to-Target-Hospital-Super-Users.html, accessed January 10, 2015.
2 For more details, see www.npr.org/2015/01/05/375201444/big-data-not-a-cure-all-in-medicine, accessed October 15, 2015.
3 For more information on the virtualization, see www.govtech.com/data/Iowa-Employs-Big-Data-to-Identify-Potential-UI-Fraud.html, accessed January 21, 2015.
4 For more details, you can search the city of Pittsburgh website for the snow-plow tracker application. A story can be seen on www.govtech.com/dc/articles/Pittsburgh-Snowplow-Tracker-Activates-When-Levels-Exceed-a-Half-Inch.html, accessed March 30, 2015.

References

Agranoff, Robert. 2007. *Managing Within Networks: Adding Value to Public Organizations*. In *Public Management and Change Series*, edited by Beryl Radin. Washington, DC: Georgetown University Press.
Bertot, John C., Paul T. Jaeger, and Justin M. Grimes. 2010. "Using ICTs to Create a Culture of Transparency: E-Government and Social Media as Openness and Anti-Corruption Tools for Societies." *Government Information Quarterly* 27 (3):264–71.
Bharosa, Nitesh, Remco van Wijk, Marijn Janssen, Niels de Winne, and Joris Hulstijn. 2011. "Managing the Transformation to Standard Business Reporting: Principles and Lessons Learned from the Netherlands." Dg.o'11, the 12th Annual International Conference on Digital Government Research, College Park, MD, USA, June 12–15.
Chen, Yu-Che, and Tsui-Chuan Hsieh. 2014. "Big Data for Digital Government: Opportunities, Challenges, and Strategies." *International Journal of Public Administration in the Digital Age* 1 (1):1–14.
Comfort, Louise. 2007. "Crisis Management in Hindsight: Cognition, Communication, Coordination, and Control." *Public Administration Review* 67 (Supplement to volume 67):189–97.
Davenport, Thomas, and Laurence Prusak. 2000. *Working Knowledge*. Boston, MA: Harvard Business School Press. Original edition, 1998 (hardcover).
Dawes, Sharon S. 2010. "Stewardship and Usefulness: Policy Principles for Information-based Transparency." *Government Information Quarterly* 27 (4):377–83.
Deloitte-NASCIO. 2014. "2014 Deloitte-NASCIO Cybersecurity Study: State Governments at Risk: Time to Move Forward." Deloitte and the National Association of State Chief Information Officers (NASCIO).
Desouza, Kevin C. 2014. "Realizing the Promise of Big Data." Washington, DC: IBM Center for the Business of Government.
Dhillon, Gurjit Singh, Vishanth Weerakkody, and Yogesh Kumar Dwivedi. 2008. "Realising Transformational Stage E-Government: A UK Local Authority Perspective." *Electronic Government: An International Journal* 5 (2):162–80.
Duncan, George, and Stephen Roehrig. 2003. "Mediating the Tension between Information Privacy and Information Access: The Role of Digital Government." In *Public Information Technology: Policy and Management Issues*, edited by G. David Garson, 94–119. Hershey, London: Idea Group Publishing.

Executive Office of the President. 2012. "Big Data Across Federal Government." Washington, DC: White House.

Fung, Archon, Mary Graham, and David Weil. 2007. *Full Disclosure: The Perils and Promise of Transparency.* Cambridge, NY: Cambridge University Press.

Goldsmith, Stephen, and Susan Crawford. 2014. *The Responsive City: Engaging Communities Through Data-Smart Governance*: San Francisco, CA: Jossey-Bass.

Hoffer, Jeffrey A., Mary B. Prescott, and Fred R. McFadden. 2002. *Modern Database Management.* Upper Saddle River, NJ: Prentice Hall.

Janssen, Marijn, Ricardo Matheus, and Anneke Zuiderwijk. 2015. "Big and Open Linked Data (BOLD) to Create Smart Cities and Citizens: Insights from Smart Energy and Mobility Cases." In *EGov 2015*, edited by Efthimios Tambouris, 79–90. Switzerland: Springer.

Kapucu, Naim. 2006. "Interagency Communication Networks During Emergencies: Boundary Spanners in Multiagency Coordination." *American Review of Public Administration* 36 (2):207–25.

Laudon, Kenneth, and Jane Laudon. 2006. *Management Information Systems: Managing the Digital Firm.* Ninth edition. Upper Saddle River, NJ: Prentice Hall.

Laudon, Kenneth C., and Jane P. Laudon. 2012. *Management Information Systems: Managing the Digital Firm.* 12th edition. Upper Saddle River, NJ: Pearson Education.

McAfee, Andrew, and Erik Brynjolfsson. 2012. "Big Data: The Management Revolution." *Harvard Business Review*, October, 60–8.

McNabb, David E. 2007. *Knowledge Management in the Public Sector: A Blueprint for Innovation in Government.* Armonk, NY; London, UK: M.E. Sharpe.

National Science Foundation. 2012. NSF Leads Federal Efforts in Big Data. Press Release, March 29, 2012. Washington, DC.

Polanyi, Michael. 1962. *Personal Knowledge: Towards a Post-Critical Philosophy.* Chicago: University of Chicago Press.

Polanyi, Michael, and Harry Prosch. 1975. *Meaning.* Chicago: University of Chicago.

Research Office of Legislative Council Secretariat. 2013. "Innovation and Technology Industry in South Korea, Israel and Belgium." Hong Kong: Hong Kong Legislative Council Secretariat.

Scholl, Hans J., and Ralf Klischewski. 2007. "E-Government Integration and Interoperability: Framing the Research Agenda." *International Journal of Public Administration* 30 (8/9):889–920.

Scholl, Hans Jochen, Herbert Kubicek, Ralf Cimander, and Ralf Klischewski. 2012. "Process Integration, Information Sharing, and System Interoperation in Government: A Comparative Case Analysis." *Government Information Quarterly* 29 (3):313–23.

Soares, Sunil. 2012. *Big Data Governance: An Emerging Imperative.* Boise, ID: Mc Press.

The Economist. 2010. "Data, Data Everywhere: A Special Report on Managing Information." *The Economist*, February 27.

The Economist. 2016. "Briefing: The New Face of Facebook." *The Economist*, April 9, 21–4.

The World Bank. 2013. "The Four Pillars of The Knowledge Economy." The World Bank. Available at: go.worldbank.org/5WOSIRFA70 (accessed November 10, 2013).

Tsoukas, Haridimos. 2005. *Complex Knowledge.* Oxford: Oxford University Press.

United Nations. 2010. *Creative Economy Report 2010.* New York: United Nations; UNDP & UNCTAD.

U.S. Securities and Exchange Commission. 2009. *In Brief FY 2010 Congressional Justification.* Washington, DC: U.S. Securities and Exchange Commission.

U.S. Securities and Exchange Commission. 2010. "Office of Interactive Disclosure: History." U.S. Securities and Exchange Commission, last modified 01/08/2010. Available at: www.sec.gov/spotlight/xbrl/oid-history.shtml (accessed May 2, 2016).

Wagner, Christian. 2003. "Knowledge Management in E-Government." *Proceedings of the Ninth American Information Systems Conference*: 845–50.

Ward, Matthew O., Georges Grinstein, and Daniel Keim. 2015. *Interactive Data Visualization: Foundations, Techniques, and Applications.* Second edition. Boca Raton, London, New York: CRC Press, Taylor & Francis Group.

7 Digital Privacy and Digital Security Management

Introduction

Protection of digital privacy for individual citizens is foundational in earning trust. Because citizens trust government with their vital records such as social security, property, and financial information, governments have a duty to ensure the individual information privacy that citizens expect when turning over their personal information. The U.S. Government Accountability Office (GAO) has highlighted the threats to sensitive information and urged federal government agencies to strengthen the safeguards protecting sensitive information citizens have entrusted to them (GAO 2015). Earning citizen trust also requires governments to ensure accuracy of information because errors in government records, such as property records, can cause major disruption of citizens' lives. Moreover, citizens expect governments to protect their vital information not only in regular online interactions but also in the worst of circumstances, such as natural disasters or cyber-attacks. Citizens will only trust governments that can protect their vital information and preserve vital records to help them quickly reestablish themselves during disasters and cyber-attacks.

However, the digital privacy of citizens is increasingly under threat. The growing use of surveillance technologies such as surveillance cameras, biometrics, drones, and satellites allows private individuals, companies, and governments to track daily activities of individuals in an unprecedented way (Mack 2014). An increasing use of drones in civilian life has gained attention in the United States (Sherwood 2012). The pervasiveness of social media use further exposes individuals to data mining and profiling if information is not carefully guarded. The vast amount of public information put online also allows companies to create and sell personal profile information by utilizing software programs to crawl through websites.

Digital security is also under attack. For national governments, the concern is that cyber-terrorism could potentially bring down critical infrastructures such as power grids. The GAO in the United States highlighted the serious threats to cybersecurity in its 2012 report (GAO 2012a). Security breaches in government information systems or private information systems with personal information pose another threat to digital security and digital privacy. For instance, in March 2012, approximately 780,000 Medicaid patients and recipients of the Children's Health Insurance Plan in Utah had personal information stolen.[1] The scope and seriousness of these information security breaches have continued to rise. According to the *Washington Post* in 2015, the hack of the security clearance system of the Office of Personnel Management (OPM) in 2014 compromised more than 21.5 million people's records.[2]

To address these critical challenges, this chapter provides an introduction to concepts and issues on digital privacy and digital security. More importantly, this chapter discusses the regulatory frameworks, policy principles, and management strategies for protecting digital privacy and securing digital information. The next section will begin with the definition and significance of digital privacy, and will follow with the policy framework and management issues surrounding digital privacy. A description of a management strategy combining institutional and technical solutions completes the discussion about digital privacy. Discussion of digital security follows the same organization for digital privacy by starting with the definition, moving to policy and management principles and issues, and then introducing a risk-based comprehensive management strategy. The conclusion of this chapter will highlight management recommendations and explore a more integrated approach to digital privacy and security.

Digital Privacy

Definition and Significance

Digital privacy can be seen as an extension of individual privacy into the digital sphere. The United States has a long tradition of individual privacy rooted in individual rights. Warren and Brandeis' (1890) essay entitled "The Right to Privacy" is one of the early seminal pieces on privacy with the goal of protecting the "sacred precinct of private and domestic life" (1890, 195). This expectation of privacy was codified in the Privacy Act of 1974. Such a notion of privacy represents control over transactions between people and others with the goal of enhancing individual autonomy (Margulis 2003). A more modern definition of individual privacy also entails the right to control personal information, preferably after it has been disclosed to others (Margulis 2003). For instance, the Health Insurance Portability and Accountability Act (HIPAA) of 1996 has a privacy rule that regulates the use and disclosure of protected health information (PHI). HIPAA mandates that healthcare facilities that collect PHI must properly notify individuals of the use of their PHI.

Digital privacy is of growing importance with the increasing amount of personal digital information transmitted, utilized, and stored in various public, private, and non-profit organizations. The increasing adoption and use of e-government information and transactions have accelerated the collection of personal information in a digital format (Beldad 2011). Citizens are concerned about theft and misuse of personal information in digital format when it is stored, transmitted, and inadvertently made available to the general public. For instance, electronic filing of income taxes involves the electronic transmission of social security numbers in the United States or some form of national ID numbers in other countries. Sensitive income and other personal finance information are also included in the transactions. The application of government benefits such as social security, Medicare, and food stamps alike also require personal information and are later digitalized and stored in government records.

At the same time, a growing array of information and communication technologies are posing increasingly serious threats to digital privacy. Examples include surveillance cameras that can collect video footage of individuals' activities (Mack 2014); Google Maps that can show satellite images of an individual's property; Facebook that stores personal/group pictures and information; location-based technologies that can track our movements via phones, etc. The use of big data gathered from social media, sensors, and mobile devices, or even for academic and research purposes, could have serious privacy implications (MIT Big Data Initiative (bigdata @casil) 2015). These exposures and the possibilities for combining the information to create personal profiles for sales or marketing purposes constitute an invasion into our digital privacy.

Moreover, the e-government movement towards integration of information and services creates growing concerns about digital privacy. The existing laws and regulations tend to take a more cautious approach to data linkages between governmental agencies for privacy purposes. For instance, the Social Security Administration (SSA) does not have an active data link to the records of the same individual at the Internal Revenue Service (IRS). However, the increasing linkage and sharing of information from various agencies to provide citizen-centric services is likely to lead to concerns about digital privacy if there are no additional safeguards for potential profiling as the result of such linkage.

Policies and Management for Digital Privacy

One of the main policy issues for digital privacy is the balance between the public's "right to know" and an individual's "right to privacy" (Garson 2006, 75). An increasing amount of personal information is being collected by government and then stored and shared in a digital format—such as home address, social security number, tax, medical information, etc.—leading to numerous benefits associated with easy access to such information in the form of information-sharing among governments. These benefits include better law enforcement and improvement of public services, among others. Nevertheless, such information-sharing makes it easier than before to create a profile of an individual simply based on electronic records available to government. For instance, police officers can gain access to drivers' licenses, criminal records, or Federal Bureau of Investigation (FBI) files through a portal accessing various databases. If information is not accessed carefully with proper safeguards, there is a risk associated with violating individuals' privacy.

Another tension between privacy and access deals with the information made available on government websites. For the purpose of transparency and efficiency, governments strive to make public records available online. However, such transparency, if not carefully monitored, may inadvertently make personal and proprietary information available to the public and increase susceptibility to secondary use and profiling of individuals (Kulk and van Loenen 2012). One example of such tension is that the county treasurer offices in some states in the United States make property information searchable online. The intent was to improve information access to property information, which is deemed as public records that citizens and businesses can request from local governments. Instead of paying a personal visit to government to request such information and experience lengthy wait times, citizens and businesses can gain instantaneous access, verification, and even analysis. However, this constitutes invasion of personal privacy as people can search the information on the ownership of a particular piece of property. An added complication is the growing power of internet search engines and applications that even allow an information consolidation company to integrate all public records online to create personal profiles for many individuals and then to sell them for profit.

The management challenge for public managers is to strike a dynamic balance between privacy and access in the digital era. Such a balance in protecting digital privacy is a moving target depending on the capability of current technologies intruding into personal digital privacy. The European Union's legislation on the protection of personal data is an example of striving to find that balance by specifying the conditions under which personal information should be used and shared.[3] A higher challenge is to find a third alternative that protects individuals' privacy and improves access to information at the same time. The overarching goal is to find ways to maximize both privacy and access.

Another challenge involves managing individuals' expectations of digital privacy. Individuals tend to expect a high level of privacy protection from government because of their fear of identity theft and potential intrusion by others into their private lives. However, digital privacy is not viewed by government as an absolute right, but instead as an important right whose exercise needs to be balanced with other rights (right to information) or other policy goals (Cullen 2009). For instance, e-mail correspondence between government employees and citizens can be considered public communication, so government employees cannot have any expectation of privacy. It is the responsibility of public managers to develop an e-mail policy that balances the right to privacy and the right to public information. The challenge is to effectively manage citizens' expectation of privacy in their communication with government.

Protection of digital privacy will face additional challenges in the future. The push for increased access will further heighten the risk of the loss of privacy as the result of sharing, transmitting, and disseminating personally identifiable information (PII) in digital format (Kulk and van Loenen 2012). The move to open government data, as seen in the Data Accountability and Transparency Act (DATA Act) in the United States, will continue to put pressure on governments to provide more detailed information (such as raw data sets) to the public. Moreover, the ability of government to collect information via the use of surveillance technologies for public safety and national security poses another threat to individual privacy (Mack 2014). Lastly, there will be an increasing need for a more coordinated approach between the protection of digital privacy and assurance of digital security in the digital age because a main source of the loss of digital privacy is security breach of a government information system with citizens' personal information—as seen in the data breach of the U.S. OPM.

Protection of Digital Privacy

Principles and Regulations of Digital Privacy

Protection of digital privacy should begin with a set of principles that articulate a coherent policy on digital privacy. One such principle for digital privacy would be to err on the side of over protection, requiring all personal information (such as home address and social security number) to be stricken from any publicly available electronic documents. Another principle is informed consent for the release and sharing of personal information (such as name, digital images, or security tapes) beyond intended purposes. The exceptions would only be granted on the ground of protecting public interests such as national defense and public safety.

One main principle of information privacy protection is to grant individuals control of personal information. In the United States, several regulations provide individuals some control over their personal information. The Freedom of Information Act establishes the right of individuals to access information from the government about themselves. The Family Educational Rights and Privacy Act permits some control over disclosure of personal information. For a student or a guardian of a minor student, this Act provides access to educational records concerning the student as well as the right to challenge the accuracy and completeness of these records. The Criminal Justice Information System Statute (enacted in 2011) provides individuals with the ability to access, inspect, and correct their information in the system.

Use limitation principle, as established for the protection of personal information, is also a relevant principle (OECD 1980). This principle establishes that personal information should not be used for any purpose other than what is intended in the collection of personal information. For instance, personal information collected through registration for a public event should not be shared beyond what is relevant to that event. The United Kingdom's Personal Data Protection Act of 1998 has a similar principle, stating that personal data should be used for the purpose specified.[4]

Additional privacy policy principles can be seen in the United Kingdom's Personal Data Protection Act of 1998. For instance, one principle states that personal information should not be kept longer than necessary and be up-to-date. This reduces the risk of exposing personal information through prolonged storage by government and ensures the accuracy of personal information. All these policy principles articulated in the protection of personal information are likely applicable to the protection of digital privacy by including both paper and digital formats in the government's stewardship and use of personal information.

These digital privacy policy principles should be codified into a government-wide policy. A government should have a policy document that clearly states the privacy principles it adheres to, the exceptions to privacy protection, and the reasonable expectation of privacy with specific reference to digital personal information. At minimum, such a policy should state when personal information will be collected, how it is used, and the conditions under which personal information will be shared—such as in the privacy policy by the U.S. Federal Trade Commission.

As an illustration, the State of Utah's privacy policy for users accessing their official website is instructive.[5] This policy identifies what PII (such as name, address, social security number, etc.) it collects. It also specifies what information is automatically collected when someone is accessing its website, such as IP address. This policy then states how the information is used. For instance, access and use information is utilized for improving the website and online services. The information is employed for official state business only. The policy also specifies the conditions under which PII is shared and the laws and regulations governing information-sharing. Noteworthy is a special section on children's information. Such a policy also makes reference to information security and information integrity, as well as the responsibilities of a third party having access to the information.

Institutional and Technical Solutions to Digital Privacy

The implementation of these digital privacy principles can take the form of institutional mechanisms and technical solutions, as suggested by Duncan and Roehrig (2003). Institutional mechanisms articulate the processes and procedures for governmental agencies to uphold any digital privacy principles. Technical solutions are specific ways for using information and communication technology to safeguard personal information. As noted before, protection of digital privacy is usually a balancing act as there is a trade-off between digital privacy and information access (including information-sharing among governmental agencies). A proper combination of institutional mechanisms and technical solutions has the potential to maximize both the protection of digital information privacy and the sharing of information for better public services.

Institutional mechanisms are foundational in keeping up with a growing array of emerging threats to digital privacy. A rudimentary form of such institutional mechanisms is to require a routine check of privacy concerns on government information published online via websites or other social media outlets. For the dissemination of government information, a government agency can designate a privacy advocate to act on behalf of the individuals whose privacy could be compromised as the result of government actions (Duncan and Roehrig 2003). A possible invasion of digital privacy falls under the purview of this privacy advocate. An ombudsman could play a similar role, but might be more reactive in nature as he/she handles complaints.

A governmental agency can establish a privacy review board, especially if the agency's main responsibility is to produce and disseminate PII. The responsibility of this board includes examining the release of public government information and ensuring that individuals' confidential information is not revealed. A good example is the U.S. Census Bureau's Microdata Review Panel, which is charged with reviewing policies for the dissemination of public-use microdata files. The goal is to protect individual privacy. The U.S. National Center for Education Statistics has a Disclosure Review Board that has a similar charge (Duncan and Roehrig 2003, 112). Moreover, Section 208 of the United States E-Government Act of 2002 also has a privacy impact assessment (PIA) requirement for the collection, maintenance, or dissemination of PII as a result of deploying new or substantially changed technology. For instance, the Privacy Office at the Department of Homeland Security (DHS) has conducted a PIA of the DHS State, Local and Tribal Fusion Center Initiative.[6]

Another solution is to incorporate a privacy program in a government agency or the entire government enterprise that can identify the PII in government as well as coordinate the efforts throughout the entire government to protect the PII under its stewardship. The GAO serves as an example of such a program. For its privacy program, the GAO has established a Privacy Office with a Chief Agency Privacy Officer (CAPO) supported by a Records Officer, Management Analyst, and an advisor from the GAO Office of General Counsel. The privacy office has identified more than ten information systems under its management that have stored PII. A privacy threshold has been discussed and delineated with coordinated efforts to provide privacy training to implement developed privacy safeguards. Moreover, such a privacy program has subjected itself to periodic review to identify opportunities for further improvement (Office of Inspector General at GAO 2015).

The most extensive institutional mechanism is forming a national body that oversees all government information to protect individual privacy, such as having a national data and access protection commission. These commissions can regulate information gathering and dissemination by government. For instance, Australia and New Zealand have Privacy Commissioners, and the United Kingdom has a Data Protection Registrar (Duncan and Roehrig 2003, 113). These institutional mechanisms provide an ongoing review of privacy policies to keep up with advances in information and communication technologies. Such review mechanisms are of growing importance in an era of open government and in light of the increasing capabilities of software programs and applications alike to create personal profiles with the potential to invade individual privacy.

There are technical solutions for governments to protect citizens' digital privacy; the most basic is to de-identify citizens when personal information such as race, gender, age, or income is released. Some of the practices include assigning identification numbers other than social security numbers. Additional attention is given to the potential to re-identify an individual due to tabulated data with a small count in a cell. For instance, if a cell in a table on a particular census track shows only one Asian man with the status of orphan, then the privacy of that person is compromised (Duncan and Roehrig 2003, 115). A more sophisticated technical solution involves the use of a specialized software program to scramble information to preserve the pattern of information and prohibit re-identification of any single individual or establishment in a census tract.

Technical solutions are likely to evolve with new threats to digital privacy. The examples introduced here are for illustrative purposes rather than being intended to present a comprehensive picture. For instance, an enterprise software program can operationalize privacy rules to filter individual privacy information before such information can be made electronically available to employees or customers/citizens. For data linkages across governmental agencies, the creation of an employee identification number and implementation of an automatic filter to screen out any personal information during the data-sharing process are recommended. Moreover, the introduction of an identity management system can be beneficial for enforcing policy and principles of privacy protection and for personalization of privacy settings (Priem et al. 2011).

Digital Security and Cybersecurity

Definition and Significance

Digital security has three key components: confidentiality, integrity, and availability (Bishop 2002). Confidentiality refers to the ability to have confidential exchanges of information and/or transactions. Encrypting information is a way to ensure confidentiality so that, in the event a message is intercepted in transmission, it will not be deciphered. Confidentiality is also about the protection of personal and private information. Personal information that citizens give to governments should remain confidential and only be used for the purpose of completing a particular transaction such as applying for a permit, renewing a driver's license, or getting government benefits. The inclusion of confidentiality in the definition of digital security articulates its connection with digital privacy, which shares the goal of confidentiality for protecting personal information.

Integrity refers to data quality for government information. If there is a data error in a government information system, citizens suffer the consequences. Integrity is also important in some of the mission-critical governmental operations. For example, the accuracy of the location information on an underground water main is especially critical when digging takes place in an area that is likely to cut into the water main. The last component of digital security is availability, which is essential for business continuity. For instance, it is important for governments to operate continuously in times of crisis/emergency. One mechanism for ensuring business continuity for government websites is to have a set of proxy servers in a remote site to safeguard mission-critical information and to keep governments functioning, even in the event of state capitals being destroyed.

Digital security has garnered growing recognition of its importance with the growing number and scale of digital/cybersecurity threats to government. According to a report by the U.S. GAO (2012b), the number of cybersecurity incidents among 24 key agencies has increased more than 650 percent over the last five years. Facing the continuing growth of information security incidents (tenfold growth over the last seven years), there is a call for greatly increased security efforts by the federal government to protect sensitive information (GAO 2015). Moreover, there have been enduring concerns about protecting our critical infrastructure, such as electric power grids, nuclear power plants, and defense facilities that are increasingly connected to an electronic network (GAO 2012b). The concerns about digital security are likely to increase because future warfare and terrorist activities will likely focus more on cyber targets.

Digital security has also commanded the attention of chief information officers (CIOs) when the growing use of mobile devices poses new threats to government networks. CIOs at the state and local levels have a difficult time coping with the proliferation of personal iPads and smart phones that connect to secure networks (Opsahl 2011). Recently, state and local government employees in the United States have become more accustomed to the idea of using mobile devices such as Blackberries, smart phones, and iPads/tablets for their professional and personal dealings. These mobile devices, although convenient for communication, pose security threats due to the networks they are connected to and because of potential leaks that may result from engaging in personal activities on the same device that has access to government networks.

Cybersecurity has become a more widely used term in the U.S. Federal Government than computer security and digital security. Cybersecurity entails securing the entire cyberspace that is a global domain consisting of "internet, telecommunications networks, computer systems, and embedded processors and controllers" as stipulated in the CNSSI-4009 (National Institute of Standards and Technology (NIST) 2013, 62). This broader notion is consistent with the increasing use of networks for government services, the increased capability of wired and wireless telecommunication infrastructure, increasing adoption of mobile and connected devices, and growing interdependence of various networks and information systems. Cybersecurity places greater emphasis on cyberspace as a whole with interconnected networks, systems, processors and controllers, while digital security focuses on securing digital information. Also, the notion of cybersecurity has a stronger connection to national security concerns.

Policy Principles and Management for Digital Security

There are several information security laws, regulations, and plans at the federal level in the United States. Part of Presidential Decision Directive No. 63 requires the development of an internal information assurance plan. Another law, the Computer Security Act of 1987, requires NIST and the National Security Agency (NSA) to develop security requirements for technology areas, including operating systems, database systems, firewalls, smartcards, biometric devices, the web, intrusion detection, Public Key Infrastructure (PKI), Virtual Private Network (VPN), etc. More recently, the main piece of legislation has been the Federal Information Security Management Act (FISMA) of 2002, which is part of the Electronic Government Act of 2002. FISMA specifies the responsibility of each federal agency to protect the digital security of its information systems and data.[7] The National Cyber Security Division in the DHS provides resources and coordination for the implementation of digital security at these individual agencies. This Division has three main program areas to secure cyberspace and protect America's cyber assets, including the national cyberspace response system, federal network security, and cyber-risk management program.[8] The Cybersecurity National Action Plan, unveiled by the White House in 2016, outlines a national strategy that establishes a national commission, modernizes information technology (IT) systems, empowers Americans to secure their online accounts by partnering with major technology firms, and invests heavily in cybersecurity (White House 2016).[9]

The principle of digital security policy as dictated by FISMA as well as the Cybersecurity National Action Plan is one of risk management. A risk-based principle first recognizes that the policy goal is not risk elimination but risk minimization, given the allocated resources because resources are not infinite and risk can never be eliminated. Such a principle also implies that the number of resources allocated should be commensurate to the severity of the risks an organization needs to mitigate. For instance, the government information system running critical infrastructure such as power grids should receive a large proportion of the digital security resources, as the failure of such a system has dire consequences.

One main policy challenge stems from the trade-off between digital security and information access. Digital security is about creating barriers to unauthorized access to information. These barriers can be in the form of keeping parts of a secured database scattered in various and undisclosed locations, such as some of the database for the Department of Defense in the United States. A higher barrier is to further disconnect these portions of a large database from any telecommunication networks, but such high-level security will limit access to information and its use. Public managers need to be aware of this trade-off to make an informed policy decision on the level of digital security that strikes a balance between access control and use.

Maintaining a process orientation is an important management issue for digital security. The risk-based approach mentioned earlier requires periodic review of risks and adaptation to new and emerging threats. Digital security is compromised by the lack of rigorous implementation of security safeguards. Therefore, it is important to focus on integrating digital security measures into standard operating procedures. This process orientation also allows monitoring of emerging security threats and then addresses them appropriately. Such monitoring and adaptation makes an information security system resilient (Deloitte-NASCIO 2014).

Understanding threats is another critical management issue for digital security because awareness is essential for successful implementation. A management team needs to know that threats to digital security can come from either external or internal sources. Such distinctions will help with the development of an appropriate response plan. External threats via the internet and other networks are typically associated with cybersecurity. Attacks on cybersecurity may be launched by criminal groups trying to attack systems for monetary gain, such as the use of ransomwares to extort money from victims. Such attacks could also be the result of the recent development of cyber tools for information-gathering and/or espionage activities (Reddick 2012, 217). Software attacks such as viruses, worms, macros, and denials of service belong to the category of external threats. Other types of external attacks include the use of malware, a Trojan horse in a software program, "war driving" to intercept information from a wireless network, and logic bombs to initiate a programmed destructive action. Information extortion such as blackmail of information disclosure constitutes another external threat. The top three external cybersecurity threats of state government CIOs include malicious code, hacktivism, and zero-day attacks (Deloitte-NASCIO 2014).

Internal security threats are mostly related to human behavior. It has been argued that humans are the weakest link in the defense against threats to information security. In fact, end-user errors are the main source of information security problems according to a survey of state agencies in Texas (Reddick 2009). The causes of these human errors are lack of a rigorous information security policy and poor implementation of such policies. Moreover, errors can occur due to the lack of appropriate information security measures as embedded in government information systems. Rudimentary errors are weak and persistent passwords and lack of virus protection software. Another internal threat is sabotage launched by disgruntled employees of an organization. The authorized access to data presents an opportunity to such employees to breach information systems to download critical information. Understanding possible sources (internal and external) of digital security threats helps raise the saliency of the issue among public managers and lays the foundation for devising plans for securing digital assets.

A critical goal of digital security is to achieve business continuity (Laudon and Laudon 2015, 278; GAO 2012b). In the event of a disaster, government plays a vital role in ensuring evacuation as well as the preservation of records and the continuing functioning of information systems. Natural or manmade disasters can present a serious threat to digital security, especially to the availability of mission-critical information and computer systems (GAO 2012a). Fires, floods, earthquakes, and lightning can damage hardware and equipment that support the function of servers. For instance, a sustained power outage can bring down critical information systems. Flooding can cause permanent damage to databases or data servers that store critical government and citizen information. Some state governments have adopted the best practice of off-site back-ups for vital records. Moreover, some governments have maintained a facility with a duplicate set of databases and servers that can keep all the mission-critical systems functioning even when the primary ones are destroyed by disaster.

An Integrated Approach to Ensure Digital Security and Cybersecurity

Protection of digital security requires a multi-pronged approach with risk management at the core (Chang and Lin 2007; Bauer and Eeten 2009). Although the nature and severity of the relevant risks may change with the advance of new technologies, the risk management approach has been regarded as an industry standard and has been relatively stable over time. Most organizations in the public and private sectors subscribe to a risk-based management approach (I. T. Governance Institute 2001; Laudon and Laudon 2010; GAO 2012b). As a framework for the entire country, the U.S. Cybersecurity National Action Plan also upholds the need for a risk management approach (White House 2016).

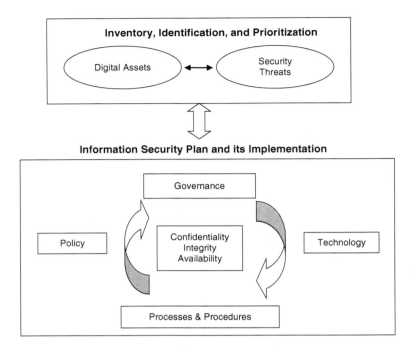

Figure 7.1 A Comprehensive Information Security Management Strategy

The overall scheme of the risk-based multi-pronged approach is illustrated in Figure 7.1. One of the first steps in risk management is identification and prioritization of digital assets. For the U.S. Federal Government, the most critical assets are infrastructures such as electric power grids, national security information, and financial systems. Local and state governments are more concerned about vital records for citizens, and financial and human resources systems for their basic operation. This concern has been justified by a security breach in the South Carolina state government in 2012 that exposed over three million social security numbers along with more than 300,000 credit and debit card numbers. Low-priority digital assets are those considered as public records, such as government information on public services and events. These are more routine services and basic information rather than mission-critical data for the organization. These types of digital assets can be low on the list for receiving funding for digital security measures.

The next step is to identify possible threats to high-priority digital assets. One perspective advocates distinguishing internal from external threats while considering both sources of information security threats. The probable external and internal threats were listed earlier in the chapter. Such a distinction is productive in devising an appropriate digital security policy and measures for the nature of threats identified. External threats call for digital security measures that protect the electronic exchange of information via the internet between the governmental agency and its stakeholders. Internal threats could stem from the sabotage behavior of disgruntled employees and/or employees not following information security protocols and measures. Managers call for more rigorous internal digital security processes and procedures that prevent human errors and malicious behavior of employees.

With the growth in interconnectivity of various systems and devices via wired and wireless telecommunication infrastructure, it is important to identify information security threats that include telecommunication infrastructure, networks, information systems, data, and processes. The trend of increasing use of wireless networks, platforms, and devices utilizing these wireless networks has created a new set of information security vulnerabilities that governments need to be concerned about (Deloitte-NASCIO 2014). Digital security threats may result from inadequate updates of security patches for the intranet, inherent information system vulnerabilities, poor data quality, and lack of information assurance processes. For high-stake digital assets, measures should be comprehensive to address possible vulnerabilities through the scrutiny of both perspectives. For instance, a financial information system with mission-critical information should run on a private network with a security clearance system (internal threats combined with attention to network elements) and install an intrusion-detection system for cyber-attack (external threat with attention to information systems).

After digital security risk identification and prioritization, public managers need to develop and implement a comprehensive digital security plan that has many critical elements, as shown in Figure 7.1. The overarching goals of such an information security plan should be confidentiality, integrity, and availability (CIA) as indicated in the middle of the four elements. These three goals have been the cornerstone of information assurance (GAO 2012b; General Accounting Office 2003). Confidentiality ensures that only authorized personnel have access to privileged information and it also provides the needed information security foundation for digital privacy. Integrity is about the quality and accuracy of information that an information security system aims to ensure. Availability is the assurance of business continuity even in the event of disaster or major catastrophe.

Overall, this plan needs to first outline the principle of risk management with prioritization of digital assets, identification of threats, and development of security measures proportional to the priority and threats. As such, this plan will serve as a framework for development and implementation of security measures. Moreover, this plan communicates the security measures and expectations of digital security to the key stakeholders so they understand what measures should be put in place to secure digital information and what they can expect regarding the security of their information. For example, a government agency needs to make sure that a transaction with a citizen is secure by implementing layers of information security measures to protect the transmission of personal information. Effective digital security needs to address the information security threats introduced by the use of social media (Public CIO 2011).

For governance, this information security plan needs to include a clear delineation of roles and responsibilities, both in the development of policy as well as the implementation and evaluation of digital security measures (I. T. Governance Institute 2001). The current practice of state governments is to have a dedicated position for a chief information security officer (CISO) to oversee the entire information security plan and its implementation for the state government (Deloitte-NASCIO 2014). Such a CISO typically reports to the CIO for the state. Leaders and executive-level management should be involved in making digital security decisions, and such decisions should align with an organization's strategic plan. More specifically, digital security needs to have the support of the main policy-making body of an organization (i.e. Congress, state legislature, city council for a municipality, or board for a company), as it requires building a security culture and significant resource commitment. Such action is critical to address the disconnect between resource allocation and information security that is evident in the public sector (Deloitte-NASCIO 2014). Executive-level support and attention should be directed to all other elements of a comprehensive strategy such as development of a security policy, building an information security infrastructure, etc. (I. T. Governance Institute 2001). The creation of a CISO position is productive in overseeing various components of such a comprehensive strategy.

For information system security policy, it is important to translate the parameters of the assessed risks and their associated costs into specific policy. Such policy provides a clear ranking of the information risks, acceptable security objectives, and the mechanisms to achieve these goals (Laudon and Laudon 2015, 277). The policy should have sections on security clearance structure, information access, access to networks, social media use policy, wireless device use policy, and other policies that ensure information security. The mechanism of using digital security to secure digital privacy can also be articulated to help achieve the goal of confidentiality. Moreover, this policy needs to include a section on business continuity and disaster recovery for ensuring the availability of information systems and the information residing in these systems.

A digital security process and procedure guided by the security policy is another integral element of an overall strategic plan. Such a process requires monitoring digital security vulnerability on a regular basis. The discipline of periodic assessment is critical to keep pace with the growing sophistication of cyber-attacks (Deloitte-NASCIO 2014). Assessment should combine both information systems and humans to monitor implementation of digital security processes and procedures. Receiving security updates from the National Cyber Security Division in the Department of National Security is an example of such monitoring. Moreover, this process should conduct a comprehensive review of various aspects of the overall risk management strategy—including policy, technology, and training—to see how various components need to be updated. Such a review also involves scanning emerging digital security threats and solutions so security measures will be up to date.

Training and education are paramount in ensuring digital security since humans are usually regarded as the weakest link of digital security. Therefore, the focus should be on education and training for individuals in the organization so they will be aware of digital security issues and follow digital security protocol (I. T. Governance Institute 2001; Radl and Chen 2005). Minimally, government employees need to be trained to perform some basic risk-management functions such as updating passwords, securing their laptops, and never allowing unauthorized people to access critical files. For high-level security required by the Department of Defense and major financial institutions, education and training on digital security should be even more rigorous. It could involve a complete ban on the use of USB drives and securing all the machines that have a connection to critical data and files.

Technology is also an integral element of the overall strategy, especially to keep pace with the increasing sophistication of cyber-attacks and proliferation of interconnected devices and systems. Digital security technologies include authentication, biometrics, intrusion detection, and many others. At the most basic level is access control technology, which allows only authorized users to gain access to government information systems. These include an access control protocol and password for controlling access. A more elaborate identity management and authentication system keeps track of legitimate users and their access and use privileges. Each access will first require the user to authenticate him/herself. Such authentication can be done with passwords (single or double sets) and/or supplemented with added layers of biometrics and other authentication measures. There is a move toward enterprise identity and access management (IAM) that allows for multi-factor authentication and secures the entire enterprise composed of interconnected information systems (Deloitte-NASCIO 2014).

For external threats via the internet, firewalls, intrusion detection systems, and antivirus and antispyware software are effective (Laudon and Laudon 2015, 281–3). Encryption of information transmitted over the internet is an important digital security measure. It protects against personal/private information being stolen in the process of transmission. Examples include the uses of Secure Sockets Layers (SSLs) and Secure Hypertext Transfer Protocol (S-HTTP). The use of VPNs for some of the more secure transactions is also popular. Incoming requests from the internet for resources in the private network need to pass firewalls first. Policy rules for firewalls govern which request is legitimate and which is not. Intrusion detection systems (IDS) allow an active scan of the various connected information systems, information requests, and the transmission of information. A more rigorous adoption of wireless information security protocol as part of this IDS is necessary to address emerging threats. Antivirus measures and anti-spyware are useful. To keep pace with the emerging sophistication of ransomware, malware, and other new hacking tools, it is critical to update the information security technology portfolio to keep up with the emerging trends (Deloitte-NASCIO 2014).

A unified information security threat management system is designed to integrate all the digital security tools for ease of management and implementation (Laudon and Laudon 2010, 316). This integrated system should be guided by information security policy with the supporting governance structure to make timely decisions that keep pace with the growing complexity of the information security landscape and the sophistication of cybercrime and cyberwarfare. Such a unified system should aim to cover the entire enterprise rather than several information systems. The need to take an enterprise approach is grounded in the growing connectedness of various information systems; cyber-attacks can exploit the weakest defense of several connected information systems. Moreover, such a system should take into account both digital and physical threats to information security to be effective.

Conclusion

Individual digital privacy needs to be balanced both with easy access to public information and with the need for national security. Protection of individual privacy should be managed in a way that recognizes the trade-offs between these policy objectives. Ultimately, such trade-offs should be the decision of the community, striking a balance that reflects community values. Moreover, citizens should understand what expectations are reasonable given the trade-offs being made so public managers can reach a mutual understanding with citizens that promotes trust in government.

Institutional solutions are fundamental in the protection of digital privacy. An individual, committee, or board needs to conduct periodic reviews of digital privacy protection measures to ensure that digital privacy policies are properly implemented and keep pace with recent developments in technology. Before a data set is released to the public, such as the one for the U.S. Census Bureau, care should be given to a digital privacy review that examines possible threats to digital privacy as the result of profiling via possible data linkages. In addition, technical solutions, such as an identity management system that allows for rigorous authentication and access control based on an established digital privacy policy, will assist in implementation. A well-functioning identity management system is likely to minimize the tension between competing policy objectives in advancing digital privacy.

Digital security is concerned with the confidentiality, integrity, and availability of information and supporting information systems. Increasing digital security usually comes at the expense of ease of access, as security is typically built by having layers of barriers to unauthorized access to the information. The level of digital security needs to be balanced with its cost. In response, the federal government has adopted a risk management approach that places more restrictions on information deemed as high risk and makes low-risk information items more accessible. This approach also prioritizes digital security resources and allocates more for information with the highest digital security risks, such as the risks associated with a failing critical information infrastructure.

Overall, a digital security plan should be risk-based and include the components outlined in Figure 7.1. Inventory, identification, and prioritization of digital assets and threats to digital security help develop the needed background information for a comprehensive digital security plan. Such a plan needs to incorporate an active governance body, a well-articulated policy, rigorous processes/procedures, and appropriate technology for successful implementation. A rigorous process should raise employees' awareness of digital security for any public organization/services. Training is also a critical component of a proper process and procedure, as digital security is only as good as the weakest link in the defense for digital security.

Digital privacy is only possible through security that protects the confidentiality of personal information. Public managers should strive to maximize digital privacy and security while minimizing access restriction. A risk-based approach is productive for both digital privacy and security because only limited resources are available for addressing privacy and security issues; consequently, prioritization is necessary. Governance and technology are integral to a digital privacy and security plan. A governance structure and timely review will allow privacy and security measures to evolve with new concerns and technological advances. Such adaptability is critical in the era of social media, mobile devices, and digital society.

Notes

1 It was deemed to be a hacker who accessed the Utah Department of Technology Service's server. For more details, see www.healthcarefinancenews.com/news/top-10-data-security-breaches-2012, accessed August 20, 2012.
2 For more details, visit www.washingtonpost.com/news/federal-eye/wp/2015/07/09/hack-of-security-clearance-system-affected-21-5-million-people-federal-authorities-say/, accessed July 20, 2016.
3 For more details, visit europa.eu/legislation_summaries/information_society/data_protection/l14012_en.htm, accessed November 1, 2012.

4 For more details, see en.wikipedia.org/wiki/Data_Protection_Act_1998, accessed June 10, 2012.
5 For more details, see www.utah.gov/privacypolicy.html, accessed June 28, 2012.
6 For more details, visit www.it.ojp.gov/default.aspx?area=privacy&page=1287#contentTop, accessed August 23, 2013.
7 For more details, visit csrc.nist.gov/groups/SMA/fisma/index.html, accessed October 22, 2013.
8 www.dhs.gov/national-cyber-security-division, accessed October 13, 2013. Please note the web link no longer works and is for information only.
9 For more details, visit www.whitehouse.gov/the-press-office/2016/02/09/fact-sheet-cybersecurity-national-action-plan, accessed September 7, 2016.

References

Bauer, Johannes M., and Michel J.G. van Eeten. 2009. "Cybersecurity: Stakeholder Incentives, Externalities, and Policy Options." *Telecommunications Policy* 33 (10–11):706–19.

Beldad, Ardion D. 2011. "Trust and Information Privacy Concerns in Electronic Government." PhD Dissertation, Enschede, University of Twente.

Bishop, Matt. 2002. *Computer Security: Art and Science*. Boston, MA: Addison-Wesley.

Chang, Shuchih Ernest, and Chin-Shien Lin. 2007. "Exploring Organizational Culture for Information Security Management." *Industrial Management & Data Systems* 107 (3):438–58.

Cullen, R. 2009. "Culture, Identity and Information Privacy in the Age of Digital Government." *Online Information Review* 33 (3):405–21.

Deloitte-NASCIO. 2014. "2014 Deloitte-NASCIO Cybersecurity Study: State Governments at Risk: Time to Move Forward." Deloitte and the National Association of State Chief Information Officers (NASCIO).

Duncan, George, and Stephen Roehrig. 2003. "Mediating the Tension between Information Privacy and Information Access: The Role of Digital Government." In *Public Information Technology: Policy and Management Issues*, edited by G. David Garson, 94–119. Hershey, London: Idea Group Publishing.

Garson, David. 2006. *Public Information Technology and E-Governance: Managing the Virtual State*. Sudbury, MA: Jones and Bartlett Publishers, Inc.

General Accounting Office. 2003. "Security: Counterfeit Identification and Identification Fraud Raise Security Concerns." Washington DC: General Accounting Office.

Government Accountability Office (GAO). 2012a. "Cybersecurity: Threats Impacting the Nation." Washington, DC: Government Accountability Office.

Government Accountability Office (GAO). 2012b. "Information Security: Weaknesses Continue Amid New Federal Efforts to Implement Requirements." Washington, DC: Government Accountability Office.

Government Accountability Office (GAO). 2015. "Information Security: Federal Agencies Need to Better Protect Sensitive Data." Washington, DC: Government Accountability Office.

I. T. Governance Institute. 2001. "Information Security Governance: Guidance for Boards of Directors and Executive Management." Rolling Meadows, IL: The Information Systems Audit and Control Foundation.

Kulk, Stefan, and Bastiaan van Loenen. 2012. "Brave New Open Data World?" *International Journal of Spatial Data Infrastructures Research* 7:196–206.

Laudon, Kenneth C., and Jane P. Laudon. 2010. *Management Information Systems: Managing the Digital Firm.* 11th edition. Upper Saddle River, NJ: Prentice Hall.

Laudon, Kenneth C., and Jane P. Laudon. 2015. *Essentials of Management Information Systems.* 11th edition. Boston: Pearson Education.

Mack, Timothy C. 2014. "Privacy and the Surveillance Explosion." *Futurist* 48 (1):42.

Margulis, Stephen. 2003. "Privacy as a Social Issue." *Journal of Social Issues* 59 (2):243–61.

MIT Big Data Initiative (bigdata@casil). 2015. "Big Data Privacy Scenarios." Boston, MA: MIT.

National Institute of Standards and Technology (NIST). 2013. "Glossary of Key Information Security Terms," edited by Richard Kissel. Washington, DC: National Institute of Standards and Technology.

OECD. 1980. Recommendation of the Council Concerning Guidelines Governing the Protection of Privacy and Transborder Flows of Personal Data. Paris, France: OECD.

Office of Inspector General at GAO. 2015. "GAO's Privacy Program." Washington, DC: Office of Inspector General at the Government Accountability Office.

Opsahl, Andy. 2011. "CIOs Cope with Personal iPads and Smartphones on Secure Networks." *Government Technology* 24 (8).

Priem, Bart, Ronald Leenes, Alea Fairchild, and Eleni Kosta. 2011. "The Need for Privacy-Enhancing Identity Management." In *Digital Privacy*, edited by J. Camenisch, Ronald Leenes and D. Sommer, 53–71. Berlin, Heidelberg: Springer-Verlag.

Public CIO. 2011. Cyber-Security Essentials for State and Local Government. e.Republic white paper.

Radl, Alison, and Yu-Che Chen. 2005. "Computer Security in Electronic Government: A State-Local Education Information System." *International Journal of Electronic Government Research* 1 (1):79–99.

Reddick, Christopher G. 2009. "Management Support and Information Security: An Empirical Study of Texas State Agencies in the USA." *Electronic Government, An International Journal* 6 (4):361–77.

Reddick, Christopher. 2012. *Public Administration and Information Technology.* Burlington, MA: Jones & Bartlett Learning.

Sherwood, Christina Hernandez. 2012. "Everyday Drones." *Government Technology*, August, 12–17.

Warren, Samuel, and Louis Brandeis. 1890. "The Right to Privacy." *Harvard Law Review* 4 (5):193–220.

White House. 2016. Fact Sheet: Cybersecurity National Action Plan. Washington, DC: White House.

8 Management of ICT Performance for Digital Governance

Introduction

The management of information and communication technology (ICT) performance in the public sector calls for a broader perspective to evolve with technological advances and innovations in digital governance. The conventional perspective on government ICT performance tends to focus on internal operations such as information technology (IT) service to support the use of computers and information systems by government employees. The increasing importance of delivering public information and service online and providing online transactions with citizens necessitates the evaluation of ICT performance from the perspectives of a variety of users (including citizens, businesses, non-profit organizations, and other governments). A shift in focus from internal to external is needed to respond to government becoming more digital in providing information and service.

Another impetus for a broader perspective of ICT performance is the growing use of digital means for democratic governance as well as for the production and delivery of public service (Chen and Hsieh 2009; United Nations 2014). In response to the prevalent use of social media by citizens, governments increasingly utilize social media to provide information to citizens (Mergel 2013b; International City/County Management Association (ICMA) 2011; Grimmelikhuijsen and Meijer 2015). Governments also interact with citizens on social media and other online platforms to engage citizens in providing policy ideas and/or voicing their policy preferences and concerns. Enabled by the availability of citizen service information systems and apps for interfacing with such systems, citizens can provide public service information as well as submit service requests on their smart phones to engage in co-production of public service information and service (Clark, Brudney, and Jang 2013).

The confluence of mobile technologies, social media, the internet of things, and big data creates a rising expectation for government ICT performance. The experiences that citizens have with e-commerce will likely impact their evaluation of government ICT performance when using such e-commerce experience as their reference point. As a result, governments may be burdened with explaining a gap in performance between the public and private sectors.

The connection between ICT performance and public values has grown stronger. The Obama administration has utilized ICT as a means to enable open government to foster transparency, participation, and collaboration (Orszag 2009). The U.S. Data Accountability and Transparency Act (DATA Act) passed by Congress in 2014 also signaled a commitment by the U.S. government to increasing transparency of government financial and operational data by making it machine readable and accessible online.[1] The U.S. Federal Government's IT expenditure was made accessible online as early as 2015. Moreover, organizations in the civil society and individual citizens also link public values to ICT performance. Overall, the performance of ICT use can be measured by the extent to which such use can further advance public values such as transparency and accountability by addressing the online aspect of these core public values (Cresswell, Burke, and Pardo 2006).

For ICT performance, a contemporary definition needs to adapt to the ever-expanding technology portfolio of government. Governments need to add mobile and connected devices (i.e. tablets, iPads, sensors) to their measurements of ICT performance. The utilization of social media for communication, outreach, and engagement is also a growing aspect of ICT performance. With increasing computing and communication power, governments also need to change their perspectives to incorporate the inclusive notion of cyberinfrastructure—enabling them to go beyond devices and networks to include storage and computing capabilities (National Science Foundation (NSF) 2007).

This chapter addresses the "what and how" of ICT performance. In addition to a more inclusive and contemporary definition of ICT performance in the public sector, this chapter discusses the management of financial and human resources as well as needed project and program management to further improve ICT performance. To facilitate the improvement of government ICT performance, this chapter provides public managers with a performance management strategy.

To achieve the goals of this chapter, the next section delineates enduring and emerging aspects of ICT performance. Next follows a discussion of managing financial and human resources to provide the support for improving ICT performance. Following that is a delineation of the project and program management skills and strategies that support the effective implementation of ICT projects. This chapter will then introduce an ICT performance management strategy for continuously improving ICT performance for advancing public values. Lastly, this chapter will discuss future trends of ICT performance management to guide future development and adaptation for digital governance.

Performance Measurement for Government ICT Service

Conventionally, the assessment of IT has tended to focus on input and output of IT services and less on the quality of service provided. The ICMA has recommended performance measures such as central IT expenditure per workstation and ratio of workstations to the total number of jurisdiction employees. Technology investment (i.e. IT expenditure per workstation) is an input measure. Such measures could also include other technology investment in purchasing hardware, software, and services. The availability of IT services (workstation or devices per employees) counts as an output measure for the investment. These services could include various capabilities such as transactions on government websites, online payments, and geographic information system (GIS) applications.

A contemporary measure of ICT performance needs to place more emphasis on service quality. An objective service quality measure would be the average amount of time to respond to an IT service call and/or the resolution of an IT issue. Another objective performance measure of an e-government information system would be server uptime (i.e. 99.99 percent of the time) for website and online transaction services. Subjective measures call for human judgment. For service quality, user/customer satisfaction with the service experience has been widely used (Morgeson and Petrescu 2011). Performance measures of user satisfaction could be about the satisfaction ratings that government agencies give to received IT services in areas such as e-mail, IT equipment, network storage, and operation and maintenance (Desouza 2015). For citizens, such measures could involve their satisfaction with performing a particular task online with government (i.e. renewing a driver's license online).

Performance measures should include the ever-growing cyberinfrastructure and social media service platforms. The increasing processing speed of computers, the maturity of wired and wireless telecommunication networks, the rapid development and deployment of cloud computing and services—coupled with the exponential growth of smart phone/devices in the last decade—necessitate the expansion of traditional IT service to a more inclusive one of cyberinfrastructure (NSF 2007, 5). Cyberinfrastructure goes beyond a single organization to consider a network of service providers and how computing, data, and networks come together to provide ICT service. Moreover, the utilization of social networking sites/services such as Facebook, Twitter, and Instagram should be incorporated into ICT service performance portfolios. This is particularly relevant given the rise of social media over the last decade as well as the growing use of social media by government for the provision of government information and service (Zavattaro and Bryer 2016; Mergel 2013a).

E-government website performance evaluation provides insights into websites as main channels for providing government information and service. These include usability (navigation/organization), information relevance/quality, customer service/responsiveness, and website usage performance and growth (Morgeson 2012). Usability is best evaluated by the users. The diversity of users that e-government websites serve requires governments to consider people with disabilities and/or various native languages. Another measure of performance of e-government websites is the provision of relevant and quality government information such as actual information on permit applications and emergency notifications. Responsiveness is another measure of ICT performance with the rising expectations for e-government websites as well as governments as a whole (Goldsmith and Crawford 2014). The reach and use of government websites as measured by views and transactions are important measures of ICT performance. For instance, e-government service can be measured by the percentage of eligible users using the service (i.e. percentage of e-filings of personal income taxes).

With the prevalent use of social media by governments, social media metrics are a critical part of government ICT performance. One basic principle of measuring social media performance is the ability of such platforms to achieve agency/program missions. For instance, for U.S. open data initiatives, social media performance is measured by transparency, collaboration, and participation (Mergel 2013b, 122–44). More specifically, the number of Twitter followers or "likes" on Facebook can be measures for the reach of social media. Participation can be measured by click-throughs and the number of tags. Direct feedback can be measured by the number of times the content appears in the media. Satisfaction can be measured by sentiment analysis of social media posts. The number of return visits and referrals can be used to measure loyalty and brand awareness (Mergel 2013b, 143).

ICT performance measurement should move beyond output to include outcomes and periodic review (Chen and Zhang 2012). Most of the existing e-government performance measures tend to focus on input (expenditure) and output (the presence and sophistication of websites and social media). Much more emphasis is needed, however, on outcomes in order to be consistent with the evolution of performance measurement in government (Hatry 2006; Poister 2003). Outcome measures for e-government websites should include, but not be limited to, cost-saving, responsiveness, and satisfaction. Outcome measures of civic engagement and interactivity should include the diversity and reach of social media/apps use as well as the quality of comments and feedback received via such engagement. Moreover, successful performance measurement should conduct periodic reviews. This is more particularly the case for ICT than other areas of public service. The fast-changing landscape of technology demands a shorter time horizon for updating performance measures that are meaningful for measuring outcomes and impact.

The performance of ICT is ultimately measured by the advancement of public values. Such a public-value focus should define the "return" in

160   *Management of ICT Performance*

"return on investment" (ROI). When citizen participation in democratic governance is a core public value, the impact of ICT performance should be measured by, for instance, the number and quality of online channels and forums available for online participation, their use, and adoption and use of the comments from online participation (Chen and Zhang 2012). Similarly, transparency as a public value would require measuring ICT performance by the number of government data sets available online to increase the public's understanding of government activities. Whether these data sets are machine-readable is another important performance measure. Although the specific techniques and measures may evolve over time, connecting these impact/outcome measures of ICT performance to public values will need to be an enduring strategy.

Resource Management for ICT Performance

Having adequate resources is foundational for the continuous effort needed to improve the performance of ICT for digital governance. There are two types of resources: human resources and financial ones. Human resources are the people with the relevant skills and knowledge to succeed in the design and implementation of digital governance projects. Financial resources are the financial investments made in these digital governance projects.

Human Resource Management for ICT Performance

The recruiting and retention of talent for high-performing digital governance projects have been enduring challenges. Surveys of e-government efforts have consistently ranked the lack of people with technical expertise as one of the top two challenges for e-government (ICMA 2004, 2011). In the United States, governmental agencies at all levels of government need to compete with the private sector for ICT talents. For the same IT skill sets, corporations are in a position to pay 50 percent, or sometimes two to three times, more than their public-sector counterparts. Another related challenge is the need for government to navigate complex hiring regulations that cause delays and create unnecessary burdens. Firing staff with outdated skill sets is difficult with the legal protection offered to government employees. Complicating government retention, corporations are actively seeking ICT talents that have extensive experience in government, especially at the federal level. In addition, the challenge of limited or nonexistent training budgets makes it particularly difficult for government employees to keep up with the rapid development of new technologies and emerging IT challenges.

Leveraging public service motivation is an established way of recruiting and retaining talents to work in the public sector. Studies of public service motivation point to the value systems of those who thrive on working for governments (Belle 2012; Perry 2000). These could be feeling that they are making a direct impact on the community or offering a service that is meaningful to them. In addition, understanding public service motivation assists in targeting the segment of populations that are willing to offer their talents without seeking the same financial rewards available in the private sector. These are people who have had role models in their lives for providing public service who instill public service values in them.

Another way of recruiting and retaining IT talents for government is to increase the scope of responsibilities and to offer training opportunities. Governments typically are in the position to offer a wider range of responsibilities and experiences than their private-sector counterparts for people with the same skill set. For instance, a chief information officer (CIO) for a large city can oversee operations covering thousands of employees and serving a population of over one million people with a wide range of legacy systems to cutting-edge software applications. In addition, governments can increase investment in training. Such training might be technical training for non-technical people as well as more advanced technical classes for their IT employees.

To address the challenge of limited access to IT talents to work inside government, IT outsourcing has become a main vehicle for leveraging a broad IT talent pool to continuously improve the performance of e-government and digital governance projects. Outsourcing government services to the private sector has been a growing trend in the United States, over several decades dating back to the early 1990s, with the National Performance Review by the Clinton Administration to make government more efficient and effective. The outsourcing of ICTs follows this general trend. More importantly, the growth of cloud-computing and rapid advancements of various information technologies have made the strategy of accessing resources outside government more compelling.

The outsourcing of ICTs can address the need for IT talents in several ways. Outsourcing ICT service helps government agencies gain access to state-of-the-art technology services and talents (Chen and Perry 2003). The fast-paced development of ICTs makes access to state-of-the-art technology even more important as any skill set that the government acquires via hiring can become obsolete in several years. Another main benefit of such outsourcing is cost-sharing with other governments/corporations to financially sustain a talent pool that keeps pace with recent technological developments. Such arrangements allow government agencies to hire top talents based on projects and/or by hours. This practice is much more affordable than hiring these talents full-time as government employees.

To realize the full potential of outsourcing for ICT performance, government needs to retain internally the core competence to independently assess the cost and quality of these outsourcing projects (Chen and Perry 2003). Otherwise, information asymmetry between government and contractors would result in loss of control and ineffective monitoring of service quality. Moreover, the use of service-level agreements is another means to drive performance in an IT outsourcing arrangement. As complexity of outsourcing projects increases, there is a growing need for a relational approach (Brown, Potoski, and van Slyke 2013).

Several additional methods are available for addressing the talent challenge to drive ICT performance. In the United States, the existence of a Cybercorp scholarship program allows government to secure recent graduates of university information assurance programs to serve in government. The students who receive the scholarship for undergraduate and graduate education have a service obligation to work for government in the area of cybersecurity. State and local governments can offer internship opportunities as a way to recruit talents when recent graduates in IT fields have advantageous knowledge of the newest technologies.

Forming partnerships with university and non-profit organizations is another productive avenue to leverage ICT talents to improve digital governance performance. Increasingly, governments work with university research centers and laboratories to develop and test innovative ways of utilizing information technology for improving public service. Another practice is to form partnerships with foundations/corporations that can offer e-government and digital governance services such as search engines, fiber optic networks, and IT innovations. Moreover, governments are increasingly leveraging volunteer software programmers and designers of online experiences via working with Code for America and other non-profit organizations. The use of various online platforms can also aid in gaining access to ICT talents in broad sections of society.

Financial Resource Management for ICT Performance

Governments have struggled to locate and secure funds for e-government and/or digital governance projects. In the United States, surveys of local governments have consistently indicated lack of funding as one of the top two barriers to e-government (ICMA 2004, 2011). Lack of funds is also an impediment to hiring IT talents to implement e-government projects. At the state level, modernization of e-government services has faced the challenge of securing enough funds for major system upgrades. The U.S. Federal Government also requires a significant amount of budget appropriation to implement IT modernization projects for its agencies.

In the United States, a variety of funding options have been available (Rocheleau 2006, 134–9). Government can utilize and combine various funding sources to finance a digital governance project. IT expenditure typically comes from general funds; from these general funds, governments can decide how much money to allocate to IT and the items to purchase for this purpose. Sometimes, another funding option is the creation and management of funds dedicated to the improvement of ICT services. Such funding could be a dedicated fund for e-government that draws from the tax revenue generated from charging fees on telecommunication companies. These kinds of special purpose funds can help create secure funding sources for e-government. Issuing bonds and utilizing capital improvement funds are also viable options. Capital improvement funds are particularly useful for telecommunication infrastructures, such as fiber optic networks, and smart transportation infrastructures that require large initial investments.

For e-government services, charging user fees is a common way to generate the financial resources needed (Chen and Thurmaier 2008). User fees can be charged to cover the cost of information system development as well as on-going maintenance and upgrades. In addition, user charges can help off-set the additional charges of third-party financial institutions, such as credit card fees. Moreover, a "self-funding" model can levy fees to fully cover the cost of the production and delivery of e-government service over the e-government system's lifecycle (Gant and Gant 2003). This funding option does not require budget allocation from the general funds for an e-government service that benefits a particular segment of the population such as builders, contractors, and home-owners applying for building permits.

Public–private (non-profit) partnership is another model for financing digital governance service. Technology companies or their foundations are willing to donate technology services in exchange for notoriety and/or future market opportunities. Google currently offers free services for cities to advertise government services and businesses in their communities as well as providing Google Fiber for qualified communities.[2] Using a partnership model, IBM has helped pay for demonstration projects to bring technology to government, such as the sustainability project in Dubuque, Iowa.[3] Such partnerships can extend beyond corporations and are increasingly formed between non-profit organizations (foundations) and governments. For instance, community foundations can assist in providing funds needed to upgrade ICT services as an integral part of improving services.

Public finance principles and public values assist in deciding the level of user charges as well as in the choice of financing options (Chen and Thurmaier 2008). The benefit-received principle is applicable in deciding the amount of user charges. Such user charges can be set at the level of covering the shared cost of providing information and service online as an additional mode of public service. Another important principle is the consideration of externality in deciding whether a service can be offered with reduced or no user fees involved (Chen and Thurmaier 2008). For those e-government systems that benefit beyond one service (i.e. an online payment engine), user fees should be reduced by the amount that is commensurate to the positive externality of such an e-government service. Moreover, since government operation is paid for by taxpayer dollars (from individuals and corporations), some public information and service should be free-of-charge.

To achieve public values that define ICT performance, government needs to first decide on value metrics for determining the mix of financing options and their implementation. For digital governance projects that achieve the values of equity, effectiveness, and efficiency, general funds are a logical main source for financing. For a component of such projects that have online credit payment options, it is best to charge user fees for the credit card payment option. The more such a project promotes equity by reaching a broad cross-section of the community, region, or nation, the more it is sensible to cover the majority of the cost by tax revenues. To align financing with democratic principles and externality, a digital governance project that more strongly promotes civic engagement and democratic governance should have greater priority for financing from general funds.

Government and foundation grants are good funding sources for state and local governments to launch and implement their digital governance projects. In addition, specific NSF grants and foundation grants have targeted smart city initiatives.[4] One grant has funded building a smart city research consortium to share knowledge and resources. For more basic research such as big data, the U.S. NSF has made grants available to promote the establishment of big data research hubs that would help government build their big data analytics capability and cyberinfrastructure. For digital governance, the MacArthur Foundation via its Opening Governance Research Network Grant, for one example, leverages academia to design and implement 21st-century solutions to keep pace with technological advances.

The growth of online platforms and digital technologies provides new and innovative ways of financing digital governance projects. The crowdfunding model (i.e. Kickstarter) allows citizens and foundations to engage the public to donate money to a worthwhile project that advances public value. Such a project could be an app that enables emergency notifications to reach mobile devices and then provide information on where to go and what to do by pulling information from relevant organizations in the public, private, and non-profit sectors. Moreover, co-production is an increasingly significant model to lessen the financial burden on governments as well as achieve some core public values. In the United States, volunteer citizens contribute their time and skills to help track weather or natural disasters, find new species, or report/share community issues and solutions to governments and each other to improve public service in their communities. Volunteer software programmers and online platform designers, either individually or via non-profit organizations, contribute their time and expertise to add value to government data such as the ChicagoWorksforYou project that makes 311 data available for the public to access a ward-by-ward view of service delivery in Chicago.

Project and Program Management for ICT Performance

Government IT projects have a high failure rate as a result of various unique challenges posed to IT projects in the public sector. The failure rate is more than 50 percent for large IT projects when failure is defined as one of the following conditions: over budget, delay, and/or lack of functionalities.[5] Some major projects have had significant implications both in terms of public service and costs. One of the most cited examples is the U.S. Federal Bureau of Investigation's (FBI) failure to modernize its case system while costing more than US$100m with the price tag of hundreds of millions of dollars without the delivery of appropriate functionalities (Eggen and Whitte 2006).

The challenge facing government IT projects is multifaceted, especially in comparison with experiences in the private sector. Fragmentation of governance and a multitude of authorities has made IT projects that require cross-departmental and cross-boundary collaboration particularly challenging (Yang, Zheng, and Pardo 2012; Gil-Garcia et al. 2010). Another challenge is the short-term perspective driven by short election and budget cycles. A new administration, political appointees, and new chief administrators are all likely to create new initiatives that alter the priorities of an on-going IT project. In addition, the public sector has accountability rules and regulations, such as procurement rules, that impose restrictions on adapting to these changing priorities.

Project Management for ICT Performance

The discipline of project management is foundational for the success of government IT projects (Garson 2006, 349–68). Such project management includes the use of tools and techniques to produce a holistic and detailed look at a project. Managing projects involves several related activities: identifying project objectives, developing tasks and their interdependence for achieving objectives, securing needed financial and human resources for completing tasks, managing deliverables and deadlines, and implementing a mechanism to track and adjust as the project progresses. A more complex project requires a higher level of resource input in planning and implementation. Project management has become a respected discipline and has been recognized as foundational for project success.

A rigorous e-government project initiation needs to be first evaluated according to its potential contribution to targeted public services and to enterprise e-government. Progressive governments have a metric for evaluating the relevance and viability of an e-government project. Examples of these criteria include costs, ability to meet service needs, technology, alignment with strategic priorities, impact on the enterprise (government-as-a-whole), benefits to citizens, and the extent of citizen participation. Greater emphasis has been placed on advancement of public values as intangible returns on investment (i.e. transparency and accountability).

Needs assessment is particularly salient in project initiation and planning to ensure the success of later implementation (Garson 2006, 350–6). In the race to put more e-government services online, there is a tendency to equate availability of e-government services with their use. Moreover, low adoption rates due to the lack of careful assessment of needs and/or pricing structures have led to project failures. A careful needs assessment is critical to ensure later adoption and use.

Before development into a more elaborated plan for funding approval, project initiation and planning can benefit from initial vetting of proof of concept; a thorough vetting includes the key stakeholders of the project. For example, for an e-government project that serves local residents and businesses, these users can be involved earlier in the planning process to ensure that key concerns are fully addressed. Moreover, planning is about anticipating contingencies (i.e. personnel changes, health issues, changing project priorities, technological changes) and developing plans accordingly. One of the challenges particularly associated with IT is rapid development of technologies that renders old technologies irrelevant in a short period of time. Planning is also about managing interdependence between projects and actively identifying ways to improve efficiency and effectiveness.

Project implementation requires continuous monitoring and active management. Such implementation requires the project team to be fully aware of the state of the project and the progress to date. Such awareness needs to extend down to the level of individual project team members and the tasks (as well as sub-tasks) of the project. An enterprise project management tool is likely to become a necessity as the complexity of the project increases. Moreover, there is an increasing need for coordination when the number of team members is large. One important element of project implementation is communication and getting inputs. Regular and effective communication of implementation issues and timely resolution of these issues are critical (Boyer 2001). For instance, agile development of software programs has highlighted the importance of timely communication and involvement of stakeholders (Sutherland 2015).

An effective project implementation needs to address the interdependent realities of various components (Pardo and Scholl 2002). On a high level, these components include simultaneous consideration of organization, personnel, funding, and technology. For digital governance projects, the technology identified and deployed is a function of the knowledge and skill of key personnel as well as the budgeted resources for the project. Organizational priorities, especially due to a change in political leadership, may result in the change of personnel and the direction of the project. The turnover of key personnel can also affect the project. A successful implementation would require active management of these components and their interdependence.

Program Management for ICT Performance

Managing projects as parts of a larger program is an effective strategy (Yardley 2002). Taking a program perspective affords the flexibility that is

Management of ICT Performance 167

sometimes needed to address both the changing and interdependent reality of organization, personnel, technology, and funding. Veterans of government IT projects speak of the importance of staying on the project path rather than the project plan. A project plan can be rigid and fail to adapt to new realities. In contrast, staying on the project path offers much-needed flexibility. Moreover, taking a program-level perspective aids in pursuing strategic alignment as well as responsiveness to external demands and changes (Yardley 2002). The U.S. Federal Government has also recognized the importance of taking a program management approach for improving the success rate of IT projects (Khan 2010).

The evolution of e-government to a higher level of integration requires the adoption of an enterprise perspective to deal with fragmentation of IT projects and silos of government information systems. An enterprise perspective requires treating individual projects, as well as the larger programs they are under, as part of the overall enterprise endeavor. The increasing emphasis on an integrated citizen service information system requires an enterprise perspective on e-government service, security, privacy, transparency, etc. Moreover, an enterprise perspective can be supported by a project/program office for the entire federal, state, or local government. For instance, the U.S. Federal Government has an Office of E-Government & Information Technology headed by the Federal CIO to develop and manage the direction of the use of internet-based technologies.

A Strategy for Effective ICT Performance Management

An effective performance management strategy for improving the use of ICT to support digital governance entails following five principles (as shown in Table 8.1). The first principle is to take a stakeholder-focused approach to understanding, measuring, and improving performance as defined by various stakeholders. Such a diversity of perspectives requires clarification, deliberation, and making necessary trade-offs of performance goals. The second principle is to align performance measures to core values with a focus on outcomes measures including both process-based and results-based. The third principle is to apply data-driven performance management and learning. It is essential to collect performance data and use it to foster learning in improving performance. The fourth principle is to take a more integrated and user-centric approach to performance management. The last principle is to leverage an agile development approach to address the challenge of delay and cost overrun prevalent in digital government projects.

Stakeholder-focused Performance Management

A stakeholder-focused approach is productive for performance management of digital governance projects. For public policy and programs, a long established tradition has considered perspectives of different stakeholders

168 Management of ICT Performance

Table 8.1 Principles of an ICT Performance Management Strategy

Principle	Explanation
Stakeholder-focused	Stakeholders (including at least governments and users) need to be involved in defining and evaluating performance, as well as its active management.
Strategically aligned and outcome-driven	Performance management needs to align with government's digital governance strategy, and performance measures should reflect the alignment and focus on outcomes rather than inputs.
Data-driven performance management and learning	Data are central to managing performance and learning in performance improvement. Performance data need to reflect strategic priorities and to inform learning.
User-centric	ICT performance is judged by the end-users. User experiences and customer experiences are key.
Leveraging agile development	An agile development approach is particularly productive in adapting to changing policy priorities and the technology landscape. An agile approach reinforces stakeholder involvement, a focus on strategy, user input, and collaboration.

in public service production and delivery. These stakeholders include businesses, non-profit organizations, and other governments. From the perspective of stakeholders, digital governance projects are usually broader than most of the information system projects in the private sector. For e-commerce projects, the primary stakeholder is the paying customer. In contrast, a digital governance project with a strong emphasis on citizen participation needs to provide equal and free access to people with a diverse array of backgrounds, computer literacy, and motivations. In the United States, Section 508 of the Rehabilitation Act further specifies the legal requirements to consider people with disabilities, such as those who are visually impaired.

A stakeholder-focused approach to performance management seeks to clarify the value propositions of the proposed digital governance project and to measure the attainment of these values. A common pitfall of digital governance projects is a focus on the preferences and aspiration of governments rather than a fuller understanding of the potential users of/participants in e-government transaction services and/or e-participation opportunities. For instance, a government hosting an e-participation website can measure performance solely on the number of visits or users. From the user perspective, in contrast, there could be additional considerations as to whether relevant information is provided for the purpose of meaningful participation and whether the opinions of the citizens are included. A clarification of targeted public values (i.e. transparency and effectiveness) could answer one of the most difficult questions in performance measurements: what constitutes performance.

An important task for stakeholder-focused performance management is to articulate both the various dimensions of performance and potential trade-offs. One dimension addresses various values such as transparency, efficiency, and accountability. Developing an online service that caters to a whole range of users with various preferred channels of communication has cost implications that imply some trade-off with efficiency. Another important dimension is the potential trade-off between the interests of a collective (a network) and those of individual organizations (or individuals). For personalized digital governance service that typically demands information-sharing and collaboration across organizational boundaries, trade-offs could arise between the collective and individual organizations, especially when one organization disproportionally bears the cost.

The primary responsibilities of a digital governance manager include designing ways to engage various stakeholders with the goal of understanding their values and interests. Attention needs to be paid in particular to users and their experiences as articulated in the U.S. Federal Government's digital government strategy. Performance indicators should be developed in accordance with the priorities and values as deliberated and articulated through inputs from various stakeholders. Moreover, a digital governance manager needs to be able to map and navigate the dimensions of performance as well as the potential trade-offs. Such mapping and navigation requires managers to possess the skills to understand and articulate the shared interests of various stakeholders in performance and to deal with potential conflicts and trade-offs between dimensions of performance results.

Strategically aligned and Outcome-driven Performance Management

Digital governance performance measures should be in alignment with the public values shared by the majority of the stakeholders as well as the unique value propositions of individual stakeholders. When online citizen participation and equity are the primary values, performance measures of such online options should include both a measure of the number and nature of online participation, and a measure of equity in the representation of various segments of the population. In addition, performance measures must align with strategic goals. Strategic goals are typically developed based on the core values. For example, a strategic goal could target utilizing ICTs to deliver efficient and effective public service. An actionable objective under the overarching goal could be building and implementing an online permit system to reduce the burden and delay of business permit applications. A potential measure could include the number of days it takes to review a permit application.

The measures of performance should focus on outcomes. Consistent with an earlier discussion about ICT performance measures, the development of performance measurement has evolved to place a greater emphasis on outcomes rather than output (Hatry 2006). This shift in emphasis is particularly salient in the area of digital government when the typical evaluation criteria tend to be about outputs. Most output criteria are about availability of e-government services in terms of number and sophistication, such as those used in the United Nations e-government ranking reports (United Nations 2010, 2012, 2014). Many fewer criteria focus on the extent to which these online services and information have been utilized; even fewer are about the impact of these digital governance projects. Moreover, outcome performance measures should include both results-based outcomes and process-based outcomes. Results-based outcomes are concerned with impact, and can be further differentiated into short-term, mid-term, and even long-term outcomes (Frechtling 2007). For instance, a government open data initiative would include output measures such as the number of data sets available online. Then, short-term outcome measures would involve the number and type of data sets being downloaded. The long-term outcome measures examine whether the use of these government data actually brings in any economic and/or governance benefits.

The other type of outcome is process-based, especially critical for online public governance that emphasizes process. Such a process orientation is also salient as governments strive to provide personalized digital information and service to various stakeholders when a successful outcome is trust-building among key stakeholders that could later lead to more in-depth collaboration in information-sharing for high quality digital government service.

Data-driven Performance Management and Learning

An integral component of digital governance performance management strategies is the development, collection, analysis, and use of performance data. Development of a key performance index is critical. Such performance measures need to align with the strategic priorities of the organization to be key and improvement-focused. These measures need to be few in number to increase the ROI of time and energy for data collection. Moreover, these performance measures should incorporate some growth indicators as a way to spur innovations. For performance data collection, integrating such data collection into the standard practice of the existing information system to track performance is advantageous to reduce the burden on staff and increase the quality of information. For instance, the citizen service information system (i.e. 311) has tracked the time involved in handling a service request. In addition, it is better to increase the number of data points and frequency of data collection to understand the potential fluctuation involved.

Performance data can add value when analyzed, but analysis needs to be purposeful in measuring the state of performance against the key performance index. For instance, a city can keep track of water use and monitor the performance of sustainable water use. The real benefit of data analysis is the ability to identify the primary factors contributing to a higher level of performance. A wide range of statistical techniques and business intelligence tools could aid in such analysis. Moreover, the learning from performance analysis needs to be converted into actions. Performance management requires continuous learning and adjustment to respond to changes in internal and external conditions.

Digital governance data come from a variety of sources in a variety of formats. Citizens access government information and interact with government via various platforms, including websites, social network sites/services, apps, etc. In addition, some of the digital governance data can be monitored close to real-time by tracking online interactions, visits, information requests, and service provision. The rise of Twitter and Facebook provides another rich source of data. Using Twitter data analyzed by Klout scores, government agencies can determine whether a particular agency's social media presence is a thought leader, broadcaster or a specialist (Mergel 2013b, 135–41). The volume of digital governance performance data is likely to be large when images, biometrics, and video feeds for surveillance constitute a growing portion of government data. For information dissemination, governments can utilize data analytic tools to understand the following factors: who constitute the registered users of government information notifications and via what information-service platforms.

Communication of performance information is critical for its productive use. Being stakeholder-focused, communication of performance should include a communication plan that differentiates timing, content, and format of performance communication based on the needs of a particular group of stakeholders (Bingham and Felbinger 2002). For instance, governments can provide the details on the number and demographics of registered users for text messaging services to emergency management service agencies on a monthly basis while communicating with the public by publicizing summary information on an annual basis. For social media interactions, governments can track Facebook use and communicate the results with real-time notifications to event managers when the purpose of communication is about event promotion. Moreover, a broader approach treats performance communication as a larger part of knowledge management. Doing so will allow individuals and/or organizations to contribute and share performance information to foster innovation.

Performance management should focus on learning to enable the discovery of new and better ways to improve public service and public governance (Chen and Zhang 2012). The learning imperative is more pronounced in the area of digital governance than other areas since the ability to learn and adapt to changing technology is a necessity in the areas of digital governance. Doing so requires the cultivation of an innovation culture as well as institutionalizing innovations—such as establishing an innovation office to drive

172 *Management of ICT Performance*

performance. With the goal of improving performance, digital governance managers need to engage in double-loop learning. Double-loop learning helps managers question underlying assumptions and adapt to new realities (Argyris and Schön 1996). Such adaptation is key to utilizing innovative online channels and platforms to improve performance.

User-centric Approach to Managing Performance

Performance measurement for digital government/governance has evolved to focus more on user experience with and evaluation of an online service, as evident in the U.S. Federal Government's digital government strategy (White House 2012). This focus has several major implications for understanding and improving performance. First, performance of digital governance in its ultimate form is determined by the experience of the users. Traditional measures of digital government performance tend to focus on the availability of online information and service functionalities. However, these are merely intermediate steps to address the issue of user-centric performance. Much more needs to be done to achieve the creation of values for the users. Second, user expectations are evolving with the type and quality of service that they experience with e-commerce. Governments need to be able to keep up with development in the private sector in order to meet citizens' digital government performance expectations.

Additionally, the user/customer perspective demands the breakdown of government silos in providing customer-centric experience. Performance is not measured by individual government agencies, but rather by the quality of personalized online service for users/citizens. This requires collaboration among government agencies in sharing information, adopting the same data standards, and potentially utilizing the same system to improve performance.

Leveraging Agile Development to Improve Performance

The e-government project failure of the FBI in the United States underscores the need for an agile approach. One of the most notable e-government project failures is the FBI's unusable Virtual Case File system, not functional after over US$170m was spent on its development (Eggen and Whitte 2006). The underlying challenge for the project was addressing the changing needs of the FBI as well as fast-changing technologies. The traditional waterfall approach to information system development as initially deployed was ill equipped to adapt to these changes. The use of an agile development approach is credited with providing a cost-effective solution to the FBI's modernization needs that was finally delivered under budget and ahead of schedule (Sutherland 2015).

An agile development approach, since it addresses the fundamental challenges of digital governance, is more likely to deliver results. First, an

Management of ICT Performance 173

agile approach underscores the importance of stakeholders and solicits their early and regular involvement based on the agile software development manifesto and the principles behind it.[6] Users of government systems including those inside and outside governments need to be consulted to understand the desired functionalities of the system. Within the rigid structure of the waterfall approach, such user input is mostly solicited at the beginning for identifying requirements. In contrast, an agile development approach involves users of the information system along the way to seek feedback on their needs and preferences. Doing so will allow system developers and interface designers to obtain important input not in the abstract, but at a high-level of specificity when users review a prototype.

Agile development relies on a cross-functional, self-organized team with ample interactions (Sutherland 2015). Team members need to be trained across various functional areas to be familiar with skills involved in completing the tasks of other team members. The ability to carry out a function as needed rather than waiting for a team member is crucial in moving the project forward in a timely manner. Moreover, self-organization to address a problem is another important organizational feature of the agile methodology. This is about team members taking ownership and initiative to expedite the process of finding solutions to any issue identified by users. Frequent interactions and communication are needed to facilitate learning and self-organization for problem-solving.

Furthermore, an agile development approach raises awareness of performance and enhances learning by inspecting how projects are implemented (Sutherland 2015). The team members have regular (i.e. weekly) meetings to review the progress of the project. The goal of such meetings is to engage project members in learning how they can perform better. The ability of team members to "plan, do, check, and act" is critical to accelerate learning and improvement. In this cycle of "plan, do, check, and act," "act" refers to seeking new and better ways to achieve a project goal.

Agile development is particularly useful for the projects with a clear product/result orientation rather than a strong concern about rules and procedures. A product orientation favors flexibility in the process and self-organization as a main feature of the agile development. In contrast, an overarching concern about following the letter of the rules and procedures for software development makes it incompatible with agile development.

Conclusion

This chapter provides a current and inclusive conceptualization of performance measurement for ICTs. This conceptualization embodies the traditional measures of e-government performance (mostly input-oriented) while expanding the notion of ICT performance to encompass outcome-focused measures. Outcomes examine the actual use of the online digital governance service and users' satisfaction with it. More importantly, outcomes are about advancement of public values (i.e. efficiency, effectiveness, and transparency). The economic and societal impact of ICT is the ultimate measure of ICT performance. In addition, such conceptualization embraces the proliferation of the means of digital governance via the use of traditional websites, mobile-friendly websites, social network sites/services, text-messaging, etc.

Human and financial resources are foundational for ICT performance. This chapter discusses the challenges associated with gaining access and utilizing these resources. More importantly, this chapter offers a variety of methods that governments can pursue to recruit, retain, and utilize IT talents. These include public service motivation, increasing the scope of responsibility, and cross-training. Government can gain access to IT talents outside government via partnerships with universities and non-profit organizations, and via IT consulting and outsourcing IT service. For guidance in obtaining needed financial resources for ICT, this chapter focuses on following public finance principles in evaluating and combining a range of options including general funds, user fees, "self-funding" models, and partnerships.

The discipline and rigor of project and program management are equally crucial for ICT performance; the success of IT projects depends largely on their implementation. Rigorous e-government project management demands an assessment of needs and articulates the project's potential to reach a performance target. Project implementation requires continuous monitoring and active management to ensure success. Project managers need to understand and manage the interdependence between organization, personnel, funding, and technology. In addition, e-government program management offers high-level strategic consideration and flexibility in achieving the objectives of IT projects.

This chapter outlines a strategy for effective ICT performance management—a strategy composed of principles relevant to a wide range of digital governance projects. Effective management of ICT performance should pursue alignment with organizational strategies while focusing on outcomes rather than outputs. The process would put a strong focus on the involvement of stakeholders in defining performance and offering performance evaluation and improvement ideas. The utilization of performance data and their timely communication are integral to the strategy. Moreover, an agile development approach is central to the proposed overall strategy for driving ICT performance.

The frontier of digital governance performance management centers on several trends. First, ICT performance will place increasing emphasis on outcomes. A future-oriented ICT performance management scheme needs to define relevant outcomes as related to public values and government priorities. Second, ICT performance will become more user-centric in terms of measurement. User experiences and satisfaction will become an increasingly important measure of performance. Third, ICT performance metrics will continue to expand with the proliferation of online platforms and services such as the utilization of social networking services as well as emergency notifications. Fourth, agile methodology will be utilized for digital governance projects to increase performance. The use of methods that are more flexible and adaptive is a response to changing government priorities as well as the technology landscape. Lastly, the governance of ICT performance would need to address the interdependent reality of integrating digital governance service in various government agencies to provide personalized digital service. Digital governance needs to evolve to a higher level of information and service integration to achieve digital service personalization and advance public values.

Notes

1 For details on the DATA Act, see the publication by the White House: www.whitehouse.gov/blog/2015/05/08/better-data-better-decisions-better-government, accessed July 9, 2016.
2 For more details on Google Fiber, visit fiber.google.com/about/, accessed July 10, 2016.
3 For more details on the project, visit www-03.ibm.com/press/us/en/pressrelease/34575.wss#release, accessed July 10, 2016.
4 For more details on the NSF grants, visit nsf.gov/news/news_summ.jsp?cntn_id=136253, accessed July 10, 2016.
5 This is based on an article published in 2008 that gathered IT project failure rates from various sources. This article is published by *Portland Business Journal* and was accessed on July 10, 2016 via www.bizjournals.com/portland/stories/2008/10/20/smallb4.html.
6 For more details on the agile software development manifesto and the principles behind it, visit agilemanifesto.org/, accessed June 20, 2016.

References

Argyris, Chris, and Donald Schön. 1996. *Organizational Learning: Theory, Method, and Practice.* Second edition. MA: Addison-Wesley.
Belle, Nicola. 2012. "Experimental Evidence on the Relationship between Public Service Motivation and Job Performance." *Public Administration Review* 73 (1):143–53.
Bingham, Richard, and Claire Felbinger. 2002. *Evaluation in Practice: A Methodological Approach.* Second edition. New York: Chatham House Publishers.
Boyer, David. 2001. "ERP Implementation: Managing the Final Preparation and Go-Live Stages." *Government Finance Review* 17 (6):41–4.
Brown, Trevor, Matthew Potoski, and David van Slyke. 2013. *Complex Contracting.* New York, NY: Cambridge University Press.
Chen, Yu-Che, and Jun-Yi Hsieh. 2009. "Advancing E-Governance: Comparing Taiwan and the United States." *Public Administration Review* 69 (Supplement 1): S151–8.
Chen, Yu-Che, and James Perry. 2003. "Outsourcing for E-Government: Managing for Success." *Public Performance & Management Review* 26 (4):404–21.

Chen, Yu-Che, and Kurt Thurmaier. 2008. "Advancing E-Government: Financing Challenges and Opportunities." *Public Administration Review* 48 (3):537–48.

Chen, Yu-Che, and Jian-Chuan Zhang. 2012. "Citizen-centric E-Government Performance: Satisfaction with E-Information." *Electronic Government, An International Journal* 9 (4):388–402.

Clark, Benjamin Y., Jeffrey Brudney, and Sung-Gheel Jang. 2013. "Coproduction of Government Services and the New Information Technology: Investigating the Distributional Biases." *Public Administration Review* 73 (5):681–701.

Cresswell, Anthony M., G. Brian Burke, and Theresa A. Pardo. 2006. "Advancing Return on Investment Analysis for Government IT: A Public Value Framework." Albany, NY: Center for Technology in Government.

Desouza, Kevin C. 2015. "Creating a Balanced Portfolio of Information Technology Metrics." Washington, DC: IBM Center for the Business of Government.

Eggen, Dan, and Griff Whitte. 2006. "The FBI's Upgrade That Wasn't; $170 Million Bought an Unusable Computer System." *Washington Post*, August 18, 1.

Frechtling, Joy. 2007. *Logic Modeling Methods in Program Evaluation*. San Francisco, CA: Jossey-Bass.

Gant, Diana Burley, and Jon Gant. 2003. "Enhancing E-Service Delivery in State Government." In *E-Government 2003*, edited by Mark A. Abramson and Therese L. Morin, 53–80. Washington, DC: Rowman & Littlefield Publishers, Inc.

Garson, David. 2006. *Public Information Technology and E-Governance: Managing the Virtual State*. Sudbury, MA: Jones and Bartlett Publishers, Inc.

Gil-Garcia, J. Ramon, Ahmet Guler, Theresa A. Pardo, and G. Brian Burke. 2010. Trust in Government Cross-Boundary Information Sharing Initiatives: Identifying the Determinants. Paper read at 43rd Hawaii International Conference on System Sciences (HICSS-43), 5–8 January 2010, at Koloa, Kauai, HI.

Goldsmith, Stephen, and Susan Crawford. 2014. *The Responsive City: Engaging Communities Through Data-Smart Governance*. San Francisco, CA: Jossey-Bass.

Grimmelikhuijsen, Stephan, and Albert Jacob Meijer. 2015. "Does Twitter Increase Perceived Police Legitimacy?" *Public Administration Review* 75 (4): 598–606.

Hatry, Harry P. 2006. *Performance Measurement: Getting Results*. Second edition. Washington, DC: The Urban Institute Press.

International City/County Management Association (ICMA). 2004. 2004 E-Government Survey. Washington, DC: International City/County Management Association.

International City/County Management Association (ICMA). 2011. Electronic Government 2011. Washington, DC: International City/County Management Association.

Khan, Alyah. 2010. "Government's New IT Career Path is Critical, Sources Say: OPM Chooses Agencies for First Tests of the Program." *FCW (Federal Computer Weekly)*, December 20. Available at: fcw.com/articles/2010/12/20/new-it-program-management-career-path.aspx (accessed November 8, 2012).

Mergel, Ines. 2013a. "A Framework for Interpreting Social Media Interactions in the Public Sector." *Government Information Quarterly* 30 (4):327–34.

Mergel, Ines. 2013b. *Social Media in the Public Sector: A Guide to Participation, Collaboration and Transparency in the Networked World*. San Francisco, CA: John Wiley & Sons.

Morgeson, Forrest V. III. 2012. "E-Government Performance Measurement: A Citizen-Centric Approach in Theory and Practice." In *Electronic Governance and Cross-Boundary Collaboration: Innovations and Advancing Tools*, edited by Yu-Che Chen and Pin-Yu Chu, 422. Hershey, PA: IGI Global.

Morgeson, Forrest V., and Claudia Petrescu. 2011. "Do They All Perform Alike? An Examination of Perceived Performance, Citizen Satisfaction and Trust with US Federal Agencies." *International Review of Administrative Sciences* 77 (3): 451–79.

National Science Foundation (NSF). 2007. "Cyberinfrastructure Vision for the 21st Century Discovery." Washington, DC: National Science Foundation.

Orszag, Peter R. 2009. Open Government Directive, Memorandum for the Heads of Executive Departments and Agencies, edited by Executive Office of the President Office of Management and Budget: Office of Management and Budget. Washington, DC: White House.

Pardo, Theresa A., and Hans J. Scholl. 2002. Walking Atop the Cliffs: Avoiding Failure and Reducing Risk in Large Scale E-Government Projects. Paper read at 35th Hawaii International Conference on System Sciences (HICSS), Hawaii, January 7–10, 2002.

Perry, James. 2000. "Bring Society In: Toward a Theory of Public-Service Motivation." *Journal of Public Administration Research and Theory* 10 (2):471–88.

Poister, Theodore H. 2003. *Measuring Performance in Public and Nonprofit Organizations*. San Francisco: Jossey-Bass.

Rocheleau, Bruce. 2006. *Public Management Information Systems*. Hershey, PA: Idea Group Publishing.

Sutherland, Jeff. 2015. *SCRUM: The Art of Doing Twice the Work in Half the Time*. London: Random House Business Books.

United Nations. 2010. United Nations 2010 Global E-Government Survey: Leveraging E-Government at a Time of Financial and Economic Crisis. New York: United Nations.

United Nations. 2012. United Nations E-Government Survey 2012: E-Government for the People. New York: United Nations.

United Nations. 2014. United Nations E-Government Survey 2014: E-Government for the Future We Want. New York: United Nations.

White House. 2012. "Building 21st Century Platform to Better Serve the American People." Washington, DC: White House.

Yang, Tung-Mou, Lei Zheng, and Theresa Pardo. 2012. "The Boundaries of Information Sharing and Integration: A Case Study of Taiwan e-Government." *Government Information Quarterly* 29:S51–S60.

Yardley, David. 2002. *Successful IT Project Delivery*. London: Pearson Education.

Zavattaro, Staci M., and Thomas A. Bryer, eds. 2016. *Social Media for Government: Theory and Practice*. New York: Routledge.

9 Building Management Capacity for Digital Governance

Introduction

Identifying and developing core competencies are critical for building digital governance capacity since capacity-building requires a clear articulation of what capacity is needed. Competencies provide the specifics on the knowledge and skills needed for building the needed capacity. For digital governance, these competencies include both technical and management iterations. For instance, computer and network literacy is a technical competency while cross-boundary collaboration is management-related. Moreover, competencies are relatively universal across a variety of organizational contexts because of the focus on individual capabilities and attributes. Work competencies have several unique features. One is the competencies' link to job performance (McClelland 1973), and another is their emphasis on virtue and morality (Bowman, West, and Beck 2015).

The core competencies of digital governance need to address contemporary issues as well as seize opportunities to advance public values. In the area of e-government and digital governance, a growing need exists for integrated and personalized digital services that require managers to effectively manage across organizational boundaries to integrate information and systems. In addition, the emphasis on engaging citizens via online platforms and means continues to grow (Goldsmith and Crawford 2014; Mergel 2013). Such engagement can be in the form of providing personalized information/service to citizens or opportunities for citizens to co-produce digital services with government.

Technical knowledge is a crucial dimension of digital governance core competencies (Ni and Chen 2016). Information technology (IT) literacy allows digital governance managers to understand the basic inner-workings and functionalities of technologies in order to leverage and manage them effectively. The constantly changing technology landscape makes it exciting, though challenging, to keep up with the newest developments. Social media have matured into some of the most prevalent tools for people and government to communicate (i.e. Facebook and Twitter in the United States). The growth in artificial intelligence, the internet of things, and big data analytics (among others) requires that core competencies continue to evolve with technologies.

Another critical task is to describe and assess efforts made to develop those core competencies. The question to answer is how we are preparing effective digital governance managers to fully realize the potential of digital technologies while mitigating the risks involved. A further important question to ask interrogates the extent to which we are developing these core competencies and the opportunities to further improve. It is important to look at public administration and public policy programs that train public and non-profit managers. In addition, the on-going education provided by governments and professional associations needs to be assessed to gain a fuller understanding of developing core competencies.

In response, this chapter will first describe the core competencies of digital governance as gleaned from the literature and practice. These core competencies will include individual values and attributes as well as technical and managerial knowledge and skills. Next, the chapter describes and reviews the efforts to develop core competencies by public administration and public policy programs. The goals are to provide the reader with a variety of options for developing these core competencies and to identify improvement opportunities. The discussion then examines the efforts made by governments and professional associations to provide on-going development of these core competencies. This chapter will conclude with key lessons and opportunities to meet the challenges of building digital governance capacity.

Competencies: Individual Values and Attributes

Public values are central to individuals for shaping digital governance and help create the shared foundation for government and non-profit employees and managers to provide public service to people in the community. Public values can serve as a guide for the ultimate goals of digital governance projects. The goal of managerial work by government is to create public values; technical and managerial competencies, as well as political neutralities, are important standards to achieve these values (Moore 1995). Mechanisms exist that can create public values via the use of IT to improve efficiency and effectiveness—as well as to enable individuals by making information available or changing their environment (Cresswell, Burke, and Pardo 2006).

Public values typically include efficiency, effectiveness, and equity. For public service, efficiency is about cost-saving in the production and delivery of services. For instance, renewing vehicle registrations online saves time for people trying to renew them as well as the cost to government of maintaining the facility and staffing to process these renewal requests in person. Effectiveness is about the extent to which the goal of public policy and services is being achieved. A tax e-filing service can measure effectiveness by the percentage of people filing online. Equity is a particular concern in the public sector. For instance, equity in treatment (i.e. no age discrimination) and opportunity (i.e. being an equal opportunity employer) are salient aspects of equity in our society.

In the literature of digital governance, the list of public values extends to democratic governance, transparency, and accountability. The open government initiative by the Obama Administration highlights the importance of citizen participation and the collaboration between government and citizens for improving digital service. One of the three pillars of this initiative is transparency. The use of online service is instrumental in promoting the transparency of government operations, such as the IT expenditure of the U.S. Federal Government. The establishment of a government spending website aims to promote accountability of government to tax revenues. Table 9.1 is a summary table covering these values and individual attributes as well as the technical competencies and managerial competencies introduced later.

Several individual attributes are relevant to the development of digital governance competencies. First, fostering a high level of public-service motivation among individuals is preferable. The intrinsic value and characteristics of public service help motivate people to perform at a higher level. Such public-service motivation is instilled via social processes, personal upbringing, and reinforced by public-service experiences (Perry 2000). The second attribute is the emphasis on ethics and ethical behavior. Individuals must strive to adhere to a high ethical standard: following the code of ethical conduct at minimum and actively pursuing opportunities to advance societal interests. For instance, protection of internet privacy is one of the commonly cited ethical behaviors in computer ethics.

The next preferable individual attribute is active and continuous learning. This is particularly desirable in the area of digital governance because of the rapid advancement of IT. Individuals need to possess a high level of learning motivation and curiosity to keep up with the development. Another desirable individual attribute is being innovative. Digital governance is about finding novel ways to leverage information technologies to improve public information and service. Innovative people are able to make an impact on the quality of public service as seen in the Digital Services Innovation Center at the U.S. General Service Administration as well as civic innovation labs such as Urban Mechanics in the city of Boston.

Competencies: Technical Knowledge

Basic Concepts of Technology, Hardware, Software, and Information System Infrastructure

Information and communication technology (ICT) literacy is an important area of competencies. Governments typically have information technologies

Table 9.1 Competencies of Digital Governance Managers

Dimensions of Competencies	Sub-dimensions	Examples/Illustrations
Values and Attributes	Individual attributes	Public service motivation, active learning, innovativeness
	Values	Public interests, morality
Technical	Basic IT literacy	Hardware, software, computer
	Data, database, data analytics	Database design, database software programs
	Telecommunication, internet, and wireless technologies	Telecommunication infrastructure, internet and wireless communication protocols
	Information system development	Traditional and agile methods
	System applications	ERP, CRM
	Security and privacy	Intrusion detection system (IDS), authentication, access control
	Social media	Facebook, Twitter, Instagram
	Emerging technologies	Big data, artificial intelligence, drones
Managerial	Technology and changes in society and organizations	Sociotechnical approach
	Public administration and public service	Public service values, E-government Act
	Strategic IT/IS planning	Strategic planning, information as a strategic resource
	Management of ICT resources, performance, and risks	Managing the interplay among resources, performance, and risks
	Management of external engagement and collaboration	Digital citizen engagement and cross-boundary collaboration for citizen-centric services
	Management of digital communication, open data, and digital coproduction	Portfolio approach to digital communication, utilization of open data for digital co-production

such as legacy systems and cloud-based application services that span over several decades. It is particularly important to understand the whole range of technologies, rather than merely the latest, to manage such a diverse portfolio of technologies. ICT literacy implies a basic understanding of the essentials of ICTs. First is an understanding of basic terms such as technology, hardware, software, and components of a computer as well as an information system. A computer has hardware such as the central processing unit (CPU), random access memory (RAM), hard drive, and display. The key software systems include the operating system (I/O) and various applications (i.e. word-processing, spreadsheets, presentations, etc.). Although the specifics and functionalities vary, these are the basic components that a decision-maker needs to know to make an informative purchase decision. An information system is a broader concept. In addition to hardware and software that support an information system's functionalities, an information system also includes data and communication networks for the data to be transmitted. More importantly, an information system needs to accommodate organizational and managerial aspects in conjunction with technology to be effective (Laudon and Laudon, 2012, 18). Knowing these indispensable components allows people participating in or leading a digital governance project to be more effective.

Data, Databases, and Data Analytics

The second topic of ICT literacy covers data, databases, and, more recently, data analytics. A basic understanding of data fields, data definitions, and data standards is important as data are the building blocks of an information system. The data hierarchy—ranging from bit, byte, and field, to record, file, and database—is a useful concept to understand the various levels of building blocks. A database typically includes more than one file. From the perspective of business intelligence and data analytics, it is important to understand metadata while performing analysis and interpretation. Metadata documents the data sources, definitions, file formats, and any changes in data definitions and other factors (Hoffer, Prescott, and McFadden 2002). An interpretation can be flawed if metadata are not being properly consulted. For instance, crime data as shown on a heat map could be misleading when violent crimes and non-violent crimes are combined together to generate a total count for each neighborhood.

In addition, a fundamental understanding of the basic database design principles, as well as the popular types of databases, provides a working vocabulary for an effective digital governance manager. For the last few decades, the dominant design of databases has been a relational database design. This type of approach establishes entities (files) and links them together with shared key fields. Relational database designs have proven much more efficient and accurate than flat file systems in terms of retrieving information from the database for services and decision-making (Hoffer, Prescott, and McFadden 2002). Online services and business intelligence are all built on the foundation of databases. Although the landscape of relational databases is likely to change, Oracle and MS SQL have been mainstays for large-scale corporate database systems over the last several decades. MS Access has been similarly useful for small organizations. MySQL is an open-source system that has been used mostly in academia and some public and non-profit organizations.

More recent development has occurred in the area of data and databases. There are a growing number of data types including images, videos, communication data (i.e. cell phone communication records), and social media contents (photos, videos, posts/reposts, tweets/retweets, tags, etc.). These require a lot more storage capability to manage and more bandwidth for transmission. In addition, these data are typically unstructured and require new methods for data management. For instance, Hadoop has been developed as a method to manage unstructured data in a distributed environment with a variety of formats and to generate business intelligence as needed (White 2015).

Telecommunication, Internet, and Wireless Technologies

Telecommunication infrastructure, enabling the delivery of services provided by e-government information systems, is the backbone of any e-government service. The transmission of data can travel over a long distance via wired media such as fiber optics, coaxial cables, phone lines, and others. Ethernet cables allow computers to connect inside a building or a business complex. Wireless communication networks constitute the foundation for cell phone service and consist of communication standards, a central facility for routing, and towers to boost the signals for transmission and relate these signals over long distances. Recently, there has been a revival of satellite phone service transmitting signals via a constellation of satellites that offer global coverage even in remote areas without tower service (*The Economist* 2016a).

For digital governance, understanding the basic working of the internet for better governance is essential. The internet requires that participating organizations and individuals have an identifiable address to send information back and forth, as well as following the communication protocol (TCP/IP). For ease of understanding and organization, all the digits assigned to IP addresses need to be mapped to domains and governed by the Internet Corporation for Assigned Names and Numbers (ICANN). The transmission of wireless data to enable smart/cellular phones to access internet content and telephony needs to follow Wireless Application Protocol (WAP), which includes application, session, transaction, security, and transport layers.[1]

The last two decades have marked tremendous growth in wireless infrastructure in terms of both bandwidth and reach. The coverage of wireless networks has reached many areas of the world. In the United States, according to the Pew Internet and American Life Project, smart phone ownership has doubled from 35 percent to 68 percent over a four-year period from 2011 to 2015.[2] In China—with more than 688 million internet users as of December 2015—over 90 percent of them (620 million) access the internet via their mobile phones, according to the China Internet Network Information Center (CNNIC), the official organization conducting an annual internet use survey of the Chinese population (CNNIC 2016). Some African countries have chosen to leapfrog the development of telecommunication infrastructure by skipping the wired version and moving directly to wireless ones for considerations of cost savings and service reach. What is likely to happen is that the speed and bandwidth of wireless networks will continue to grow. Fourth and fifth generation wireless networks are either already deployed or coming to the market (capacity of 4G or 5G). Some of the more application-intensive cloud computing capabilities, as a result, will not require a wired connection. A wireless connection will be sufficient to run bandwidth-intensive processing.

A promising area of future growth is the internet of things. More and more devices (such as those with global positioning system (GPS) mapping and routing services) and objects (such as cars, water meters) will be connected to the internet with an automatic and continuous transmission of information. As a result, new governance issues will spring up due to the explosion of IP addresses and the need for their organization (i.e. IPv6 for U.S. Federal Government). Moreover, communication infrastructures are needed to support the introduction of billions of devices to the wireless networks.

Information System Development

A core component of any digital governance (e-government) project is the information system that provides the service digitally. An effective digital governance manager needs to understand the general method deployed for information system development to facilitate coordination and project management. One conventional information system development method is the so-called waterfall method (Sutherland 2015). Although there are variations in the steps and components involved in this waterfall method, the system development lifecycle typically begins with the analysis of information system needs, then moves to system design; next is development, including programming and testing; then comes the final production and on-going maintenance (Laudon and Laudon 2012, 494–501).

There are tools for enhancing or expediting the traditional system development cycle. The use of "user cases" helps system analysts and project managers understand the information system requirements from users' perspectives to guide and expedite the system development process and to ensure that the production information system actually meets the needs of the users. Another tool is rapid prototyping as a way to gather user input for quick revision and user acceptance (Laudon and Laudon 2012, 508–9). The use of fourth-generation languages is helpful for developing system/software applications with nonprocedural language. This is particularly useful for building simple applications for data analysis and reporting purposes.

An agile development approach fundamentally challenges the conventional wisdom of the traditional system development method (i.e. waterfall method) (Sutherland 2015). In an agile approach, the emphasis is on intensive collaboration between users and developers throughout the entire process; such an approach focuses on problem-solving, uses prototypes (even simple ones) to understand and communicate functionalities, and uses short, frequent interactions to bring agile adaption to development. The U.S. Federal Government has launched an initiative called 18F to utilize the agile method.[3] This agile approach is particularly useful for adapting to the changing needs of users and gathering the real (not imaginative) concerns/expectations of all stakeholders.

System Applications

A digital project manager needs to be well-versed in the area of effective information system applications. In terms of business functions, each functional department (business unit) tends to have a preferred information system of its own. For instance, a finance department has a financial management information system with financial management and accounting capabilities. A human resource information system allows managers to handle performance evaluation, payroll, and benefits, among other tasks (Reddick 2012). Moreover, there are production systems for particular functions that track and automate any public works projects. The ability to manage service requests is also important.

Geographic information systems (GIS) constitute a particularly important type of information system for a large number of governments at all levels. Government assets, as well as clients of government service, typically have a specific physical location associated with them. These include infrastructures such as roads, lights, sewers, water mains, electric/phone lines, houses, buildings, parks, campuses, and many other physical properties. Planning is an important function of government in order to manage resources for meeting current and future infrastructure and public service needs. GIS are a powerful type of information system to serve that planning purpose. These systems have been used widely, especially for local governments and a selected set of the state agencies overseeing assets and planning.

For e-government and digital governance, the real advances have been made in the area of utilizing enterprise resource planning (ERP) systems that integrate disparate information systems (traditionally housed in various functional departments) into one. An ERP system integrates the functions of human resources, finance, and other departments together to provide an enterprise (government-as-a-whole) view of assets and resources and, more importantly, how such integration of these resources aids in providing better government service.

Digital government 3.0 challenges digital governance managers to provide personalized e-government services that extend beyond Government 2.0, placing a greater emphasis on interacting with citizens using social media. To achieve a personalized service, corporations use an integrated system to manage all their interactions with customers; such a system is usually called a customer relationship management system (CRM). A good number of local governments in the United States have similar versions of CRM under the coined term CiRM (Citizen Relationship Management). The best versions offer various channels of communication (phone, apps, social media, in person) and integrate the information from various sources to provide a citizen-centric view of all the government–citizen interactions and personalized government service information. More importantly, an effective CiRM integrates all the information and service requests and records them in a single system. Utilizing such CiRM, citizen service representatives are able to offer information across the entire government in a personalized way.

Security and Privacy

Information security is foundational for IT literacy. Computer security has been an established field of study as early as the 1980s. The increasing prevalence of networks and the internet, along with client-server architecture, has introduced new layers of information security. Over the last decade, the proliferation of connected smart phones and devices (iPads, etc.) has further introduced another variety of information security issues. Government operation has become increasingly digital, utilizing a spectrum of digital tools for critical infrastructure and its service operations. Consequently, information (cyber) security has increasing salience in basic IT literacy for all public managers.

One area of information security notably related to government is the protection of critical infrastructure that is run by a Supervisory Control and Data Acquisition (SCADA) network. A SCADA network contains computers and applications that run critical infrastructure such as electric grids, power plants, reservoirs, bridges, water mains, and others. Computer security in this area is particularly salient in the public sector as opposed to in the private sector.

Digital privacy is another important area that builds on information security. Only when information access is properly secured only for authorized personnel can digital privacy policy be implemented. Digital privacy is an extension of personal privacy. It allows citizens to protect their own personal information (such as financial and health information) against unauthorized use and dissemination. Caution needs to be taken with government open data to make sure that no personal information is inadvertently being leaked.

A more encompassing concept that addresses security, privacy, and information needs is the notion of information assurance. As defined by the U.S. Federal Government, the three pillars of information assurance that any information security measures should aim to achieve are confidentiality, integrity, and availability. Confidentiality is about making sure information can only be accessed by authorized personnel so that the confidentiality of both organizations and individuals is protected. Integrity is a concept that addresses information use. Information needs to be accurate and valid for the purpose of making any decision. The last pillar is availability. This speaks to business continuity, especially in emergency situations when governments serve as the last line of defense. Availability of information is what information security needs to aim for: making critical information available at a critical time.

Social Media

IT literacy in the 21st century requires a rigorous social media component. In 2016, Facebook claimed to have 1.6 billion unique registered users around the world.[4] This number is about half of the total internet population, which is slightly over three billion.[5] Twitter has become an established tool used by government to get important messages out at times of emergency. Social media platforms and services have become the main source of information for people to get information, communication, and coordination via their mobile devices.

Public managers need to develop literacy on the technology of social media, including the basic services of social networking sites. The use of blogs and Wiki—along with Facebook, Twitter, Instagram, and others—are particularly relevant. More importantly, effective management of social media by government is about putting these media in the context of a variety of communication channels (Mergel 2012). Public managers need to know how to acquire and analyze social media posts as part of record management, possessing knowledge competencies such as familiarity with the Library of Congress archive as well as understanding and using tools for data analytics (Mergel 2013).

Emerging Technologies

Public and non-profit managers focusing on public service need to understand emerging technologies as part of their IT literacy. These emerging technological trends can first emerge in the private sector and then appear in the public sector. A good way of classifying these technologies is to group them in terms of capabilities rather than by a specific technology utilized. One category would be in the area of telecommunication, which will bring fifth-generation wireless communication technologies to the market place, enabling many technologies relying on such connectivity. Another area is the growth of the internet of things, which brings a new array of connected devices to improve service while introducing a new source of network vulnerability.

Big data and big data analytics have shown promise in predicting earthquakes and generating big discoveries (National Science Foundation

188 *Building Management Capacity*

(NSF) 2007, 2012; XSEDE 2014). Growth has also occurred in artificial intelligence, especially in the area of service science, where the knowledge accumulated from deep learning will allow robots to respond effectively to service inquiries and to offer personalized service. Virtual and augmented reality are likely to impact the ability of service personnel to solve problems in the field. Also, these realities offer a way of learning that is closer to real life. The landscape of emerging technologies will continue to evolve.

Competencies: Management Knowledge

Managerial knowledge is critical in ensuring that the utilization of ICT serves its purpose for the public sector and society as a whole. More importantly, these managerial concepts and skills allow managers to use ICTs to advance public values. Such knowledge and skills begin with a general understanding of the role of ICTs in society and organizations, as well as the role of public institutions in shaping IT use and vice versa. After reviewing the role of ICTs, this section will cover various components of the digital governance framework proposed by this book, including managing digital engagement and collaborating with external stakeholders—as well as managing internal resources, performance, and risks.

Technology and Societal/Organizational Changes

Digital governance managers need to understand the interplay between technology and societal changes. Knowing the role of IT in society will aid in deploying and effectively utilizing IT in government. Garson (2006, 5–6) has identified four perspectives on the role of IT in society: (a) technological determinism, in which technology profoundly shapes the world along with government; (b) reinforcement theory, in which IT reinforces the position of advantageous members of a society; (c) sociotechnical theory, which suggests the paramount role of system design in shaping the impact of technology on society; and (d) system theory, in which technology rather than humans plays an important role in system design.

Most of the leading scholars and practitioners subscribe to the sociotechnical perspective of ICTs' role in society. Through purposeful information system design, the resulting ICT and its use are more likely to serve the values of society. For instance, new ICTs afford people new and lowcost ways to share information, coordinate, interact, and communicate with government. These ICTs also introduce a much higher level of transparency to government operation as more and more government information is put online. Society, on the other hand, can shape the information system design by providing a guiding value framework. These two forces appear to co-evolve as individuals in our society are using more technology and accessing the internet more than ever before. The sociotechnical perspective also implies that the most impactful use of technology in government typically is to combine such use with administrative reform. In this context, IT is an enabler of new and better processes for service production and delivery.

Public Administration and Public Service: Values, Institutions, and IT Policies

Digital governance managers need to understand public service values and various public-sector institutions, as well as policies governing ICT. These managers need to be fully aware of the value system that defines the public sector. Moreover, managers must be familiar with the discussion surrounding the publicness of public-management information systems, which includes understanding the layers of considerations from economic and political authorities in the distal environment to personnel and organizational behavior concerns in the work context subject to public scrutiny (Bozeman and Bretschneider 1986).

The Clinger-Cohen Act provides a framework for managing information and IT as a resource in U.S. Federal Government. Understanding the intent of the Act, as well as keeping up with the training required by the Act, is crucial for digital governance managers. Adherence to the Act includes having a C-level position in government to oversee the use of IT to enable other functions and treating information as a strategic resource to aid in achieving agency missions. A related piece of legislation, the E-government Act of the United States, provides the institutional framework "to improve the management and promotion of electronic government services and processes" to increase citizen access to government information and service by establishing a federal chief information officer (CIO) overseeing the entire federal government and by pursuing the utilization of internet-based IT.[6]

Strategic IT/Information System for the Public Sector: Treat Data as a Strategic Resource

Strategic IT/information system planning, another core management competence of effective digital governance managers, corresponds to the strategic layer of the overarching framework for effective digital governance proposed in Chapter 2 of this book. This strategic planning has two aspects. First, it requires digital governance managers to focus on the outcomes of the development and implementation of any public management information system or e-government service. The deployed IT should always serve a public purpose and advance a public value rather than existing solely for the purpose of using something new. Award-winning e-government services are usually part of a larger strategic government IT plan.

Another way to ensure effective and strategic IT/information system planning is better management of the process, a process that in the public sector typically faces the challenges of short planning time horizon, competing priorities, and a multitude of stakeholders (Dufner, Holley, and Reed 2002). An effective IT planning process can leverage the knowledge and skills of general strategic planning that includes multiple steps and considers strengths, weaknesses, opportunities, and challenges (Bryson 2011). An effective process includes the following factors: inclusion of the specific technologies deployed and awareness of how such technologies are able to advance the service, as well as achieve goals and objectives.

Management of ICT Resources, Performance, and Risks

Previous chapters have offered a detailed account of managing information and IT as a resource. Effective digital governance managers need to have the knowledge and skill to manage ICT accordingly. At minimum, digital governance managers must possess the basic literacy of technical information and communication technology as mentioned in the technical knowledge part of this chapter. Such basic literacy allows them to understand the technology involved and the related technical capabilities. For information resource management, the ability to align the priorities of the ICT to those of the entire government enterprise is critical. The role of IT should encompass enabling and/or transforming the business practices of government with the goal of providing citizen-centric (user-centric) digital service and engagement opportunities.

Performance management has clearly identified goals and focuses on achieving these goals. Digital governance managers need the knowledge and skills identified in the ICT performance management chapter, and, furthermore, they must follow the principles for successful implementation. Such performance management requires frequent reviews and assessments to adapt to changing policy priorities and technological developments. Another related area is risk management. In the case of ICT performance management, risks involve digital security and privacy, and risk assessment should be part of vetting and approving a digital governance project. Digital security is a crucial component of such risk assessment. For government, compliance with privacy regulations is simply meeting the minimum requirement, and more needs to be done both in risk assessment and mitigation. Linked to ICT performance, there are implementation risks associated with the implementation of any digital governance project. A rigorous performance management approach (i.e. agile development approach) could help mitigate some of the risks involved.

Management of External Engagement and Collaboration

Digital governance managers need to acquire the knowledge and skills to manage online engagement with citizens and other stakeholders—this engagement begins with a working knowledge of the spectrum of stakeholders that interact with government. In contrast to the almost exclusive focus of the scholarly literature in public administration on e-government service to citizens, a significant portion of e-government service is actually geared toward supporting businesses and non-profit organizations. For instance, business license renewal and business registration, as well as obtaining permits, are e-government services to businesses. Moreover, for federal and state governments, the main customers or stakeholders that they need to interact with when providing digital government service are lower-level governments. For instance, a state-wide educational information system run by a state department of education serves all the school districts in the state.

Knowing the major regulations and rules overseeing government actions with stakeholders is equally important. For posting information online, Section 508 of the Rehabilitation Act in the United States governs how information is presented to serve people who are visually and/or hearing impaired. At minimum, this legislation requires alternative text for images to enable the use of a text reader to read a description of the image for the visually impaired. A one-click font enlargement option is also useful for the elderly population with weakening eyesight. Civil rights compliance requirements dictate that digital service needs to be non-discriminatory. Moreover, the E-government Act of 2002 provides a basic e-government framework for federal government and includes an information security requirement for federal agencies to establish an information security program (Federal Information Security Management Act (FISMA)).[7] Privacy impact assessment is also required under the E-government Act of 2002 for the implementation of any new or substantially changed technology that deals with personally identifiable information (PII).[8]

Additionally, a modern digital governance manager needs the knowledge and skills to provide customer-centric service experiences. With rising levels of service personalization, being customer-centric is increasingly the overarching strategy of American government. Such a customer-centric focus is the main direction of the U.S. Federal Government's digital government strategy as well as a priority in state and local governments. For managers, their responsibility is to instill a customer-centric culture for service. This customer-centric focus is supported by some evidence of the positive effect of developing customer-service culture on improving the efficiency of e-government services (Bhattacherjee 2000).

In addition, the study of service science is important in understanding how to provide service in a way that generates the highest level of customer satisfaction (Maglio, Kieliszewski, and Spohrer 2010). Working as an interdisciplinary team with people trained in software development, behavioral science, and a particular area of business, along with the customers, is one way to bring in all the relevant perspectives to design and implement a user-centric digital government service (White House 2012).

Management of Digital Communication, Open Data, and Digital Co-production

Digital communication, especially utilization of social media and mobile apps, is an increasingly important area of digital governance competence (Mergel 2012). Public and non-profit managers should receive training on how digital communication should be conducted for routine events and service (Mergel 2013). Moreover, they need to be trained on how to utilize these digital channels in the event of an emergency. The use of Twitter and text-messaging alert services have shown promise in delivering emergency information in a timely and effective manner. Moreover, digital communication should be managed as a portfolio (Dumont 2013). Communication over social media has the advantage of reaching out to a broad section of the population. However, a disadvantage is the short time span that such information stays accessible to people who receive it. Another trade-off of using social media is the lack of information depth/details. In contrast, blogs and websites are more effective as on-going stable access points to present in-depth information. In addition, websites have the comparative advantage of including transaction-based service (i.e. online payment and more) that is less available via social media. As is evident on many award-winning websites, these sites generally have a strong coordination with social media outlets to form a coordinated online communication and digital service strategy.

Managing open government data is another key core knowledge area of a competent digital governance manager. The Open Government Initiative of 2009 has ushered in a new era of open government data in the United States. The Data Accountability and Transparency Act (DATA Act) of 2014 has gradually increased the amount of government financial and expenditure data available online. What is also qualitatively different from the past open data efforts is that such data have currently become machine-readable. Data being machine-readable is consistent with the semantic web, also touted as Web 3.0. Digital governance managers must understand trends and development as well as how to develop an open data strategy. These managers need to have working knowledge about open records laws and regulations. Moreover, they need to understand the needs of the community in terms of relevant data sets and formats, as well as the necessary documentation to make them useful. Additional details of the open data effort are presented in Chapter 4 on open government.

The synergy of open data and open collaboration is another area of future growth. For instance, New York City (NYC) has an annual BigApps competition that is powered by NYC's open data effort. This competition uses technology and 311 data (city service data) to address challenges such as affordable housing, civic engagement, and waste management.[9] Digital governance managers need to develop knowledge and skills about how to engage the community to add values to open data. Having an annual apps competition is one viable option. Hackathons, as organized by civic groups or Code for America, are another way of bringing open data and open collaboration together. A digital governance manager needs to know how to design or participate in these events to add values to government data and open data efforts while mitigating potential risks in privacy and misinformation.

Capacity Building by Public Affairs Education Programs

Capacity-building Approach

Programs educating public and non-profit managers are in a position to provide the basic literacy for digital governance. In the United States, public administration, public affairs, and public policy degree programs (mostly graduate programs) are at the core of offering curricula to train current and future managers of public service. The focus on providing public services—with governments at the center of the activities—while achieving public values is what makes these educational programs particularly suitable for public governance. Most of these programs are at the graduate level, granting advanced degrees in public affairs and public administration. Therefore, the discussion will focus on public affairs programs and the Network of Schools of Public Policy, Affairs, and Administration (NASPAA) that serves as the accreditation body of these programs offering public affairs education.

The approach to building ICT competence has two dimensions as seen in Figure 9.1. One applies to the management focus of the e-government courses offered in Master of Public Affairs (MPA) and/or Master of Public Policy (MPP) programs and whether these courses are required or elective. At the most basic tier of ICT competence course offerings is a one-elective course option. An example of this type of course is an e-government course that covers technical and managerial competencies. Alternatively, when this e-government course is a required core course, it reaches every student enrolled in the program. The number of courses covering ICT competencies increases when an MPA/MPP program has a concentration in the area of information management or IT.

The other dimension of the approach to building competencies discussed in the previous section is the degree of focus on technical knowledge. Among the top-ranked public affairs programs in the area of information and technology management, Carnegie Mellon University clearly emphasizes being technical (i.e. programming) with in-depth knowledge about various technologies and software development. On the other end of the spectrum is a strong focus on information and information management as seen in the Government Information Strategy and Management concentration at the University at Albany/SUNY. The primary focus of this program is on information policy and strategic information use with less concern for technical knowledge.

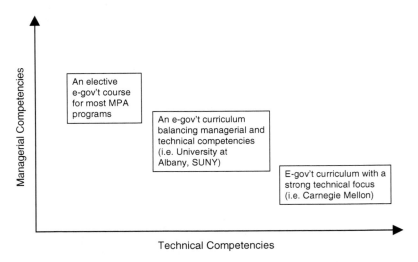

Figure 9.1 Dimensions of Digital Governance Competencies for MPA/MPP Programs

The State of ICT Competence Training via Public Affairs Education

A recent systematic survey of MPA programs in the United States suggests a limited effort to educate current/future public and non-profit managers to leverage ICTs in order to provide high quality and personalized digital service. One of the most comprehensive studies to date on public affairs course offerings is by Ganapati and Reddick (2016a). They collected data from more than 100 principal representatives of public affairs programs that belong to their accreditation body (NASPAA) on their 2013–14 academic year information. Slightly less than half of the programs that responded offered an IT/e-government course. Among those programs, more than half of them only offered this course as an elective, and less than half of them had a required IT/e-government course (Ganapati and Reddick 2016a, 274). The majority of all the MPA programs that responded did not have an IT/e-government course. Either some of the topics in a standard IT/e-government course are being covered as components in other courses, or such topics are not being covered at all. The survey of syllabi for more than 164 MPA programs also supports the notion that less than half of the MPA programs that responded did not even have a single IT course on offer (Mauldin 2016, 189).

Offering a concentration in e-government or information management is rare among MPA programs in the United States. The survey of 164 MPA programs by Mauldin reveals that around 6 percent of them (nine in total) have an IT concentration (Mauldin 2016, 188). The actual total number is likely to be around 12–15 programs among the 240 MPA programs listed under the NASPAA (both accredited and non-accredited). At minimum, all the top ten MPA programs ranked in the area of information and technology management have a concentration (Mergel 2016).

The topics covered in these e-government and IT courses have shown a broad coverage of the issues related to e-government. According to a survey of IT syllabi of 57 MPA programs, e-government (service provision and e-procurement), privacy, infrastructure, cybersecurity, GIS, and the digital divide are topics covered by at least one-third of the courses analyzed. The next most frequently covered topic is social media with around 25 percent of those syllabi examined. This topic is followed by big data, cloud computing, and cloud funding in terms of frequency covered by these syllabi (Manoharan and McQuiston 2016).

MPA alumni and their employers agree on the IT knowledge and skills that are significant for MPA graduates to succeed in their jobs (Christian and Davis 2016). The top five IT knowledge and skills are about basic IT literacy and, more importantly, knowledge of the values, institutions, rules and regulations involved in the implementation of IT. More specifically, general computer literacy and the use of basic applications (i.e. word-processing and spreadsheets) are the most important technical skills. The rest of the top five skills are management in nature. These include understanding organizational policies and procedure on computer (cyber) security; protection of the workplace from technology risks (viruses, malware, social engineering); understanding the policies and procedure of record retention, including data from social media sites; and transparency and accountability issues related to IT.

The Gap in IT Education in MPA/MPP Programs and Factors Affecting the Gap

Offering IT training for current and future managers who provide public service is important for several reasons. First, governments are increasingly using online channels as the primary means of communication with citizens, residents, visitors, businesses, and other governments. The growth of internet use has made online the default option for citizens searching for information. The adoption of websites is 100 percent for federal and state governments. Even at the local level, the adoption rate was at 97 percent based on a national survey of local governments published in 2011 (International City/County Management Association (ICMA) 2011). Another reason to provide training is the growth of social media use and the growing presence of mobile device use. Moreover, ICT is integral to almost all aspects of government operation. From financial management systems, e-mail, websites, and service-tracking databases, to basic word-processing tools, governments rely on these systems to perform basic services for their citizens and customers. Such utilization of technology in government is prevalent regardless of the size and scope of government operation (Shark 2016). To be effective, public managers need to have basic IT literacy as well as understand the applicable laws and policies for the use of IT in public service.

While government adoption has increased over the last two decades along with the rapid advancement of technology, the number of MPA/MPP programs that offer an IT course has barely increased, or even decreased, depending on the source and scope of data collected. Based on a content analysis of 170 NASPAA member schools, only 16 percent have a required IT course in their curriculum (Christian and Davis 2016, 165). That figure is a decrease from 1989 when 26 percent of the NASPAA member schools required such a course (Cleary 1990). This decrease is even more significant given the context of the rapid advancement of internet technologies and social media, and the prevalence of mobile devices between the two different time points (1989 and 2015).

Furthermore, there is a gap between IT skills required by employers to be successful and what has been taught in MPA programs (Christian and Davis 2016). Based on an alumni survey covering 84 MPA programs, a study by Christian and Davis (2016) shows that at least one-third of the respondents did not feel that the MPA program provided the needed IT knowledge and skills. Those who did not have the opportunity to take an IT course in their MPA programs registered a higher percentage (45 percent) of responses indicating they did not have the needed IT training and skills from their programs (Christian and Davis 2016, 165). In addition, it is challenging for these MPA alumni to receive IT training. Close to half of them indicated that they are required to study independently without any financial assistance from their employers or help from their peers or IT staff. The survey respondents stated that it is a significant burden to acquire relevant IT training by themselves.

One of the contributing factors to the widening gap in IT training among the MPA/MPP programs is the lack of specific program accreditation standards for IT since 2009 (Ganapati and Reddick 2016a). NASPAA changed its competence standard from a specific standard on IT to a universal standard in 2009. The specific one prior to 2009 was the NASPAA Standard 4.21 that required a component for information management, technology application, and policy as a common curriculum requirement (NASPAA Commission on Peer Review and Accreditation 2008, 9). The new universal competence language introduced in 2009 allows each program flexibility in designing the curriculum as long as it can achieve five universal competencies. The new standard does not have any specific language or requirements for teaching IT, especially for the core courses. The lack of a requirement from the accreditation organization (NASPAA) leaves individual programs and schools to decide whether or not to even offer an IT course for accreditation purposes. As a result, strong incentives are lacking for MPA/MPP programs to prioritize IT courses when competing with other priorities (Christian and Davis 2016; Ganapati and Reddick 2016a, 2016b; Ni and Chen 2016).

Another contributing factor to the widening gap is the lack of resources to support IT training in MPA/MPP programs. This lack of supporting resources has two aspects. The first deals with the recruitment and retention of instructors who are qualified to teach these IT courses (Ganapati and Reddick 2016a). These talents tend to command a higher salary requirement as they have the option of going to a management and business school where the pay is higher. It is much more challenging for a program housed in traditional political science departments or colleges of liberal arts and sciences to offer a competitive salary package to attract and retain these talents. Another aspect is the support of labs, software programs, and other components of the technology environment that support an adequate level of IT training. A program needs to provide these resources for sufficient IT training.

Presenting further difficulties, the rapid advancement of technology creates a "moving staircase" problem for the IT curriculum in MPA/MPP programs (Rocheleau 2004). ICT knowledge continues to evolve and expand at a much higher rate than other subject areas (i.e. organization theory, research methods), creating an issue following the first wave of internet technology and the use of government websites for both information and service. More recently, social media has significantly changed how citizens access information and the need for government to communicate with them (Zavattaro and Bryer 2016). In 2016, Facebook commanded 1.6 billion registered users throughout the world (*The Economist* 2016b) and was the most dominant information-sharing platform in the United States. A new wave of technologies is emerging and maturing, including cybersecurity, the semantic web (Web 3.0), the internet of things, apps for shared economy, big data, virtual reality, and artificial intelligence, just to name a few. The moving staircase problem requires faculty members in an MPA/MPP program to engage in continuous education at a much faster rate, and typically with their own resources, to keep up with new developments.

Bridging the ICT Knowledge and Skill Gap in MPA/MPP Programs

One important first step in addressing the ICT knowledge and skill gaps is to identify and categorize the ICT competencies that are necessary for an MPA/MPP program to offer. The previous section on such competencies including values, individual attributes, and technical and managerial knowledge and skills, is a response to such a call for competence identification. Moreover, the U.S. Federal Government's report entitled 'Clinger-Cohen Core Competencies and Learning Objectives' provides an important guide on the topics that federal CIOs are expected to learn and be skillful at. These include the broad aspects of relevant policy, process, and organization as well as information resource strategy and planning. Such knowledge also includes operational areas such as performance assessment, project and program management, capital investment, acquisition, and knowledge management (CIO Council 2012). Another main source of competence is input from people in the field, including MPA alums, employers, and practitioners (Christian and Davis 2016). The curricula for certified public manager programs around the country are another rich source of information on the knowledge and skills needed for managers working on or participating in digital governance projects (Shark 2016).

These sources, along with faculty in public affairs programs, provide useful information on what ICT competencies to include and which competencies are needed to keep up with the new technological development. The role of ethics and personal attributes such as innovativeness are important additions to the list of IT technical and management skills. The Clinger-Cohen core competencies have introduced recent additions that are indicative of emerging technical and management concerns such as IT program management, cybersecurity, and cloud computing (CIO Council 2012, 1). A survey of city CIOs conducted in 2015 has pointed out the increasing relevance of cybersecurity as a main concern for those in these positions (*Government Technology* 2015, 13).

Significant institutional push/support is needed to bridge the gap. Although it would be ideal for NASPAA to require IT courses for accreditation purposes, at minimum, reference documents should be created to articulate the essential role of IT for all aspects of government operation. As a result, IT competence should be a foundational area, and clear documentation on its coverage is needed. Institutional support should also take place at the program level. A demand made from government officials for IT training by an MPA/MPP program can be an important and effective institutional push. The experience of Turkey's MPA education suggests the relevance of such a push from government officials (Yildiz, Babaoğlu, and Demircioğlu 2016). Alignment between the curricula of individual programs and national priorities in science and technology can be productive. The experience of South Korea suggests that such a push/support from national government is one of the main factors for 80 percent of its MPA programs providing IT training as opposed to less than 50 percent in the United States (Park and Park 2006).

Another effective strategy to address the gap is to establish a minimum requirement for the topics covered to develop basic IT competencies for all students. A flexible design of how to accomplish this goal is desirable. It could be in the form of an e-government course or a required competence course with a different title. Programs that wish to introduce a more sophisticated curriculum could benefit from the scheme developed by Dawes (2004). This scheme uses the basic competencies as a foundation and then builds more advanced topics upon that. Each program could offer courses that emphasize a different aspect of the range for the IT curriculum. Some programs might have a stronger technical focus like those of Carnegie Mellon University, ranked #1 in the area of information and technology management in 2012. Some programs can place a stronger emphasis on management, as exemplified by the University at Albany-SUNY program. Moreover, these IT skills and knowledge should be core competencies for the growing emphasis on innovations in the public sector. In terms of connecting to a broad base of interests, these skills and knowledge can be framed as innovations in public service because innovations are typically enabled by innovative technologies.

There are several ways to address the issue of obtaining a vibrant pool of instructor talents to support a robust IT course or even a complete curriculum. Some of the more innovative universities and MPA programs have developed clusters or courses/curricula supported by an interdisciplinary group. A joint appointment model allows a faculty member to contribute to both MPA programs and another management/technology program. This model helps mitigate the salary issue and, more importantly, provides a larger pool of talents. Some universities even establish university-level research groups or centers to provide a rich pool of instructor talents to support IT curricula with depth and breadth and that can keep up with the newest developments.

Partnership is a productive avenue for designing and delivering IT training operations for public managers. The certified public manager programs around the country are viable models to provide platforms to bring in experts from both academia and in the field to train these public managers. The instructors can be practitioners in the field or experts on a specific topic (i.e. lawyers for open record regulations). Such training programs have the flexibility to tap into talents beyond academia. In addition, some innovators have experimented with service learning that allows students to obtain field experience learning technical and managerial knowledge while trying to meet the real needs of their clients utilizing ICTs.

Capacity-building by Governments and Professional Associations

In addition to academia, governments and professional associations can build ICT competencies for digital governance managers. The training for federal CIOs is particularly instructive. The competencies and objectives of the Clinger-Cohen Act (also called the Information Technology Management Reform Act of 1996) are a good match to the competencies highlighted earlier in the chapter with a stronger emphasis on management competencies. The new competence areas introduced in 2012 include "IT governance, IT program management leadership, cybersecurity/information assurance strategies and plans, social media, cloud computing, and open government" (CIO Council 2012, 1). The established competencies cover policy, organization, strategic planning, performance management, knowledge management, and project management, among others. Table 9.2 provides a comprehensive list of these areas with specifics.

Table 9.2 CIO Core Competencies

Main Competence Area	Examples of Subareas
Policy and Organization	Department/Agency missions, organization, functions, policies, and procedures; Governing laws and authorities; Federal government decision and policy-making processes; Linkages and interrelationships between Agency heads and their Chief Executive Officers; Intergovernmental programs, policies, and processes; IT governance
Leadership and Human Capital Management	Key CIO leadership attributes; Professional development and career planning; Competency performance and management; Partnerships and team-building; Personnel performance management; Attracting, motivating, and retaining IT personnel
Process and Change Management	Organizational development; Process management and control; Quality improvement models and methods; Business process redesign/reengineering models and methods; Cross-boundary process collaboration
Information Resources Strategy and Planning	Information Resource Management (IRM) baseline assessment analysis; Interdepartmental, inter-agency IT functional analysis; IT planning methodologies; Contingency and continuity of operations planning (COOP); Monitoring and evaluation methods and techniques
IT Performance Assessment: Models and Methods	Government Performance and Results Act (GPRA) and IT; System development decision making; Measuring IT success; Defining and selecting effective performance measures; Evaluating system performance; Managing IT reviews and oversight processes
IT Project and Program Management	Project scope and requirements management; Project integration management; Project time, cost, and performance management; Project quality management; Project risk management; System lifecycle management; Software development, testing, and implementation; Vendor management; IT program management leadership
Capital Planning and Investment Control (CPIC)	CPIC best practices; Cost benefit, economic, and risk analysis; Risk management models and methods; Weighing benefits of alternative IT investments; Capital investment analysis models and methods; Business case analysis; Investment review process; IT portfolio management

Table 9.2. (continued)

Main Competence Area	Examples of Subareas
Acquisition	Acquisition strategy; Acquisition models and methodologies; Post-award IT contract management; IT acquisition best practices; Software acquisition management; Supply chain risk management in acquisition
Information and Knowledge Management	Privacy, personally identifiable, and protected health information; Information accessibility; Records and information management; Knowledge management; Social media; Web development and maintenance strategy; Open government; Information collection
Cybersecurity/Information Assurance (IA)	CIO Cybersecurity/IA roles and responsibilities; Cybersecurity/IA legislation, policies, and procedures; Cybersecurity/IA strategies and plans; Information and information systems threats and vulnerabilities analysis; Information security controls planning and management; Cybersecurity/IA risk management; Enterprise-wide cybersecurity/IA program management; Information security reporting compliance; Critical infrastructure protection and disaster recovery planning
Enterprise Architecture	Enterprise architecture functions and governance; Key enterprise architecture concepts; Enterprise architecture interpretation, development, and maintenance; Use of enterprise architecture in IT investment decision-making; Enterprise data management; Performance measurement for enterprise architecture
Technology Management and Assessment	Network, telecommunications, and mobile device technology; Spectrum management; Computer systems; Web technology; Data management technology; Software development technology; Cloud computing; Special use technology; Emerging technology

Source: CIO Council (2012).

This table serves as a resource for selecting or modifying topics for training CIOs and/or IT managers.

The Federal CIO Council also maintains an information resource page for information-sharing and knowledge management, including resources on IT policy, accessibility, digital government service, open data, and a general document library. Moreover, the council's training also involves a mentoring program and training opportunities in key priority areas of e-government such as IT symposiums, solution challenges activities, and reports.

At the federal level, the Senior Executive Service Program run by the U.S. Office of Personnel Management (OPM) is a training program for public managers that work in various functional areas. The Senior Executive Service Program trains senior public administrators who serve right under presidential political appointees to link to the rest of the workforce in almost all federal agencies. These senior executives need to develop five core qualifications. The ones relevant to information technology are: (a) under number 3 covering technical credibility; and (b) under number 4 including technology management. It is clear that technology management involves utilizing technology to achieve results as well as securing access to and security for technology systems. The main development mechanism includes at least 80 hours of formal training and a four-month developmental assignment with a mentor.

The National Association of State CIOs (NASCIO) is the premier training body and resource for state CIOs as well as any digital governance managers working at the state level. Given the federal administrative system in the United States, a separate entity is needed to address the diverse needs of state governments as separate jurisdictions (states' rights). Federal government is only involved in interstate governance. NASCIO offers both annual conferences and a resource website to serve digital governance managers working at the state level. NASCIO's annual national conferences provide all state-level digital governance managers with the latest information on pertinent policy and management issues, and best practices. The themes and training provided address state and federal government priorities. Given that large state governments have multiple departments (i.e. Department of Education and Department of Transportation) and most of the medium and large departments have a CIO, the number of CIOs in state governments is relatively large.

Another way that NASCIO serves state governments' ICT training needs is the production of white papers and management reports for digital governance topics that are salient to digital governance managers. Such reports could be compiled in partnership with IT companies that have expertise in a particular area (i.e. CISCO for network security). The NASCIO website has a collection of more than 150 publications. More importantly, the contents are current and written in a style that is informative and relevant to state government CIOs. For instance, in July 2016, NASCIO published a report on the internet of things to explore its values and vulnerabilities. In addition, NASCIO leverages the collective wisdom of the CIOs to capture the ICT priorities facing them. The results of their annual survey provide important data on the priority areas for digital governance managers. For instance, cybersecurity, cloud services, mobility, broadband, and IT procurement are the top five priorities identified by state CIOs at the end of 2015 as technology priorities for 2016 (NASCIO 2015).

Local governments are served by a variety of professional organizations and IT service providers. A large number of city and county governments are served by the ICMA. Although this organization does not have a separate professional association dedicated to CIOs, ICMA does organize national conferences that bring in IT service providers and experienced managers to discuss the best practices for IT management, open data, GIS, civic engagement, etc. The National Association of Counties (NACo) in the United States serves county governments to address various current and future challenges.

In addition, other professional associations and training programs serve small local governments. For a small municipal government with a clerk as the chief administrative officer, the International Institute of Municipal Clerks is a premier institute serving these personnel. An annual international conference provides training on the salient issues as identified by these clerks. Cybersecurity, for example, was one of the featured topics in 2016. Certified public manager programs in various states also offer ample opportunities for training (Shark 2016). Public affairs schools at a university (i.e. the University of North Carolina) can serve as the main institutional base for a certified public manager program. For some land-grant universities with an outreach component, these outreach offices can recruit faculty members and practitioners to offer relevant ICT training.

In terms of trade journals, e-Republic's *Government Technology* and *Public CIO* magazines offer people interested in IT at the state and local levels information about the most recent application of technologies, the latest trends, and management challenges and solutions. The content is available via the magazine websites. Moreover, e-Republic has conducted annual rankings of city and county government websites. Local governments can learn about the innovative practices of their peer local governments to leverage information technologies while minimizing the risks. For local and state governments wishing to understand internet users, the Pew Internet and American Life Project website offers valuable resources on annual internet penetration rates by demographics. In addition, the site provides information on social media use, e-government service use, use of mobile devices, and other topics to help government understand the demand side of digital governance.

Conclusion

The capabilities of modern digital governance managers need to include education on public values. These public values include, but are not limited to, standard values such as efficiency, effectiveness, equity, and ethics. Public values such as transparency, accountability, and democratic governance are becoming more salient in the realm of digital governance. An aptitude for learning and innovation is crucial for cultivating capabilities that keep up with technological advancements. Moreover, technical knowledge and skills are important. These include basic IT literacy, information system design and development, security and privacy, social media, and emerging technologies.

For those who assume more managerial responsibilities, these managers need to first have an understanding of the relationship between technology and changes in society and organizations. An understanding of strategic IT planning and how to use such a strategic planning process is essential to realize the potential of IT in achieving public values by aligning IT priorities with organizational ones. Consistent with the proposed digital governance framework of this book, a digital governance manager needs to master the knowledge and skills to engage external stakeholders for collaboration to produce and share public information and service. Internally, this manager needs to manage ICT resources and risks while maximizing performance.

The NASPAA schools and programs are at the forefront of providing public and non-profit managers with the technical and managerial knowledge to leverage ICTs for advancing public values. However, a collective examination by scholars in the field of public affairs education has identified a continuously widening gap between the level of ICT training by these programs and the demand for ICT skills and knowledge in the field. Such an increasing gap highlights the importance of strengthening ICT education in these programs. Offering a core course that provides basic ICT technical and management knowledge and skills seems to be the minimum necessary. Various programs could provide additional ICT training in technology and management that better fits their needs and priorities via either program investment in the training and/or synergistic training arrangements with other disciplines and programs.

Moreover, on-going education and training for in-service public and non-profit managers are particularly relevant in a rapidly advancing area of expertise with a shorter lifecycle of knowledge. Various governmental agencies, as well as supporting national associations, are foundational to identifying key priorities and needs as well as providing educational resources for the purpose of meeting these training needs. The Senior Executive Service Program at the federal level and certified public manager programs supporting mostly state and local government employees are critical components of training digital governance managers.

Looking into the future, several challenges can be turned into opportunities. The first challenge is to maintain a comprehensive coverage of ICT competencies ranging from values/attributes to technical and managerial competencies. This challenge requires major resource commitment and leadership support to maintain the breadth and coverage of ICT capability development. The second challenge is to incentivize NASPAA schools and programs to make ICT education a priority, especially when there has no longer been a specific standard for training IT in the core curriculum for accreditation purposes since 2009. The last challenge is to find ways to keep pace with rapid advancements of technologies in terms of technical contents as well as ever-expanding ICT portfolios to manage.

The opportunities lie in the transformational power of combining ICTs and administrative reform to advance public values. Comprehensive competence-building is an investment that will pay dividends in advancing efficiency, effectiveness, equity of production, and delivery of public information and services. MPA/MPP programs can seize the opportunities of investing in their students and leveraging partnerships with other disciplines to ensure comprehensive coverage. The resource commitment and leadership challenge can be addressed by articulating the need to serve students and add values to public service. Citizens, customers, and other stakeholders are likely to raise their levels of expectation when they have become accustomed to getting newer and high-quality online service from e-commerce and technology companies. The constantly expanding innovative frontier requires these MPA/MPP programs to move with the times. In addition, academic institutions, along with government agencies and professional associations, should make the investment in recruiting talents and providing them with support for continuous education. Grant opportunities are available in science and technology from the Federal Government in the area of science, technology, engineering, and math (STEM) education, as well as emerging technologies such as smart city, big data, and other areas of ICTs. Linking ICT education with innovation is likely to ensure sustained support to keep pace with fast-changing technologies.

Notes

1 For more details, see www.protocols.com/pbook/wap/, accessed on July 24, 2016.
2 For more details, see www.pewinternet.org/2015/10/29/technology-device-ownership-2015/, accessed on July 24, 2016.
3 For more details, see www.govtech.com/federal/Feds-Hope-to-Inncubate-Innovation-with.html, accessed July 25, 2016.
4 The statistic was reported in the April 9, 2016 version of *The Economist*. Accessed online on July 25, 2016: www.economist.com/news/leaders/21696521-mark-zuckerberg-prepares-fight-dominance-next-era-computing-imperial-ambitions
5 See www.internetlivestats.com/internet-users/, accessed July 10, 2016.
6 The E-Government Act of 2002 in its entirety is accessible at www.gpo.gov/fdsys/pkg/PLAW-107publ347/pdf/PLAW-107publ347.pdf, accessed July 26, 2016.
7 For more information, see www.it.ojp.gov/PrivacyLiberty/authorities/statutes/1287, accessed July 28, 2016.
8 For more information, see www.it.ojp.gov/PrivacyLiberty/authorities/statutes/1287, accessed July 28, 2016.
9 For more details, see bigapps.nyc/p/challenges/, accessed August 10, 2016.

References

Bhattacherjee, Anol. 2000. "Customer-centric Reengineering at the Colorado Department of Revenue." *Communications of the Association for Information Systems* 3 (16):1–43.

Bowman, James S., Jonathan P. West, and Marcia A. Beck. 2015. *Achieving Competencies in Public Service: The Professional Edge*. London and New York: Routledge.

Bozeman, Barry, and Stuart Bretschneider. 1986. "Public Management Information Systems: Theory and Prescription." *Public Administration Review* 46 (Special Issue):475–87.

Bryson, John M. 2011. *Strategic Planning for Public and Nonprofit Organizations: A Guide to Strengthening and Sustaining Organizational Achievement*. Fourth edition. San Francisco, CA: Jossey-Bass.

China Internet Network Information Center (CNNIC). 2016. Statistical Report on Internet Development in China (January 2016). Beijing: CNNIC.

Christian, P. Cary, and Trenton J. Davis. 2016. "Revisiting the Information Technology Skills Gap in Master of Public Administration Programs." *Journal of Public Affairs Education* 22 (2):161–74.

CIO Council. 2012. 2012 Clinger-Cohen Core Competencies & Learning Objectives. Washington, DC: CIO Council.

Cleary, Robert E. 1990. "What do Public Administration Masters Programs Look Like? Do They do What is Needed?" *Public Administration Review* 50 (6):663–73.

Cresswell, Anthony M., G. Brian Burke, and Theresa A. Pardo. 2006. "Advancing Return on Investment Analysis for Government IT: A Public Value Framework." Albany, NY: Center for Technology in Government.

Dawes, Sharon. 2004. "Training the IT-Savvy Public Manager: Priorities and Strategies for Public Management Education." *Journal of Public Affairs Education* 10 (1):5–17.

Dufner, Donna, Lyn M. Holley, and B. J. Reed. 2002. "Can Private Sector Strategic Information Systems Planning Techniques Work for the Public Sector?" *Communication of the Association for Information Systems* 8:413–31.

Dumont, Georgette. 2013. "Transparency or Accountability? The Purpose of Online Technologies for Nonprofits." *International Review of Public Administration* 18 (3):7–29.

Ganapati, Sukumar, and Christopher Reddick. 2016a. "An Ostrich Burying Its Head in the Sand? The 2009 NASPAA Standards and Scope of Information Technology and E-Government Curricula." *Journal of Public Affairs Education* 22 (2):267–86.

Ganapati, Sukumar, and Christopher Reddick. 2016b. "Symposium Introduction: Information Technology and Public Administration Education." *Journal of Public Affairs Education* 22 (2):156–60.

Garson, David. 2006. *Public Information Technology and E-Governance: Managing the Virtual State*. Sudbury, MA: Jones and Bartlett Publishers, Inc.

Goldsmith, Stephen, and Susan Crawford. 2014. *The Responsive City: Engaging Communities Through Data-Smart Governance*. San Francisco, CA: Jossey-Bass.

Government Technology. 2015. "Year in Data: CIO Priorities." *Government Technology*, 13.

Hoffer, Jeffrey A., Mary B. Prescott, and Fred R. McFadden. 2002. *Modern Database Management*. Upper Saddle River, NJ: Prentice Hall.

International City/County Management Association (ICMA). 2011. Electronic Government 2011. Washington, DC: International City/County Management Association.

Laudon, Kenneth C., and Jane P. Laudon. 2012. *Management Information Systems: Managing the Digital Firm*. 12th edition. Upper Saddle River, NJ: Pearson Education.

Maglio, Paul P., Cheryl A. Kieliszewski, and James C. Spohrer, eds. 2010. *Handbook of Service Science*. New York: Springer US.

Manoharan, Aroon, and James McQuiston. 2016. "Technology and Pedagogy: Information Technology Competencies in Public Administration and Public Policy Programs." *Journal of Public Affairs Education* 22 (2):176–86.

Mauldin, Marcus D. 2016. "No MPA Left Behind: A Review of Information Technology in the Master of Public Administration Curriculum." *Journal of Public Affairs Education* 22 (2):187–92.

McClelland, David C. 1973. "Testing for Competence Rather than 'Intelligence'." *American Psychologist* 28 (1):1–14.

Mergel, Ines. 2012. "Manager's Guide to Designing a Social Media Strategy." Washington, DC: IBM Center for the Business of Government.

Mergel, Ines. 2013. *Social Media in the Public Sector: A Guide to Participation, Collaboration and Transparency in the Networked World*. San Francisco, CA: John Wiley & Sons.

Mergel, Ines. 2016. "Big Data in Public Affairs Education." *Journal of Public Affairs Education* 22 (2):231–48.

Moore, Mark H. 1995. *Creating Public Value: Strategic Management in Government*. Cambridge, MA: Harvard University Press.

NASCIO. 2015. "State CIO Priorities for 2016." Lexington, KY: National Association of State CIOs.

NASPAA Commission on Peer Review and Accreditation. 2008. General Information and Standards for Professional Masters Degree Programs. Washington, DC: National Association of Schools of Public Affairs and Administration (NASPAA).

Ni, Anna Ya, and Yu-Che Chen. 2016. "A Conceptual Model of Information Technology Competence for Public Managers: Designing Relevant MPA Curricula for Effective Public Service." *Journal of Public Affairs Education* 22 (2):193–212.

National Science Foundation (NSF). 2007. "Cyberinfrastructure Vision for the 21st Century Discovery." Washington, DC: National Science Foundation.

National Science Foundation (NSF). 2012. NSF Leads Federal Efforts In Big Data. Press Release, March 29, 2012.

Park, Hun Myoung, and Hanjun Park. 2006. "Diffusing Information Technology Education in Korean Undergraduate Public Affairs and Administration Programs: Driving Forces and Challenging Issues." *Journal of Public Affairs Education* 12 (4):537–55.

Perry, James. 2000. "Bring Society In: Toward a Theory of Public-Service Motivation." *Journal of Public Administration Research and Theory* 10 (2):471–88.

Reddick, Christopher. 2012. *Public Administration and Information Technology*. Burlington, MA: Jones & Bartlett Learning.

Rocheleau, Bruce. 2004. *Teaching IT in Public Administration: The Moving Staircase Problem*. Presentation at the American Society for Public Administration's 2004 annual conference.

Shark, Alan R. 2016. "The Information Technology Gap in Public Administration: What We Can Learn From the Certified Public Manager and Senior Executive Service Programs." *Journal of Public Affairs Education* 22 (2):213–30.

Sutherland, Jeff. 2015. *SCRUM: The Art of Doing Twice the Work in Half the Time*. London: Random House Business Books.
The Economist. 2016a. "A Tale of Technology: Highs and Lows." *The Economist*, July 2.
The Economist. 2016b. "Briefing: The New Face of Facebook." *The Economist*, April 9, 21–4.
White House. 2012. "Digital Government: Building 21st Century Platform to Better Serve the American People." Washington, DC: White House.
White, Tom. 2015. *Hadoop: The Definitive Guide*. Fourth edition. Sebastopol, CA: O'Reilly.
XSEDE. 2014. XSEDE: PY1-3 Comprehensive Report (July 1, 2011 through June 30, 2014). Illinois: XSEDE Office.
Yildiz, Mete, Cenay Babaoğlu, and Mehmet Akif Demircioğlu. 2016. "E-Government Education in Turkish Public Administration Graduate Programs: Past, Present, and Future." *Journal of Public Affairs Education* 22 (2):287–302.
Zavattaro, Staci M., and Thomas A. Bryer, eds. 2016. *Social Media for Government: Theory and Practice*. New York: Routledge.

10 Conclusion, Trends, and Strategies of Digital Governance

This concluding chapter first aims to summarize the key ideas presented in this book. The goal is to highlight the unique perspective and contribution of this book to digital governance and its management. More importantly, this chapter will identify and describe the trends of digital governance over the next three to five years. The objective is to guide the reader into developing a forward-looking perspective on building relevant knowledge and capacity. These trends are enhanced data and cyberinfrastructure, personalized public information and services, open data and governance, innovation, and protection of digital security and privacy. The final part of this chapter outlines the strategies for digital governance in the 21st century in correspondence to these major trends. It offers strategies and specific management practices for leveraging information and communication technology (ICT) to advance public values and provide better public service.

Managing Digital Governance: Resources for Managers

Rise of Digital Governance and a Framework for Public Managers

Digital governance is considered the next stage of evolution in the utilization of ICTs to provide better public information and service. There are several defining features of digital governance as distinct from earlier stages of e-government development and digital government. Digital governance signals a significant increase in the role of citizens/residents in shaping policy as well as the production and delivery of public services via online means such as participatory online platforms, social media, apps, and other channels. People in the community play the roles of customers, citizens, and partners in the public sphere empowered by digital technologies. The rise of citizens in the digital realm can be attributed to the rise of wireless connectivity, smart phones, social media, cloud computing, and big data.

Another defining feature of digital governance is the use of a collaborative and integrated approach to solving societal challenges. Digital governance's purpose is to leverage technological innovations to organize and govern to better address contemporary and future societal challenges. It takes a collaborative approach that goes beyond the jurisdictional boundary of individual governmental agencies or governments. Complex contemporary public problems such as the environment, transportation, healthcare, public safety, and emergency management are cross-boundary. Digital governance creates the unique opportunity to provide low-cost options to facilitate the coordination and collaboration of individuals and organizations in the public, private, and non-profit sectors to collectively solve societal challenges. To be effective in addressing these challenges, integration of the information and service is critical to provide personalization and opportunity for improvement.

The advancement of new ICTs will continue to push the envelope in terms of presenting challenges and opportunities for creating and advancing public values. The expectations for government in harnessing digital technologies and communication technologies will continue to rise; this rise of digital governance underscores the need for public managers and executives to acquire knowledge and skills to succeed in the 21st century.

The digital governance framework outlined in Chapter 2 offers an integrated and comprehensive system to plan and manage digital governance in response to rapid advancement of ICTs. This framework focuses on the perspective of digital governance managers in leveraging ICTs to deliver public values. Managers can assume the titles of chief administrative officers (CAOs), chief information officers (CIOs), information technology (IT) managers, innovation officers, or executive directors of any collaborative initiatives for public service.

This framework is comprehensive in simultaneously considering the external and internal factors and linking them together in an integrated way. In the era of digital governance, there is a critical need for engaging stakeholders outside government via digital means in civic engagement and cross-boundary collaboration. The digital governance imperative seeks novel and effective uses of ICTs to enhance meaningful and productive collaboration and interactions with these external stakeholders to advance public values.

The critical internal areas for digital governance managers to consider are resource management, risk management, and performance management. Resources include information and financial, human, and technological resources for the manager to leverage. The main considerations of risks particularly pertinent to digital governance include digital security and digital privacy. Performance management encompasses the methods and discipline of project and program management to drive performance while utilizing the relevant resources and minimizing the risks involved.

The strategic and policy layer covers the digital governance plan and institutions that guide both the priority area as well as the linkages between internal and external factors. The main vehicle is the utilization of a strategic IT/information system planning process to identify the priority components of resource development and focus on collaboration with external stakeholders. For instance, a local government can use a strategic IT planning process to select open data as a digital governance priority. Then, this government can build the human capital and technical capability for improving the quality of government data as well as for designing and implementing collaborative mechanisms to enhance the impact of open data.

Public Service Focus: Digital Opportunities, Opening Governance, and Citizen-centric Service

Public digital governance focuses on advancing public values. The values of equity, transparency, accountability, and democratic governance are fundamentally different from the notion of profit maximization and customer-focus as prevalent in the private sector. Chapters 3–5 explore these unique challenges and opportunities facing digital governance managers in engaging and interacting with external stakeholders for public service.

Since the rise of digital technologies inevitably creates digital divide between those who have the access and skills to leverage these technologies and those who do not, the initial environmental scanning for a digital governance manager involves collecting information about the access and skill challenges facing the users of digital technologies. The collection of such information forms the basis for crafting digital interaction and inclusion strategies while promoting equity in the digital realm. The imperative of government and public service managers is to serve all citizens/residents rather than just serving only paying customers as corporations do.

Digital divide is more than the divide in access to IT (Mossberger, Tolbert, and McNeal 2008), and the variety of digital divides is likely to grow with the introduction of new technologies. Traditionally, digital divide has been understood as the divide in internet access. In the contemporary digital landscape, there are differences in access to broadband, smart phones, computers, and software programs. For instance, access to computer and software programs (i.e. word-processing) is critical for someone to prepare a resume for job applications. Moreover, the roots of these divides are economic, educational, and cultural in nature (Mossberger, Tolbert, and McNeal 2008). For instance, the level of education is strongly associated with both a higher level of internet access and more career-related internet use. In addition, one cultural explanation for the lack of e-government use can be attributed to a distrust of government among some minority groups.

Effective strategies for digital inclusion and opportunities need to be grounded in understanding the types and sources of digital divide. Overall, digital inclusion and opportunities need to address digital divide on two levels. On the basic level, digital inclusion and opportunities need to provide access. On this level, basic wired and wireless internet access is the most basic requirement in assistance centers or other crucial public places. Broadband internet and basic word-processing software programs are a necessity in public libraries and other government-sponsored centers to address the basic digital divide. On a more advanced level, a coordinated effort to address economic, cultural, and educational barriers to the utilization of ICTs must be prioritized (Mossberger, Tolbert, and Stansbury 2003). Moreover, there is a need to confront motivation issues to extend beyond just provision of access (Helsper 2012). Incentives are needed for people to make the switch from being non-internet users to internet users. An example of coordinated efforts is to have a digital opportunity center that offers internet access, computer training, and social activities to assist disadvantaged populations in rural areas and/or inner cities.

Open government and open data are guided by the unique obligations of government to advance core societal values of democratic governance such as transparency, accountability, and civic engagement. Ultimately, governments need to address citizen needs as well as the concerns and interests of other stakeholders in society, and ICTs offer opportunities to advance these core societal values. The Obama Administration's Open Government Directive utilizes a range of technologies, data/information resources, and online platforms to advance the values of transparency, participation, and collaboration (Orszag 2009; Evans and Campos 2013). Other efforts have been made by the legislative branch, state and local governments, and other entities in society to advance these values.

The first pillar of the Open Government Directive is transparency (Orszag 2009). The Obama Administration has made open data a priority with the establishment of data.gov to release government data to the society at large, which ushered in an online user-friendly environment to gain access to government data sets with raw data. The Data Accountability and Transparency Act (DATA Act) in 2014 in the United States was the first targeted piece of legislation to advance government transparency with IT. This Act provides the impetus for the development of data standards to enhance standardization and comparability of financial and operational data of federal agencies. Such data will be made available for public viewing and to download. A major enhancement has been to make the data machine-readable for easy access and analysis.

The second pillar is participation—with the focus on participation via digital communication channels such as websites, online platforms, and online enhancement of democratic participation. The inclusion and analysis of comments on proposed federal regulations electronically, also known as e-rulemaking, is an example of participation via digital means. An e-petition is another mechanism for democratic participation of citizens in the United States.[1] The United Kingdom also has an e-petition platform for citizens to initiate policies.[2] Elected officials also utilize various social networking services such as Facebook, Twitter, and YouTube to provide opportunities for citizens to participate. Such utilization of online participation platforms and services also takes place at the state and local levels to gather citizen inputs.

The third pillar is collaboration with the emphasis on digital means. Digital co-production is an emerging phenomenon, with collaboration between governments, volunteers, and non-profit organizations (Clark, Brudney, and Jang 2013; Linders 2012). In the case of non-profits, the interactive information service available on the "ChicagoWorksforYou" government website relies on a non-profit, Smart Chicago, to engage both volunteer programmers and the City of Chicago. In the case of New York City, annual BigApps competitions leverage government open NYC 311 data and private/philanthropic donations to enlist software programmers and interface designers to develop apps. Another collaboration can take the form of government posing a public policy/service challenge online and seeking broad participation from all demographics of society to generate policy solutions. The Challenge.gov website of the federal government, as well as some state agencies' similar efforts, are examples of such direct collaboration between government and citizens (Evans and Campos 2013).

These three pillars of the Open Government Directive are supportive of one another. Effective government innovation in leveraging ICTs to deliver public values tends to incorporate two or three of these pillars. For instance, the combination of open data (transparency) and digital co-production (collaboration) allows governments to make low-cost, citizen-centric websites, and/or government service apps. The combination of open data and citizen participation allows the consideration of a diverse range of views and opinions, and invites crowdsourcing solutions to complex public problems.

Citizen-centric service is one of the guiding principles of effective digital governance. The focus on citizens is a strategic direction of digital governance that is considered the highest form of e-government. Being citizen-centric requires a high level of integration of information and service across departments, governments, and even sectors to provide personalized service in health, mobility, education, and other government services. Such a citizen-centric focus involves personalization of online platforms, communication channels, and content to be user-friendly and beneficial to citizens; this type of strategic focus allows a digital governance manager to develop and organize internal components of the digital governance framework to foster productive interactions and collaboration with external stakeholders.

This book has a broad and multi-faceted notion of being citizen-centric that is consistent with the essence of digital governance as emphasized by this book. Citizens play multiple roles when interacting with governments and society at large (Thomas 2012). Citizens can play the role of citizens who have both rights and duties to be productive members of a democratic society. That includes voting and participating in public affairs and the duty to uphold the core values of the society they live in. Citizens can be partners with government in digital coproduction as mentioned previously. Citizens can be customers of government services as individual residents, business owners, or members of non-profit organizations.

The overarching strategy of being citizen-centric has several components. First, a digital governance manager needs to seek and secure political and administrative support for citizen-centric digital governance efforts. This includes fostering a culture of customer service and transparency. Second, such a manager needs to build and facilitate cross-departmental and inter-organizational collaboration in information-sharing and service collaboration to provide the needed information to offer personalized information and service. Lastly, being citizen-centric requires digital governance managers to engage citizens to understand their needs, gather their inputs, and invite collaboration with them in user innovations to continuously improve service.

Information/Knowledge, Risks, and ICT Performance Management

Information and knowledge are central for achieving the strategic vision of digital governance, empowering public managers and other stakeholders to make better public service decisions. Quality government information is a precondition for any success of open government data. ICTs play a supportive role to improve the quality and relevance of information, as well as managing government knowledge for better public service.

Information is about giving meaning to data to make them useful for public purposes. In the public sector, regulatory information, such as building safety and food safety, protects the safety and health of the public. Public service information, such as advertisement of community events and notification of upcoming elections, assists with public governance. Knowledge involves adding value to information such as business intelligence on areas of service improvement and the generation of creative content for the creative economy. Advancements in information and knowledge are continuing to be made in the areas of big data, data analytics, and data visualization. For instance, virtual reality is an increasingly popular way to visualize information.

The principles and strategy of managing government information are enduring while technologies are constantly changing. The over-arching goal of public service information and knowledge is to improve public service and advance public governance. For information management, digital governance managers need to adhere to the principles of stewardship and usefulness (Dawes 2010). Governments need to protect information with which all members and organizations of the society entrust government. Such stewardship implies archiving and ensuring quality and availability of information to be a good steward. In addition, stewardship is comprised of information security and protection of personally identifiable information. Usefulness entails the need for information interoperability to benefit stakeholders relying on government for information—and for treating information as a strategic resource for government as an object or subject of public policy.

Knowledge management needs to adhere to the same principles of stewardship and usefulness while also aligning itself closely to the strategic goal of an organization. In the information economy, knowledge about business intelligence constitutes the competitive advantage of an organization (Chen, Chiang, and Storey 2012). Successful knowledge management requires matching the knowledge management strategy to the type of knowledge. An emphasis on mentoring programs, workshops, retreats, and conferences is more productive for tacit knowledge. For explicit knowledge, it is better to automate the acquiring, capturing, and sharing of knowledge with the assistance of data analytics techniques and artificial intelligence. A conscious effort to convert paper-based knowledge to digital forms will advance government's ability to leverage information and knowledge resources for digital governance.

Risk management of digital governance primarily concerns digital privacy and security. Fundamentally, the protection of digital privacy and assurance of cybersecurity are about engendering citizen trust in government. Digital governance managers need to invest the time and effort internally to ensure the protection of online privacy and security while interacting with stakeholders via online platforms and digital channels. This is a particularly challenging area of digital governance because cybersecurity is only as strong as the weakest point of the entire front of the defense. Threats to individual privacy and cybersecurity have recently evolved to be more sophisticated as the increased interconnectivity of various information systems has made every organization more vulnerable (Deloitte-NASCIO 2014; Government Accountability Office (GAO) 2012).

Digital privacy primarily entails managing the balance between the right to know and the right to privacy. Citizens have the right to know about how governments utilize the resources that governments manage. Citizens also have the right to privacy in terms of personally identifiable information to maintain a cloak of privacy in society. Neither "right to know" nor "right to privacy" is absolute. Digital privacy typically involves balancing risks and benefits: digital governance managers need to manage the risks involved while maximizing the benefits to the society. Cybersecurity manages the risks of security breaches on government and corporate information systems that maintain information on critical infrastructure, personally identifiable information, and any national security data.

The overarching approach to digital privacy and security is a risk management one, which involves the identification of critical digital assets and vulnerability for security and privacy protection purposes. Then, government needs to invest in the technology and processes to focus on high-value digital assets to minimize risks. In the public sector, managing risks of digital privacy and security benefit from economy of scale and extensive collaboration and information-sharing. Given that the defense for online security and privacy is only as good as its weakest link, it is beneficial for various governmental agencies, as well as different levels of government, to pool their resources and information in a collaborative approach to managing risks.

ICT performance management covers all aspects of a government's utilization of ICT to advance public values. Consequently, ICT performance management must be broad in scope to cover the areas of information knowledge management and risk management. The goal is to organize these information and technology resources while minimizing risks. Performance management of ICTs needs to pay special attention to human and financial resources, which are regarded as the two main barriers to e-government (International City/County Management Association (ICMA) 2011).

The core of ICT performance management lies in its discipline and approach, and its focus should be on the method utilized to drive performance. One area of growing attention and relevance is the utilization of agile development methods in response to the changing needs and short budget cycle of public-sector information and communication technology. Agile development has produced some success stories and support from innovation-minded public executives (Sutherland 2015). In addition, ICT performance management involves the discipline and methodology of project management while attending to the program-level consideration of being more adaptive to changing circumstances.

An effective strategy of ICT performance, as Chapter 8 of this book suggests, has several components. Such performance management needs to be stakeholder-focused, especially given the context of government information and service with a multitude of stakeholders. Next is the strategic alignment with the mission and goals of government with a focus on outcomes rather than outputs. Such performance improvement needs to be based on data while taking a learning perspective. In addition, performance should implement a user-centric (citizen-centric) approach as articulated in the U.S. digital government strategy. Lastly, agile development processes provide productive methods to achieve desirable results.

Capacity-building for Digital Governance

This book aims to offer relevant contents and programs for building capacity for digital governance in order to address the challenges facing digital governance managers of the 21st century. The contents of this book provide an in-depth analysis and review of relevant knowledge and also offer practical strategies to be effective in managing ICTs in the 21st century. The digital governance framework provides a comprehensive picture for digital governance managers to consider in developing resources and capacity internal to organizations, engaging and collaborating with external stakeholders, and establishing linkages between internal and external factors.

Fundamentally, capacity-building for digital governance managers develops competencies that include values and individual attributes, technical knowledge and skills, and managerial capabilities. The understanding and upholding of public values such as efficiency, effectiveness, and equity are important for digital governance managers to guide their efforts in advancing these values (Ni and Chen 2016). The advances in internet and wireless technologies further enable these managers to advance values such as transparency, accountability, and democratic participation.

Technical concepts and skills include: (a) basic concepts of technology; (b) hardware, software, and information system infrastructure; (c) data, databases, and data analytics; (d) telecommunications, internet, and wireless technologies; (e) information system development; (f) information system applications; (g) digital security and privacy; (h) social media; and (i) emerging technologies.

Managerial competences lie in managing the relationships between technology and the changes in organization and society. Digital governance managers also need to understand values, institutions, and IT policies in the context of public administration and service. Moreover, an effective digital governance manager conducts strategic planning by treating information as a strategic resource. Internally, such a manager focuses on the management of information, risks, and performance. Externally, an effective manager has the knowledge and skills to enhance digital communication, open government data, and engage various stakeholders for digital co-production.

The need for developing these competencies is particularly urgent and salient in the 21st century. The gap between the skills a digital governance manager needs to possess to be effective and the amount of training she/he receives via a university educational program continues to widen (Ganapati and Reddick 2016). At minimum, a required course in the core curriculum of a Master of Public Administration (MPA)/Master of Public Policy (MPP) program should offer a broad overview of the technical knowledge, management issues, and best practices for building basic literacy in digital governance. Institutional support from the accreditation institution (the Network of Schools of Public Policy, Affairs, and Administration (NASPAA)) is critical for incentivizing a university MPA/MPP program to offer digital governance courses (Ganapati and Reddick 2016). Moreover, senior executive programs, certified public management programs, and professional associations can provide in-service training for any public and non-profit employees wishing to leverage ICTs to improve public service and advance public values.

Trends of Digital Governance

There are five trends of digital governance, based primarily on observation and analysis of the efforts in the United States. These trends aim to depict

218 *Conclusion, Trends, and Strategies*

the major current and future developments in the area of digital governance with the time horizon of three to five years (see Figure 10.1). These include: (a) data and cyberinfrastructure; (b) personalization of public information and service; (c) open government data and open governance; (d) innovation in digital governance; and (e) protection of cybersecurity and digital privacy. Figure 10.1 offers an illustration of these trends for forward-looking planning and monitoring for future development. This section will describe the main aspects of these individual trends and the driving forces behind them. It will also address relationships between these trends, with data and cyberinfrastructure playing a central role in enabling the other trends.

Data and Cyberinfrastructure

Digital governance managers are likely to see more data, more digital data, and more strategic use of data/information. Both the amount and variety of data have continued to rise (*The Economist* 2010). The rise of social media and smart phones has added a huge amount of data in picture and video format. The further development of the internet of things will bring

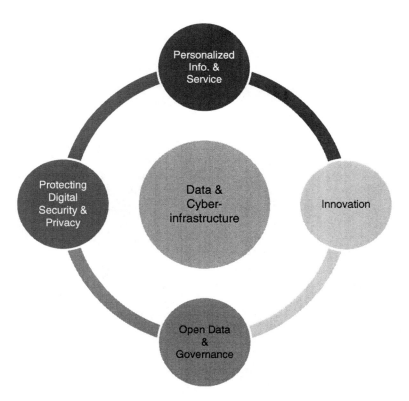

Figure 10.1 Trends of Digital Governance

in much more data when billions of devices begin to generate and transmit data in higher frequencies. Government's scientific exploration in such areas as climate, geomatics, seismic activity, and deep space exploration—as articulated in the big data program in the United States (Executive Office of the President 2012; National Science Foundation (NSF) 2012)—has further added to the amount of data. Data will become more digital in their format because of the continued development of e-government by converting paper-based data to digital format, as well as new data that are born digital. The increase of machine-readable data has also fueled the conversion of data into digital format for ease of distribution and manipulation to add to public values. Moreover, the strategic use of digital data for service improvement and citizen engagement in government will continue pushing the trend of digital data.

Big data will continue to be on the rise and display its relevance in the public sector. Big data initiate qualitative differences in the volume of data, velocity of data coming in, and the variety of data formats (Soares 2012). Equally promising is the improved veracity of data; big data have shown promise in the areas of disaster response, fraud detection, mobility management, and government service analytics. The successful big data projects are able to convert big data into big insights by leveraging big data analytics tools. Continuing innovations and maturity in this big data area will be driven by addressing the challenges of data storage, distributed processing, dissemination, and data analytics. New governance challenges associated with big data, particularly the use of big data to evaluate public service performance, will arise (Lavertu 2016).

The growth in digital data and the need for a distributed process to handle big data makes the development and operation of cyberinfrastructure an imperative. Traditionally, governments have tended to concern themselves with isolated information systems that connect various users via a telecommunication infrastructure to access the same system. The rise of cloud computing and big data ushered in the need for distributed computing with devices and servers connected to the cyberinfrastructure. The NSF in the United States has led the way in creating a high-speed, state-of-the-art cyberinfrastructure for scientific discovery (XSEDE 2014). It sets the standard for distributed computing. Moreover, NSF-sponsored cyberinfrastructure projects serve as examples of government-led innovations in partnership with national labs and universities.

Cyberinfrastructure also requires providing digital opportunities to disadvantaged populations and the organizations serving them (XSEDE 2014), filling the gap in the private sector that does not see the needed economy of scale to make profits for their telecommunication, internet, and computing service investments. A variety of government programs attempting to address this issue are fueling the development of cyberinfrastructure. These programs include laying fiber optics networks to connect rural and remote communities for internet access and connectivity.

Moreover, there are programs aimed at providing training and education at libraries and digital opportunity centers for people to leverage such cyberinfrastructure.

Big forces will continue to push the fast addition of digital data and the development of cyberinfrastructure to leverage these data. Advances in ICT will continue to drive the volume, velocity, and variety of data as defined in big data. Governments around the world and at all levels will continue to evolve in using digital information to accelerate innovations and provide better services. Cyberinfrastructure is key to that innovation strategy, and the development of cyberinfrastructure also aids in addressing digital divide and providing digital opportunities to disadvantaged populations.

Personalized Public Information and Service

Personalized digital public information and service is another prominent trend. The use of ICTs has been integrated into more and more government operations. The ubiquitous nature of IT use is a requirement for moving to Government 3.0 (Creative Government Planning Division 2013). The use of internet technologies, websites, social media, and apps serves the purpose of providing increasingly personalized government information and service over digital channels. Constant connectivity, the ubiquity of technology, and user-centric approaches have symbolized the next stage of evolution of e-government and digital governance.

Personalization implies the ability to meet the need of users with a wide range of preferences and characteristics. Users have varying preferences for different modes of online access such as apps, social media, mobile websites, and traditional websites optimized for desktop/laptop computers. A wide range of preferences also exists in regard to languages, fonts, and presentations. For online services, various stakeholders in society wish to have different services put online. Personalization can also be about focusing on life events and providing online services to support those life events (i.e. starting a business, moving to a new town, preparing for taxes, marriage, and retirement).

The future of personalization lies in considering stakeholder needs and online platforms. For digital governance, stakeholders include citizens, residents, businesses, non-profit organizations, governments, and public servants. Stakeholders' needs vary in terms of their preferred online services. E-government services for businesses have typically involved regulatory compliance and transactions. Citizens' needs are mostly informational with opportunities for participation. Other governments are concerned about e-government systems that bind various governments together in the provision of service via online channels. With such a variety of stakeholders, the choice of platforms is also an important dimension of personalization. Some users prefer mobile access to websites due to heavy use of their smart phones. In this case, having a mobile app meets their platform needs. Other users prefer the use of social media by government for information delivery and as a gateway to online services.

Public digital governance managers can anticipate rising expectations of various stakeholders for providing digital government services. After experiencing the convenience and innovative digital services made available by big technology and media companies, users/stakeholders will expect government to deliver high-quality digital service that can keep pace with the private sector. The use of apps, particularly citizen-service information system apps (311), has opened the door for personalized government information and service. Advanced apps allow individuals to keep track of the service requests they submit and subscribe to information and online services that are relevant to them via one app to access all services across all departments and units in a government enterprise.

Open Data and Opening Governance

Open data will continue to be on the rise due to the DATA Act and the demand for transparency at all levels of government. The DATA Act requires federal government agencies to make machine-readable spending data available in 2017.[3] Governments are likely to respond to citizen demands for transparency and accountability by using technological tools. At the local level, some innovative local governments leverage open data portals to make transportation and citizen service data open to the public. For instance, Kansas City, Missouri, is one of the local governments leading the effort.

Moreover, the frontiers of open data are pushing to make data machine-readable to enable user-driven analysis and provide the public data resources to create public values or to be more economically competitive. Such open data is consistent with the development of semantic web where data rather than text are searchable and usable. The development of XBRL language has helped the Security and Exchange Commission make machine-readable financial and business data available to the public. Another frontier is Big and Open Linked Data (BOLD) that leverage big data and link them in a meaningful way to add values while making access open to all members of a society (Janssen, Matheus, and Zuiderwijk 2015). Linked data have the advantage of creating interoperability and personalized data views. Big data combines a variety of data sources and formats while accelerating the speed of data input and analysis to expedite performance evaluation and decision-making.

Opening governance will continue to evolve as a partnership model to bring various stakeholder groups together to collectively add value to open data as well as to address societal challenges. Opening governance implies a bi-directional data flow between government and other stakeholder groups. For instance, businesses contribute to government data by filing regulatory compliance data with government. Government can help businesses with planning by providing census data. The collaboration between governments and other stakeholder groups is likely to grow. For instance, complex societal problems such as climate change, healthcare, transportation, and poverty require close collaboration between non-profit organizations, businesses, and governments. The availability of low-cost communication technologies and an online collaborative environment further opens up new opportunities for collaboration among organizations across distance and time. In addition, there will be innovations in using technology to enhance personalization of opening governance to engage people with their interests. These innovations could consist of crowd-sourcing scientific endeavors to citizen scientists or providing real-time health risk information to reduce the risks of major outbreaks.

Technology-enabled Innovation

The advancement of ICTs will continue to drive innovations in government service and government-sponsored scientific discovery. For public service, national governments recognize the pivotal role of IT in driving innovations and national competitiveness (Research Office of Legislative Council Secretariat 2013). Governments striving for the next level of e-government see innovations as the engine for reaching that next level. The growing amount of data and computing power, coupled with political and administrative support, is likely to further innovation.

Government service innovations are likely to be multi-faceted. First, the pathway to innovation involves process innovation: looking at ways in which the process of producing and delivering public service can be streamlined or transformed. For instance, emergency notification can go out on social media (Twitter) to reach citizens faster and more cost-effectively than before. A second facet is the leveraging of service data and big data, as well as data analytics, for insights on service improvement (Goldsmith and Crawford 2014). The evacuation of urban populations in the event of a hurricane can take advantage of big service data and weather data to inform the development of an evacuation plan and its implementation. Third, user innovations in providing government with feedback or even designing a better process will continue to ascend. At the time of disaster response and recovery, individuals can post information on the likely issues and coordinate their response efforts.

Scientific innovation enabled by ICT will become more compelling in providing a competitive advantage. The main feature of such innovation is the utilization of sophisticated cyberinfrastructure to offer distributed computing to process big data across the network of the cyberinfrastructure. Moreover, individuals are likely to contribute more to scientific innovations. Users are particularly effective in the area of visualization and use of communication tools. The availability of open-source programming tools, as well as the organized effort of software engineers as volunteers (civic hacking efforts), is likely to spur scientific innovations.

The Need to Protect Digital Security and Privacy

Cybersecurity has risen to the top three of IT issues facing CIOs (*Government Technology* 2015). Given that government information systems are more connected than ever before and many more critical assets are connected digitally to a network, the possible damages of cyber-attacks will continue to increase over time. According to a report from New York City's Attorney General published in 2014, 22.8 million private records of New Yorkers were exposed over the last eight years. According to the *Washington Post*, in 2015, the security breach of the Office of Personnel Management in the United States exposed the personal information of 21.5 million people (one in 15 Americans).[4] That was the biggest data breach reported in history, exposing addresses, dates and places of birth, foreign travel history, and other data used to conduct background investigations by government.

Cybersecurity will become a more serious concern for national governments and individuals, and is a national defense issue when attacks can be launched via the ever-increasing connections between information systems and networks. The tools and techniques of cyber-attacks available to organized criminals, terrorists, and even other governments have become more sophisticated over time. At the same time, there are more connected devices and vulnerabilities being introduced with smart phones, tablets, and the internet of things. Moreover, individuals and small governments are increasingly victims of cybercrimes with data loss and even financial loss due to the proliferation of cybercrimes. Without a layer of cybersecurity, individuals' personally identifiable information, including financial and health data, is likely to be exposed.

The landscape of digital privacy will become more complex with increasing threats from more prevalent uses of technologies. Increasing modes of government surveillance—such as using various means to intercept cellular communication, conducting video surveillance to combat terrorist and criminal activities, flying drones to collect intelligence, and monitoring activities over social media—pose privacy threats to individuals.[5] The open government effort and the transparency of government could also introduce privacy concerns. Putting property information online with the names of owners exposes landowners. Some states, while releasing crime information to the public, could inadvertently allow people to compromise the privacy of individuals while combining other data sources to re-identify the individuals.

Privacy concerns will increase with the locational and personal data being shared on social networking sites and other services. Individuals leave a significant amount of personal information (digital traces) when interacting with one another on social media sites such as Facebook and Twitter. Tools currently available for identifying and analyzing the communication patterns and content of tweets could potentially lead to violations of privacy. The location information that some people casually share to obtain location-specific services can be a threat to their privacy. Moreover, there are privacy concerns associated with the increasing ability of corporations and organizations alike to profile individuals based on the digital traces they leave on the internet. Some organizations are developing personal profiles by combining data available online and selling them for a profit on the internet.

Strategies of Digital Governance

This section provides digital governance strategies that correspond to each of the five areas as shown in Figure 10.1. For data and cyberinfrastructure, digital governance managers need to build and leverage data and cyberinfrastructure as strategic resources for advancing public values. For open data and opening governance, a productive strategy is to pursue data standardization to make data useful and comparable, while enabling the use of these data by partnering with non-profits and leveraging cyberinfrastructure. With regard to personalized information and service, the overarching strategy is to integrate various online platforms and utilize mobile technology to deliver personalized user experiences to build trust in government. An innovation strategy will engage all stakeholders to pursue both service and scientific innovations. Lastly, digital security and privacy needs to follow a risk management strategy with close integration of various government agencies and development of human capital and tools.

Data and Cyberinfrastructure

The overarching strategy for data and cyberinfrastructure is to treat them as strategic resources. This would constitute a paradigm shift for most organizations as they typically regard data and cyberinfrastructure as a cost or result rather than a strategic priority or input. Treating them as strategic resources also implies utilizing them to achieve the strategic goals of the organization and make the organization more efficient and effective in all its operations. The mandate of the Clinger-Cohen Act in the United States serves as a good model of treating information strategically and aligning information to an agency's mission and goals while establishing CIOs as advocates for such strategic use of data and information.

A successful implementation of strategic use of data and information needs to consider policies, tools, and data standards. Policies must be put in place to guide the appropriate collection, use, and dissemination of data to advance strategic priorities. The selection and utilization of data analytics tools are equally important to increase the generation of service insights. Data standards are used to improve interoperability and data integration. Integration of service data will aid in conducting service data analytics as well as providing personalized information and service to stakeholders served by government. For instance, America's Digital Government Strategy emphasizes the need for developing common data standards and formulating data policies and tools.

Government should take full advantage of information and data as strategic resources to achieve public policy goals. In European countries, there is a notion of public sector information (PSI). PSI, such as environmental conditions and regulatory compliance, can improve the evidence-based discourse and decision-making on these main public policy issues. Transportation information can be a tool to spur innovations in mobility and provide innovative businesses to provide better mobility service.

Development of cyberinfrastructure is the other aspect of the overall data and cyberinfrastructure strategy. Cyberinfrastructure is the infrastructure that adds values to data and allows users to work individually and collectively to turn data into insights and innovations. NSF should continue to invest in its cyberinfrastructure programs to enable researchers to achieve major discoveries and breakthroughs. The creation of big data regional innovation hubs is another good example of the benefits of cyberinfrastructure for scientific innovations and discovery.[6] Cyberinfrastructure could also focus on a specific area of public service such as transportation and environmental protection. A transportation cyberinfrastructure to accelerate research on mobility, improve livability, and spur economic development is a case in point.

Moreover, governments need to pursue building cyberinfrastructure for all. The main component of a cyberinfrastructure is the telecommunication network. In the United States, relevant efforts have been made to build a high-speed network for underserved regions and communities. The U.S. Department of Agriculture awards rural development grants that support such cyberinfrastructure. At the state level, there are broadband initiatives such as the one in Iowa that connects all corners of the state to offer high-speed access even for remote rural communities. The actual building of the cyberinfrastructure can take a partnership approach. Some of the smart city initiatives are carried out as partnerships between local government and technology companies such as Google Fiber. Some small communities partner with non-profit organizations to provide free WiFi to business districts or remote villages. It is the unique responsibility of government to ensure the continuity of service and sustainability of cyberinfrastructure to serve disadvantaged populations.

Personalized Information and Services

The goal of personalizing government information and services is to earn the trust of citizens in the governments' role in advancing public values. An overarching strategy of such personalization is to be "customer-centric" by organizing resources and utilizing technology to allow users to utilize government information and services to suit their preferences. The U.S.

Digital Government Strategy aims to "[allow] customers to shape, share, and consume information, whenever and however they want it" (White House 2012, 5). This strategy principle provides details on utilization to extend beyond simple consumption by leveraging smart devices and social network websites for shaping and sharing. This customer-centric principle also reinforces the notions of convenience and autonomy. Users should be able to access information via devices of their preference and retain autonomy in shaping information.

Building a service culture in government is foundational for successful personalization of information and services. Leadership needs to build a culture of service (customer service, citizen service) to lay the necessary foundation. Public employees need to subscribe to the values of public service to provide broad-based support for these personalization efforts. In particular, personalization of information and services usually requires changes to existing business processes and bureaucratic rules. Without a change in culture, these reform efforts are unlikely to succeed.

Integration is a prerequisite for personalization, recognizing that the extent of integration varies in terms of the service in question. For full integration of citizen service information for the entire suite of local government services to individuals, a local government needs to develop a citizen relationship management system (CiRM) (similar to a customer relationship management system (CRM) in the private sector). A sophisticated CiRM integrates: (a) all interactions via all channels with the citizen; and (b) all the relevant departmental service activities rendered to that individual. Given the rise of social media, there is an increasing need for integration of information coming through various channels into an integrated environment. For instance, the City of Jacksonville, Florida, integrates social media, a mobile website, mobile apps, and a public service information dashboard to communicate with the public while offering backend support of service analytics and business analytics to achieve personalization.

Presentation is critical in achieving personalization, especially when digital media are used; usability is key to personalized presentation. The use of a Google-like search function on a government website with a strong supporting algorithm is a way to personalize information and service by increasing usability. This is much more efficient than asking citizens to spend hours going through various sections of a government website to locate the relevant information and services. More advanced personalization via presentation uses mobile apps that have stored individual preferences and subscriptions to information and services of personal interest. Moreover, presentation is also about aesthetics. The emotional aspect of personalization is as important as the functional one. An award-winning interface design pays attention to aesthetic and other human factors.

Personalization of information and service can benefit from advancing the application of technologies to serve science. On a basic level, data analytics can help identify and compile a list of the most searched and used government information and services. Such a list of the most frequently used government information and service can be adjusted according to seasonal changes of information and service needs by various stakeholders. A more sophisticated way of personalization is to develop business analytics that are issue or location specific. For instance, a predictive modeling of rodent problems in the City of Chicago is a case in point. The City can anticipate and deploy countermeasures to be effective. In the future, the use of artificial intelligence supported by all the detailed and comprehensive information on government service and history, as well as individual preferences, can be particularly powerful. Such a sophisticated artificial intelligence (AI) could take the form of a digital personal assistant attending to all the needs and preferences of an individual.

Open Data and Opening Governance

The strategy for open data and opening governance begins with the foundational work of gaining political and administrative support. The passage of the DATA Act in the United States has laid an important foundation for political support in opening federal governments' financial and operational data. With completion of its first phase in 2017, this Act will provide the momentum moving forward. Administrative support is equally critical for success and much more relevant in the implementation of open data and governance efforts. The Obama Administration's Open Government Initiative includes transparency, participation, and collaboration that support open data and opening governance. The executive orders stipulating the rules of engagement further facilitate these activities (Orszag 2009). A future strategy is to deepen support at the federal level as well as to provide assistance and support at the state and local levels by leveraging relevant policy lessons and strategies.

Another component of an open data and opening governance strategy is to further enhance the interoperability, quality, and usability of data. Governments can develop and implement common data standards across agencies. The effort by the Office of Management and Budget (OMB) and the Treasury to finalize the definitions of 57 standardized data elements to achieve the goals of the DATA Act and to create a standard data exchange is an example of such efforts to improve interoperability. As the above effort demonstrates, common definitions and data standards are critical for understanding data from various agencies and making meaningful comparisons when traditionally each agency has its unique definitions and standards. Data quality is also important because a data-driven decision is only as good as the quality of the data it is based on. Misinformation can have serious consequences (Lavertu 2016). Government needs to invest in data quality assurance. Usability of data is also key to improving the impact of open data and opening governance efforts. Making raw data available with helpful metadata aids in the use of data for analysis and service decision-making. Such raw data in a machine-readable form will help improve participation and collaboration of non-profit organizations and individuals.

The use of open data portals is another component of the strategy. An open data portal is about usability; it is a one-stop data resource and supportive environment for open data needs. A successful portal has a pleasing (icon-driven menu) and user-friendly interface on its website. Also, it contains data sets that various stakeholder groups would like to access from government to collaboratively create public values. For instance, public health information will help the society as a whole to devise evidence-based healthcare policies. In addition, such data portals need to provide metadata and any additional helpful information to assist in the authentic interpretation of government data. Biased data and misinformation may do more harm than good when made available by government. A data portal also needs to cover a wide range of areas with the opportunity for integration. For local governments, the ability to overlay transportation, environment, and service-provision information on a map, as supported by geographic information system (GIS) data, can be quite useful as seen in the City of Chicago and Kansas City, MO. Moreover, such data are best when they are machine readable to enable users to leverage software applications to add values to open data and provide new services for better public governance.

Opening governance uses collaborative governance to improve public service and solve societal problems. Collaborative governance, in turn, aims to encourage collaboration between government and other stakeholders. The City of Chicago has an open data portal to encourage civic organizations and individuals to add value to the data. Such collaboration can sometimes be best accomplished via a civic organization as the integrator/liaison between governments and other member organizations or individuals in the community. For instance, Smart Chicago is a civic organization that brings together municipal governments, philanthropic organizations/individuals, and corporations in technology-enabled civic innovations.[7] Moreover, opening governance can be further developed to cover a wide range of public concerns and service challenges. Opening governance can reach various areas of public service such as public safety, transportation, environment, and healthcare to leverage technology to understand the interconnectedness of these public services and find effective solutions.

Technology-enabled Innovation

One strategy of technology-enabled innovation might leverage the combination of a particular area of innovation and a particular model of innovation. A more sophisticated one may use a combination of more than one area and/or one model. This section will cover both the existing practices and the opportunity for future growth.

The three key areas of innovations for digital governance are public policy, public service, and science. Public policy innovation currently places a strong focus on policy ideas such as Challenge.gov and its variety at the state and local levels, where government poses a challenge and engages a broad sector of society for a solution. Future development can extend more to other stages of the policy process, including policy formulation, implementation, and evaluation. In addition, future development can be made in the level of participation and the quality of the solution. A more enticing incentive, coupled with methods for measuring impact, would foster such development.

The second area of innovation is public service. Service innovation via the use of information technology is in its infancy. The utilization of data analytics for government data and big data has shown promise in the area of fraud detection to save costs. The State of Iowa has leveraged cloud-based solutions to save millions of dollars in detecting fraudulent claims of unemployment benefits.[8] Future development of service innovation could be more creative and effective integration of various online platforms. For instance, the City of Boston's Urban Mechanics has leveraged social media and its government website to improve communication with residents about snow removal while allowing residents to cheer on snow-plow drivers.

Scientific innovation is another area of focus for technology-enabled innovation. NSF has played a significant role in spurring scientific innovations; building cyberinfrastructure to support big science is a part of this role. Other capacity-building grants are available for scientific innovation such as the big data innovation hubs and smart city grants as well as opportunities for emergency management. Future growth should be in the size of these investments in capacity-building for scientific innovation. Another growth area should provide digital opportunities in the area of scientific innovation to assist under-represented or under-served segments of the research and general populations.

An effective digital governance manager can leverage one of several models of innovation or combine two or three of them. One model for innovation is the use of crowd-sourcing to engage members of a society in developing ideas and solutions to public service challenges. Challenge.gov, as mentioned in the open data section, is an example of such a model. Another related model is user/client-based innovations that solicit innovative ideas for improving government online service. This type of model could be as simple as soliciting a service rating or feedback. It could be much more involved by forming focus groups for service innovation ideas or even collaborative platform tools for users to work together to design a better service experience.

Another important model of innovation, especially in the context of digital governance, is the development of service-learning opportunities.

Service-learning is a partnership between academic institutions and governmental/non-profit organizations to allow combining academic training and practical knowledge to spur innovation. Lastly is the establishment of an innovation park/campus to accelerate innovations by connecting academia, industry, and community together. Such an innovation center/park/campus can be university-based or run by a non-profit, and tends to exploit a niche to drive the acceleration of discoveries and their applications. For instance, Indiana University has an innovation park focusing on the niche area of bio-technology because of billions of investment dollars pumped into biotech and strong academic programs in the state.

Protection of Cybersecurity and Privacy

An effective cybersecurity strategy takes a risk management approach to achieve confidentiality, integrity, and availability. A risk management approach introduces the discipline of regularly and proactively assessing digital assets and evolving cybersecurity vulnerabilities. Such an approach recognizes that cybersecurity can be managed but not completely eliminated. A cybersecurity defense should be cost-effective and commensurate with the value of the digital assets. One of the most important areas is the protection of critical infrastructure (i.e. power grids, nuclear plants, military bases) against cyber-attacks as the cost of property damage and human lives is particularly high. Moreover, a cybersecurity strategy should focus on achieving the goals of confidentiality, integrity, and availability. Although threats and tools continue to evolve, the goals remain the same.

Cybersecurity needs to improve coordinated implementation and information-sharing to secure cyberspace. In the United States, it is important to further the coordination of cybersecurity efforts as called for in a reform proposal to the current Federal Information Security Management Act (FISMA). The development of cybersecurity standards and their enforcement should be strongly coordinated, preferably by the Department of Homeland Security. Much more coordination and standardization would ensure enforcement and a higher level of accountability. Moreover, cybersecurity information-sharing should be further strengthened, especially in a federalist system like the United States. The existence of a multi-state cybersecurity information center is a step in the right direction. The push for information-sharing is imperative given that governments are reluctant to share self-damaging security breaches.

A comprehensive government cybersecurity strategy needs to have a capacity-building component. This is particularly critical given evolving cybersecurity threats and their growing sophistication. A federal government should help build capacity at the state and local levels since the federal government tends to be much more resourceful and skillful in identifying appropriate cybersecurity measures and implementing them. Moreover, it is in the interest of the federal government to protect the interconnected government information system across jurisdictions. A cybersecurity system is only as good as the weakest link in the interconnected system. The U.S. Federal Government has provided grants to state governments to build capacity at the state level while assisting local governments within the state. Another aspect of capacity-building is to develop cybersecurity human capital. In the United States, information assurance programs sponsor students for their cybersecurity education and then recruit them to work for government. This is to ensure the human capital to keep up with evolving challenges of cybersecurity threats.

An effective online privacy strategy has several aspects. First, a digital privacy strategy needs to build on the cybersecurity measures that ensure confidentiality. Second, the need for online privacy should be at minimum balanced with the need for online transparency. Third, it is important to combine both technical and institutional solutions to address digital privacy. An institutional mechanism to review privacy implications of open data and online transparency is key to ensuring privacy. Next is capacity-building for resource-strapped governments. Building knowledge and skills for the protection of privacy in the digital age is an essential aspect of a digital privacy strategy. Lastly is the necessity to stay current on the implications of information technologies such as drones, shared economy, social media, and big data.

An Integrated Overall Strategy with Connections

As illustrated in Figure 10.2, data and cyberinfrastructure is at the center of an integrated overall strategy in response to the identified digital governance trends. At the core of data and cyberinfrastructure is building quality data, data analytic capacity, and high-performing cyberinfrastructure as a strategic resource. This reservoir of strategic resources can support all four other areas as indicated by the directions of the arrows. Moreover, the focus on data implies the measurement of progress and impact on all other four areas as a way to provide needed data for better decision-making to improve digital governance by advancing public values.

Personalized information and service constitutes a digital governance goal for the utilization of data and cyberinfrastructure. Ultimately, such personalization helps engender citizen trust. A more advanced wireless cyberinfrastructure can aid in the increasingly strong preferences for the use of smart devices in accessing personalized information and service. In addition, there are ample opportunities for cross-fertilization between personalized information and services and opening governance. The use of government service apps can be the vehicle for two-way exchanges: government providing citizens with personalized service while citizens offer government data and ideas to improve service. Data and cyberinfrastructure provides advanced data/information and digital channels for personalized information and service.

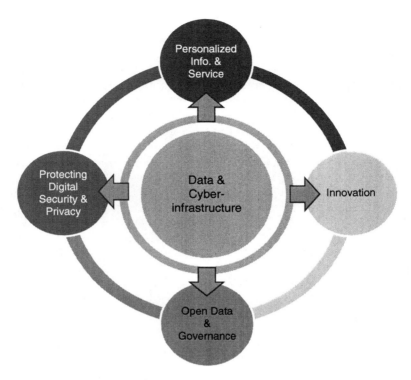

Figure 10.2 Strategies of Digital Governance

Open data and opening governance directly benefit from high quality data and advanced cyberinfrastructure. Quality data creates value when data is being made available to various groups of society. A more equitable cyberinfrastructure to support disadvantaged populations helps advance public values. Open data connects strongly to innovations in policy and service. The action of making data open can provide the needed strategic information resources to further innovations. Opening governance further advances the model of open innovations to engage citizens, businesses, non-profits, and other governments to spur innovations. The online channels and platforms (i.e. apps and online platforms) that have been created and used for opening data and opening governance can also serve as a way to provide personalized information and service.

Innovations such as big data can directly help build better data and data analytic tools. In addition, innovation in distributed cloud computing can also aid in the development of cyberinfrastructure. Innovation in civic technologies such as apps for finding affordable housing provides a personalized service to disadvantaged populations. Innovations specifically in the area of online collaborative platforms also aid in open data and opening governance. The State of Tennessee has an innovative collaborative platform that allows healthcare professionals, health service receivers, and the registered public to contribute to addressing public health issues.

Digital security and privacy can be further enhanced by better data analytics on potential threats to digital security and personal privacy. A more advanced cyberinfrastructure can also assist in the collaboration in education and training for securing cyberspace and protecting individual privacy. The development of digital security and privacy provides the necessary safeguard to open data and opening governance efforts. The attention to confidentiality in digital security and online privacy while utilizing personal information helps to engender trust in providing personalized government information and service. Digital security is essential for protecting the strategic data and cyberinfrastructure resources that power the other four areas.

Notes

1 For more details on e-petition, see petitions.whitehouse.gov/, accessed June 25, 2016.
2 For more details, see www.gov.uk/petition-government, accessed June 26, 2016.
3 For more details, see www.usaspending.gov/Pages/Data-Act.aspx, accessed July 3, 2016.
4 For more details, see www.washingtonpost.com/news/federal-eye/wp/2015/07/09/hack-of-security-clearance-system-affected-21-5-million-people-federal-authorities-say/, accessed January 5, 2016.
5 The Electronic Privacy Information Center (EPIC) has a good resource site for monitoring emerging electronic privacy concerns: www.epic.org/privacy/, accessed July 20, 2016.
6 Additional readings on such efforts can be found on the U.S. NSF website: www.nsf.gov/pubs/2016/nsf16510/nsf16510.htm, accessed July 25, 2016.
7 For more information, see www.smartchicagocollaborative.org/, accessed July 25, 2016.
8 See www.govtech.com/data/Iowa-Employs-Big-Data-to-Identify-Potential-UI-Fraud.html, accessed July 1, 2016

References

Chen, Hsinchun, Roger H. Chiang, and Veda Storey. 2012. "Business Intelligence and Analytics: From Big Data to Big Impact." *MIS Quarterly* 36 (4):1165–88.
Clark, Benjamin Y., Jeffrey Brudney, and Sung-Gheel Jang. 2013. "Coproduction of Government Services and the New Information Technology: Investigating the Distributional Biases." *Public Administration Review* 73 (5):681–701.
Creative Government Planning Division. 2013. Government 3.0: Openness, Sharing, Communication, and Collaboration. Seoul: Ministry of Security and Public Administration.
Dawes, Sharon S. 2010. "Stewardship and Usefulness: Policy Principles for Information-based Transparency." *Government Information Quarterly* 27 (4):377–83.

Deloitte-NASCIO. 2014. "Deloitte-NASCIO Cybersecurity Study: State Governments at Risk: Time To Move Forward." Deloitte and the National Association of State Chief Information Officers (NASCIO) 2014.

Evans, Angela M., and Adriana Campos. 2013. "Open Government Intiatives: Challenges of Citizen Participation." *Journal of Policy Analysis and Management* 32 (1):172–203.

Executive Office of the President. 2012. Big Data Across Federal Government. Washington, DC: White House.

Ganapati, Sukumar, and Christopher Reddick. 2016. "An Ostrich Burying Its Head in the Sand? The 2009 NASPAA Standards and Scope of Information Technology and E-Government Curricula." *Journal of Public Affairs Education* 22 (2):267–86.

Goldsmith, Stephen, and Susan Crawford. 2014. *The Responsive City: Engaging Communities Through Data-Smart Governance*. San Francisco, CA: Jossey-Bass.

Government Accountability Office (GAO). 2012. "Cybersecurity: Threats Impacting the Nation." Washington, DC: Government Accountability Office.

Government Technology. 2015. "Year in Data: CIO Priorities." *Government Technology* 28 (8):13.

Helsper, Ellen Johanna. 2012. "A Corresponding Fields Model of Digital Inclusion." *Communication Theory* 22 (4):403–26.

International City/County Management Association (ICMA). 2011. Electronic Government 2011. Washington, DC: International City/County Management Association.

Janssen, Marijn, Ricardo Matheus, and Anneke Zuiderwijk. 2015. "Big and Open Linked Data (BOLD) to Create Smart Cities and Citizens: Insights from Smart Energy and Mobility Cases." In *EGov 2015*, edited by Efthimios Tambouris, 79–90. Switzerland: Springer.

Lavertu, Stéphane. 2016. "We All Need Help: 'Big Data' and the Mismeasure of Public Administration." *Public Administration Review* 76 (6):864–72.

Linders, Dennis. 2012. "From e-Government to We-Government: Defining a Typology for Citizen Coproduction in the Age of Social Media." *Government Information Quarterly* 29 (4):446–54.

Mossberger, Karen, Caroline Tolbert, and Mary Stansbury. 2003. *Virtual Inequality: Beyond the Digital Divide*. Washington, DC: Georgetown University Press.

Mossberger, Karen, Caroline J. Tolbert, and Ramona S. McNeal. 2008. *Digital Citizenship: The Internet, Society, and Participation*. Cambridge, MA: Massachusetts Institute of Technology.

Ni, Anna Ya, and Yu-Che Chen. 2016. "A Conceptual Model of Information Technology Competence for Public Managers: Designing Relevant MPA Curricula for Effective Public Service." *Journal of Public Affairs Education* 22 (2):193–212.

National Science Foundation (NSF). 2012. "NSF Leads Federal Efforts In Big Data." NSF report.

Orszag, Peter R. 2009. Open Government Directive, Memorandum for the Heads of Executive Departments and Agencies, edited by Executive Office of the President Office of Management and Budget: Office of Management and Budget. Washington, DC: White House.

Research Office of Legislative Council Secretariat. 2013. "Innovation and Technology Industry in South Korea, Israel and Belgium." Hong Kong: Hong Kong Legislative Council Secretariat.

Soares, Sunil. 2012. *Big Data Governance: An Emerging Imperative*. Boise, ID: Mc Press.

Sutherland, Jeff. 2015. *SCRUM: The Art of Doing Twice the Work in Half the Time*. London: Random House Business Books.

The Economist. 2010. "Data, Data Everywhere: A Special Report on Managing Information." *The Economist*, February 27.

Thomas, John Clayton. 2012. *Citizen, Customer, Partner: Engaging the Public in Public Management*. Almond, NY; London, UK: M.E. Sharpe.

White House. 2012. Digital Government: Building 21st Century Platform to Better Serve the American People. Washington, DC: White House.

XSEDE. 2014. XSEDE: PY1-3 Comprehensive Report (July 1, 2011 through June 30, 2014). Illinois: XSEDE Office.

Index

311: access 90; case of New York City 90–1; as a form of integrated citizen service information system 87; for open data and open collaboration 192

agile development: for adaptation 185; for capacity building 216; core concepts 173; for ICT performance 172; needs and impact 172

big data: applications 219; definition 125; government initiatives 125; for information management 131; relevance to digital governance 27; security concerns 138; uses and challenges for government 126–7; US programs 219, 229

citizen-centric digital governance: challenges 92–6; cross-boundary collaboration 101–4; guiding public values 88; management strategies 96–107; roles of citizens 88–90

citizen-government collaboration: citizens as reporters and partners 105–6; leading and managing 106–7; as a strategy for citizen-centric digital governance 98, 109

China Internet Network Information Center (CNNIC) 1; internet use survey results 1–2; role and responsibilities 183; social networking statistics for China 2

Clinger-Cohen Act of 1996 26, 116; core competencies 197–8; as information management framework 189; mandate 224

cross-boundary collaboration: for citizen-centric services 92; 101–7; online collaboration 69; as a strategy for enhancing digital governance 26–7

crowdsourcing: examples 127–8; for generating and ranking policy ideas 69–70

cyberinfrastructure: drivers for growth 218–20; for innovation 222; relevant programs 219–20

cybersecurity: definition 114, 145; as a prominent issue 32, 223; *see also* digital security

data: as a core concept for competence 182; definition 115; growth in amount 104; management model 129; as a strategic resource 189

Data Accountability and Transparency Act (DATA Act) of 2014: impact 64, 67; mandate 192; significance 212, 227; *see also* open data

data visualization: application 129; benefits 5; concepts and examples 128–9

digital divide: in e-citizens 50–3; in e-government 48–50; nature and sources 46–8; state of the divide 43–6

digital governance: competencies of managers 179–93; definition 8–9; dimensions 9–11; features 209–10; financial resources required 29; management framework 21–37; for

Index   237

public value creation 7–8; strategies 224–33; trends 217–24
digital inclusion: an innovative approach to 57–8; programs and strategies 54–7
digital open government: implementation approach 79–82; strategy 76–7
digital privacy: definition 137; policy and management 138–40; principles and regulations 140–1; significance 138; solutions 141–3
digital security: definition 143–4; policy principles and management 145–7; protection approach 147–52; *see also* cybersecurity

e-citizens: divide in access and use 50–1
E-government Act of 2002: for open government 72; privacy impact assessment requirement in Section 208 142; as related to information security 191
e-participation 68: an area for ranking national governments 49; benefit 6; e-consultation as a type 68; e-policymaking as a type 68

Federal Information Security Management Act (FISMA): functions 145; as related to privacy 191; further reform 230

Health Insurance Portability and Accountability Act (HIPAA) of 1996 95, 137

ICT performance: measurement 158–60; project and program management 164–7; resource management 160–4; strategy for effective management 167–73
information: definition 115; management 130–1; relationship to data 115
information resource management: leadership and management strategy 129–31; principles for government 28, 117–19; strategic considerations 116
information system: applications 185–6; development 184

internet use: netizens in China 2002–15 46; total number of users in China in 2015 183; U.S. data for 2012 and 2014 45; use of government websites 52; *see also* e-citizens

knowledge management: definition and types of knowledge 116; imperative for public service 119–20; integrative processes 121–3; principles for digital governance 123–4

National Association of State CIOs (NASCIO) 202
Network of Schools of Public Policy, Affairs, and Administration (NASPAA) 193, 196, 204

open data: drivers for growth 221; use of XBRL 221; *see also* Data Accountability and Transparency Act (DATA Act) of 2014
open government: challenges 75–6; components of successful implementation 79–82; a framework 65; institutions 70–3; pillars 212–13; strategy for digital open government 76–82; trends 73–5
opening governance: applications 228; for personalized information and services 232; as a strategy of digital governance 224

performance management: systems 33; *see also* ICT performance
personalized information and service: as a strategy 225–7; as a trend 220–1; *see also* citizen-centric digital governance
Pew Internet and American Life Project 51; findings 51–2
public values: list 21–2; as purposes of digital governance 7–8

social media: growth 53; for online collaboration 69; for open government 78; statistics of use 48–9; technical knowledge as competence 187; as a tool of digital governance 209, 220; *see also* social networking

social networking: growth 2; platforms and their use 1, 4; statistics 44; use in U.S. 2012 and 2014 47; *see also* social media

strategic IT management: difference between public and private sectors 23; relevance to digital governance 22

strategic planning: for digital governance 35; strategic IT plans 22; *see also* strategic IT management

transparency: for decision-making 66; information transparency 67